Lea SWAHILI

Volume 1 of 3

A Complete Grammar

All proceeds of this book will go to needy school children in Tanga, Tanzania (where I was born, grew up and finished high school).

Other works by the author

- "Poetry: The Magic of Few Words"
- "My F-word Plan: How I Routinely Maintain Low Weight & Good Health"
- "Nine Ginans of Nine Ismaili Pirs: A Brief History of Khoja Ismailis"
- "The Willowdale Jamat Khana Story"
- "Writing [Auto] Biographies: Demonstrated by Author's Early Auto-biography"

To

Steere & Madan

And before them

Krapf

Who all, in the 19th century, brought Swahili to the bookshelves of English speakers, with the invaluable assistance of many of the local learneds of the Mrima and of the Zanzibar archipelago.

Na kwa, bila shaka, and to, without doubt,

Shaaban Robert, MBE

1909-1962

Jitu la Lugha Yetu Tamu! The Giant of Our Sweet Language!

Learn Good SWAHILI: Volume 1 of 3
A Complete Grammar

1st published: June, 2017

By Kitabu Publications, Toronto

(A division of 1304266 Ontario Inc.)

kitabupublications@gmail.com

ISBN 10: **9781548004781**

Cover Design: by the author

Karibu Kwetu!

Welcome to our place!

1 Introduction

Haba na haba, hujaza kibaba,

> Little by little, fills the measure
> [A long journey is accomplished step by step :-)]

The objective of this book is to bring a learner up to speed in using good Swahili in as reasonably short a time as possible. The keyword here is "good" as in grammatically good Swahili, for in using good Swahili it will be noticed by the locals and complimented on, enhancing the learner's overall experience in East Africa.

Why did I write this textbook? There are a limited number of Swahili textbooks out there and from a general point of view I wanted to complement that collection to increase the choice available to learners. But much more importantly than that I wanted to bring additional, very important dimensions to learning Swahili. These are:

1. A **systematic** coverage of grammar so that each grammatical entity is treated fully in one place and not scattered over different chapters.
2. **Cross-referencing** chapters and sections to answer questions that pop up in the head: "Where in the text book was or is this covered?"
3. **Examples** presented **for all** Swahili Noun **Groups**: juxta positioning examples by noun groups to clearly show them by groups and thus facilitating their comparison and contrast.
4. Though most of the books in existence do a good job of presenting the construction of words, of which verb construction is extensive, this book also shows how to **de-construct** verbs which

is NOT simply undoing the construction because of the many, many combinatorial possibilities of prefixes, etc used in construction which when encountered one must be able to parse them out not knowing how they were constructed. [See "Verb Construction & De-Construction" below.] De-construction is necessary to arrive at the meaning of a constructed word, especially of a verb, and as importantly to be able to look up words in dictionaries which ALL show entries in 'base' form i.e. NOT in their constructed form. A comprehensive use of **indexing** in chapter 22 Index of Attachments (alphabetical) facilitates this de-construction.

5. Volumes 2 and 3 are a bi-directional (Swahili-English and English-Swahili, respectively), practical, everyday **dictionary** of over 5,500 words, with a built-in mini-**thesaurus** which is useful for finding related words including synonyms and antonyms.

Verb Construction & De-Construction:

There are nearly 150 verb prefixes, infixes and suffixes, such that their possible combinations in constructing just simple verbs (pronoun+tense+**verb-base**) is over 200. But verbs are quite often encountered consisting of:

pronoun+tense+object+**verb-base**+preposition e.g.

*a+na+tu+**let**-e-**a***, he is bringing it for us

The combinatorial total of the available prefixes, etc at each of the above positions (unbolded, separated by a +/-) is in the thousands! And many of these prefixes are homonyms! All of which require the beginner to carefully sort them out to arrive at the correct meaning of a constructed verb.

Not surprisingly then, a lot of the text herein is devoted to analyzing and understanding the construction and de-construction of verbs. Such word breakdown and analysis is a most essential aspect of learning this language. Besides revealing the sense of a constructed verb, an important corollary of de-construction is that verb bases can be extracted which is necessary for looking up their meanings, without which any Swahili dictionary, which is a very essential resource, is useless.

While word construction is dealt with throughout the book, deconstruction is tackled in chapter 11 ANATOMY OF VERBS and in detail in section 22.1 How to Use the Index Tables.

Origins of the Swahili Language:

Swahili has its origins in languages of the **Bantu** people, the natives of sub-Saharan Africa. But as is historically known, Africa has been, over most of the last millennium, much influenced by Arabic, Portuguese, Belgian, French, German and British incursions, some parts more so than others. The impact on Swahili – an oral-only language like all other Bantu languages – was that it began to be <u>written</u>, first in Arabic script, then in Roman, and many words of the foreigners found their way into the language (flagged "F" in the Dictionary in Volumes 2 and 3). But this influence was not uniform in East Africa and local dialects developed e.g. *Kiungunja*, spoken in Zanzibar, *Kimvita*, a 'war' dialect spoken in Mombasa (*vita* means battle in Swahili), and *Kiamu*, the Lamu dialect, all of which have had greater use of Arabic words than compared to *Kimrima*, the Swahili spoken in my home town of Tanga and in the Tanganyikan/Tanzanian coastal areas and which therefore was probably the least adulterated of all dialects. Tanga never became an Arab town per se (although many Omanis and Yemenis settled there, but it did become a German, then British town). Also, it was not on the caravan route from Bagamoyo to Kigoma. Yet, with Pemba Island (the main spice island of the Zanzibar archipelago) being just offshore, Mombasa just up the coast, and Pangani and Bagamoyo down the coast, some of its Swahili was influenced by these neighbours but because this was a second-hand influence its Bantu roots were more intact than of these neighbours. It is not surprising that the country's poet laureate Shaaban Robert hailed from Tanga, and to whom this book is dedicated!

The Swahili Language:

First, the **sound** of Swahili: Mid-19th century British explorer John Hanning Speke, in his journal "The Discovery of the Source of the Nile" 1863, described Swahili as being "based on euphony" (which means pleasing to the ear). The key method whereby this is achieved is by the extensive use of co-related **prefixes**, **infixes** and **suffixes** as per the rules of its noun groups. Swahili words are <u>bases</u> to which these prefixes, etc are attached. For example, from the noun base –*ti*, chair, the adjective base –*moja*, one, the adjective base –*zuri*, nice, the verb base –*tosha*, suffice, and the present tense infix –*na*-, we can construct the following sentence:

ki-*ti* **ki**-*moja* **ki**-*zuri* **ki**-*na-tosha*, one nice chair suffices*

The **ki**- prefix follows the rules of the noun group described in section 3.4 "THINGS [T]: *Kitu-Vitu*, things(s)". Read out aloud the above sentence and you will see why Speke called it euphonious. Read on and you will see more for yourself. [*This was one of the first sentences we were taught in school!]

A major distinction to note here: English and other European language speakers, who are used to inflections at the <u>end</u> of words, should notice that inflections in Swahili are for the most part in <u>front</u> of word bases, and sometimes at the <u>rear</u> too. Moreover, with verb bases, typically more than one prefix is attached at the front e.g. *ki-<u>na</u>-tosha* above in which **ki**- and -*<u>na</u>*- are attached to the verb base –*tosha*. In fact, learning Swahili grammar is ALL about learning prefixes, infixes, suffixes which get attached to word bases.

Of the use of prefixes, etc, it is in **verb construction** that it is most heavily used. It has prefixes for pronoun, tense, relative pronoun, object, preposition, etc, etc to an extent which is unmatched in English where only singular / plural and past tense changes occur in word bases e.g. she comes, they come, she came, they came but she <u>will</u> come, where the <u>future</u> is indicated by a separate word "will" and not loaded onto the verb base "come" which in Swahili it is. Accordingly, a lot of the text herein is devoted to carefully explaining verb construction – and, later, de-construction. We may generalize here by stating that Swahili grammar is entirely prefix-etc-based, which this book thoroughly covers, as we'll see.

Next, is it Swahili or **Kiswahili**? The best way to understand the difference is another similar question, is it French or *Français*? In English, the language of France is referred to as French, BUT the people of France refer to it as *Français* in their own language. In the same way, in English we refer to the language of East Africa as Swahili, BUT the East Africans refer to it as *Kiswahili* in their own language.

Regarding how East Africans refer to languages in general, there is a convention we use for it as well as for the land of that language and its people, as follows:

Ki- is the prefix for the **language**

U- is the prefix for the **land** or **territory** of that language

M- (singular) or *Wa*- (plural) is the prefix for its **people**

For example, *-gogo* is the root term for the **capital region** of Tanzania. Thus:

Kigogo, local **language** of the region [*Kiswahili*, Swahili, is the national language]

Ugogo, the **region**

Wagogo, the **people** [singular, *Mgogo*]

Next, Swahili, like all languages, has been and continues to be 'shaped' by usage. That which was spoken in Speke's time is not identical to that today which in turn continues to change. Having said that, the language core remains steady whereas the changes tend to be on the 'fringes'.

No article in Swahili: There is no article in Swahili compared to the definite article "the" and the indefinite "a" or "an" in English. It is the context that determines what article is implied. For example:

mwalimu anakuja, a teacher or the teacher is coming

There is **no gender** in Swahili, not even with pronouns:

yeye ni mwanafunzi, she or he is a student

Other characteristics: all **verbs end** in -*a*, except for those of foreign origin; the favourite **first letters** of words are *m*- and *k*- which together make up one-third of all words. There are no words with the following first letters: c (except *ch*-), q, x. **Euphonious changes** abound which we will see in this book. All words **end in a vowel** and if a foreign word did not a euphonious vowel is suffixed! But there are exceptions (very few) to this vowel-ending: *maalum*, well-known / special, *rais*, president, *takriban*, approximately / almost. An exception to this exception are the occasional variations *maalumu* and *takribani* which result from the ingrained propensity* to suffix a vowel! [*This propensity is most evident in names of people e.g. Salim becomes Salimu, Mariam Mariamu, John Joni, Paul Paulo, etc.]

Swahili-English convention used in this book:

Swahili text is presented in ***italics***, **English** in **roman**, the two texts separated by a comma, as seen in the example above.

A **prefix-** is hyphenated at the end, an **-infix-** at both ends, a **-suffix** at the front.

Optional Swahili text is shown in brackets e.g. (*mimi*). Alternative text is separated with a forward slash e.g. she / he e.g.

*a-ku-**pa**-cho*, which she / he gives you

a-, she / he, is a pronoun prefix, interpreted as she or he
-ku-, you, an object infix
*-**pa**-*, give, is a **verb base**
-cho, which, is a relative suffix [optional]
If the optional suffix is dropped we get: *a-ku-**pa***, she / he gives you, that is no suffix is attached to the **verb base.**

The order of this book: we start with a gentle introduction to prefixes, before the later chapters, especially on verbs, tackle the more complex prefixes / infixes / suffixes.

Lastly, the text is sprinkled with lots and lots of examples.

2 How to Study

Haraka haraka haina baraka,

> Hurry hurry has no blessings
> [Haste is waste]

First order of business: go through the table of contents to become familiar with the organization of this book. Grammar is covered in chapters 3 Nouns through 10 More on Verbs. Chapter 11 ANATOMY OF VERBS summarizes the Swahili verb structure, while chapter 12 SENTENCE CONSTRUCTION ILLUSTRATION shows how sentences are constructed using information from this book set. Useful topics are covered in chapters 13 Numbers, 14 Calendar, 15 Time and 16 Greeting. Chapter 17 Simple Swahili for Beginners is a very useful chapter on getting you started in using Swahili in the early going, leading into the next chapter 18 Good Swahili. Chapter 19 Pronunciation is important for obvious reasons. Chapter 20 Internet Resources is a reminder of the searchable Internet which yields additional material for practice.

In a previous version of "Learn Good Swahili", Chapter 21 Dictionary had the bidirectional vocabularies, including introductory text on it. The contents of this chapter and its bidirectional vocabularies are now in Volumes 2 and 3 of this series. This has had to be done for logistical reasons.

Chapter 22 Index of Attachments (alphabetical) has ALL of the 'attachments' (prefixes, infixes, suffixes) made to word bases for actual usage. It too has introductory and how-to-use text in it. Chapter 23 Index table of Noun Groups has attachments organized by noun groups.

Practice material is presented throughout the book with answers for each practice given at the beginning of the next.

Appendices cover more useful topics: Appendix A: Pseudo-homophones, Appendix B: Nouns/Verbs Made Up From Each Other, Appendix C: Wide-use Verbs, Appendix D: Idioms, Proverbs, Teasers, Appendix E: Correspondence, Appendix F: Widely-used *Ki-* Prefix, Appendix G: -po-infix / suffix.

At the end of the book is an index of keywords.

BEFORE moving on to another chapter / section review the highlighted (bolded) parts of the many examples in each chapter / section. Read out aloud their contents; as a matter of fact, do this for any Swahili text to get accustomed to the pronunciation and flow; you want the words to 'ring' in your head thereby aiding in their recall during usage.

The key grammatical topics, covered in the chapters and sections of this book, have corresponding indexes of their related prefixes / infixes / suffixes at the end of the book e.g. chapter 5 Verbs has a corresponding index in section 22.2 Index tables: Verb and section 5.1 Tenses has a corresponding index in section 22.3.1 Index table: 3. Verb Tense Infix.

Memorize the acronyms of all eight noun groups viz. Pp, V, xFF, T, xFV, U, Pl, G which are useful aide memoires to the noun group membership. Noun groups are presented in chapter 3 Nouns.

After completing each chapter, review its corresponding index(es) in chapter 22 Index of Attachments (alphabetical) which list(s) prefixes, etc. Use it to test yourself your recall of them. [The importance of these alphabetic indices, including a couple of combined master ones, is based on the large number of prefixes, infixes and suffixes used in Swahili and as importantly on many of them looking the same in form (homonyms)!]

For each topic, there are practice sections throughout the book e.g. Section 3.12 Practice: Nouns. The answers for each such practice are found at the start of the next practice. Before commencing the next practice, use the answers of the previous to do the reverse exercise e.g. the above nouns practice requires you to determine noun plurals. Reversing it requires you to determine the singulars of the plurals given in the answers.

For the beginner who is still learning the language and is not yet quite comfortable using it and yet wants to start using it while still learning, chapter 17 Simple Swahili for Beginners describes a much easier way to start putting things into practice. Then, over time the correct usage should be fleshed out.

The opposite, undesirable approach to Simple Swahili is getting ahead of oneself and trying to communicate at a higher – even abstract – level which is not easy to do for the first timer. I like to stick to the KISS principle: Keep It Simple *Sana - sana* meaning 'very' in Swahili, adverbs coming after verbs!

To become good at Swahili grammar, it is most important to comprehend word construction and especially verb de-construction as explained in this book. Thus, after learning say all the components of verb construction, it is important to practise analyzing and parsing constructed verbs into prefix, infixes, verb base, and suffix e.g.

maembe ya-li-yo-anguka, the mangoes they which fell

> *ya*, they = pronoun prefix
>
> *li* = past tense infix
>
> *yo*, which = relative pronoun infix
>
> *anguka*, fall = verb base

The above, to be covered in detail in this book, is only presented here to illustrate verb breakdown. Word, especially verb, construction, is the main goal in mastering Swahili.

Word **de**construction which is equally important is detailed in section 22.1 How to Use the Index Tables. Besides revealing a word's meaning, deconstruction is important in being able to look up words in a dictionary. When you come across a new word and you want to look it up in a dictionary you need to deconstruct first:

(1) **Nouns**: reduce it to its **singular** form if necessary e.g. *visu* has to be reduced to *kisu* before you can look up its meaning: knife. You should be able to do this by the end of chapter 3 Nouns.

(2) **Adjectives**: in the same way as for nouns above, reduce it to its **base** form first e.g. *mbivu* is reduced to *bivu* before looking up its meaning: ripe. You should be able to do this by the end of chapter 4 Adjectives.

(3) Similarly, for **demonstratives** and **possessives**, but not for adverbs which don't go through any transformation and are always used as-is from the dictionary, and **interrogatives** which are identical to regular statements but with a question mark stuck in at the end.

(4) **Verbs**: reducing verbs to their **base** form is a lot more work than the above processes for nouns and adjectives. It requires removing prefixes, infixes and suffixes to get to its base e.g. *anasoma* has to be reduced to *soma* before its meaning can be looked up: read. You should be able to do much of this by the end of chapter 5 Verbs and the rest of it after chapters 10 More on Verbs and 11 ANATOMY OF VERBS and in detail in section 22.1 How to Use the Index Tables.

[Keep in mind that if a word is not found in the dictionary, it could be a **derived** word of which only a selection is included in it as explained in the Dictionary in Volumes 2 and 3. Derived words are covered in a number of sections according to word type viz. 3.11 Making Up Nouns, 4.3 Making Up Adjectives, 5.12 Making Up Verbs, 6.1 Making Up Adverbs and 5.8 Verb Transformations.]

There are many summary tables in this book e.g. section 3.10 Noun Summary which collectively summarize the many complexities of Swahili and thus are very important for review and memorization. See entries under "summary" in the Index at the end. The index also has other entries useful for review and memorization such as "foreign", "generic", "making up", "noun singular-plural variations", "oddity", "tips" which can be incorporated into one's 'checklist'. The rest of the index is also useful for focussing on a topic for review e.g. "negative" which lists all the places where negatives of different parts of grammar are covered.

Learn at least a few words from the the Dictionary in Volumes 2 and 3 everyday and test your memorization of them. Much of this dictionary has examples for its entries, especially of adjectives and adverbs but also of, more importantly, verbs. Upon encountering an example, read it out aloud.

A note on usage, idioms, etc: No book of grammar can be a complete treatise on language **usage** since by definition usage is fluid, constantly moving on with new phrases, and which can only be learnt by immersing oneself into these flowing waters, orally and verbally. A simple example is where a common phrase is shortened such as in English "Later" instead of "See you later", or "Morning" instead of "Good Morning"; a Swahili example is *vipi?* how? which is a greeting between friends. [No, they did not translate it from a cowboys and Indians movie! It is a short form for "how's it going?"] But it can get increasingly tricky than these cases, for example "He is lead-footed" meaning "His heavy foot sinks the car accelerator right down to the floor" whence "He floored it!" In a nutshell (!) there are no short cuts to learning usage: you have to learn it through use! [If instead you prefer to study usage then you would need to consult additional resources such as on the Internet - see chapter 20 Internet Resources.]

Keep a pocket notebook of new words and phrases encountered, of known words recognized (or not, but should have been) which is useful feedback for self-evaluation as well as for giving oneself pats on the back for progress made :-)

Lastly read aloud whatever Swahili material you can lay your hands on, whether you fully understand it or not, e.g. read aloud from sources found on the Internet (chapter 20 Internet Resources). Go through a page a day of the bi-directional dictionary (in Volumes 2 and 3) reading aloud the examples for an entry.

Swahili club: If you can connect with one or more other Swahili learners (perhaps you are climbing Kilimanjaro in a group, or touring / volunteering together, part of a diplomatic corps, working together as expatriates, etc) you can form a Swahili club of two or more people. This can easily be done over the Internet via media like video calls, text messages, emails, etc. There are all kinds of interactions possible: sentence / phrase / headline of the day / week, questions and answers, descriptions / scenarios / narratives, etc which someone in the club shares with the others in Swahili, the rest translating into English, and vice versa. Nice phrases /

quotes / idioms can be shared and discussed. Simple word challenges e.g. a sentence with a deliberate error can be submitted by someone for the others in the club to detect and explain.

University of Cambridge, England, International Examinations (CIE): Syllabus 3162 is Swahili for GCE O Level (General Certificate of Education Ordinary Level), a junior high school level. Successfully completing the material in this book makes passing 3162 easy, while acing it is within striking distance. Why write this exam? Perhaps, one wants an independent test of accomplishment. But even if one does not write it, knowing that the material herein is suitable for doing so says it all!

Is Swahili easy to learn? The answer is the classic "Yes and No", but in this case, more than justified. The "Yes" part refers to simple Swahili, as covered in **17 Simple Swahili for Beginners**, which explains a rough-n-ready approach, using only the dictionary, while all grammar rules are put on 'pause'. The "No" part refers to Good Swahili, as in grammatically correct Swahili, where the biggest challenge is verb construction and deconstruction which is unlike any other language, to my knowledge (except kindred African languages). Nevertheless, this book thoroughly covers Swahili grammar, with lots and lots of examples, plus self-practices and their solutions, and is thus up to the "No" challenge!

Bahati njema, rafiki yangu!
Good luck, my friend!

3 Nouns

Kila jambo lina chanzo,

> Every matter has a beginning
> [Everything begins somewhere]

The first thing to note about Swahili nouns is that their plurals are NOT formed in the same way as they are in English in which an "s" is added at the end of a noun. Plurals are formed differently based on the noun groups to which they belong. There are a number of major groupings of nouns. In this book they are labelled as follows:

GROUP NAME [group initials]: *Singular-Plural* (of an iconic noun of the group), followed by the **same in English**.

For example, the first group is:

PEOPLE [Pp]: *Mtu-Watu*, person(s)

mtu, meaning person, is singular indicated by prefixing *m*- to the base – *tu*.

watu, meaning persons, is plural indicated by prefixing *wa*-.

Note: nouns in the Dictionary (in Volumes 2 and 3) are given, as in all dictionaries, in their SINGULAR form e.g. *mtu* is listed, not *watu*. Their singular and plural prefixes are also given along with the noun groups they belong to :-)

The major groupings dealt with in this book are described in the sections that follow.

3.1 PEOPLE [Pp]: *Mtu-Watu*, person(s)

1: *Mtu*, person.

This is a common manner of male dressing on the East African coast. He is wearing a Swahili cap, hand-embroidered though now mostly machine-made. Muslims, especially during the fasting month of Ramadhan, wear it.

***

Watu, meaning persons or people, is the overwhelming content of this noun group. Almost all of the people and profession nouns in Swahili are found in this group. ALL singular nouns in this group begin with *m-*.

Most of the nouns in this group form their singular and plural with *m-* and *wa-* respectively e.g.

*m*toto, child
*wa*toto, children

Some variations to the above general rule

- Some nouns, beginning with *mw-*, form the plural by replacing these two letters with only a *w-*. For example:

  *mw*alimu, teacher
  *w*alimu, teachers

  But variations occur e.g.

mwandamanaji, protestor
waandamanaji, protestor [*wa*- is prefixed, not just *w*-]

And occasionally usage has both! E.g.

mwandamizi, follower
waandamizi or *wandamizi*, followers

In some words, the **-w-** is part of the root, in which case it is retained with a plural prefix **wa-** e.g.

mwakilishi, representative [from *wakili*, agent / attorney]
wawakilishi, representatives

- But in some cases an **mw-** is replaced with **wa-**:

  Mwislamu, Muslim
  Waislamu, Muslims

- A **mwi-** is replaced with **we-**:

  mwizi or **mwi**vi, thief
  wezi or **we**vi, thieves

- A couple of nouns beginning with **m-** make plurals with *mi-*:

  mtume, prophet
  mitume, prophets

  mungu, god
  miungu, gods

- Nouns to which **mwana-**, member of, is prefixed, form plurals with both:

  mwanamke, woman, literally member of the kin of *mke*, wife
  wanawake, women [*wana* and *wake* are both plurals]

  mwanamume, man, literally member of the kin of *mume*, husband
  wanaume, men [*wana* and *waume* are both plurals with the *wa-* in *waume* euphoniously dropped]

3.2 VEGETATION [V]: Mti-Miti, tree(s)

2: **Mti**, tree.

This is the *mgunga*, acacia tree. Ngorongoro Crater, Tanzania. Seen here is the tall yellow-barked 'fever' acacia surrounded by flat-topped and whistling acacias, against the background of the crater wall and its rim.

The acacia is the iconic tree of the arid plains of Tanzania and Kenya where their game parks are to be found.

***

Vegetation, meaning trees and plants, are found in this noun group. But so are some body parts and many other <u>things</u> especially non-physical. [**Tip**: the tree or plant of any produce is usually the singular name of the produce prefixed with an *m*- e.g. *chungwa*, orange, and *mchungwa*, orange tree. A few of a limited number of exceptions are *ndizi*, banana, whose plant is *mgomba*! *Mchele*, rice, whose plant is *mpunga*! and whose unhusked seed is also called *mpunga*! *Kahawa*, coffee, whose bush is called *mbuni*!]

Most of the nouns in this group form their singular and plural with *m-* and *mi-* respectively:

mmea, plant
mimea, plants

<u>Some variations to the above general rule</u>

- Nouns beginning with *mw-* or *mu-* form the plural by replacing it with *mi-*. For example:

  mwembe, mango tree
  miembe, mango trees

  muhogo, cassava plant
  mihogo, cassava plants

ALL singular nouns in this group begin with *m-*. Most *m*-followed-by-a-**consonant**[1] words [except persons[2], animals[3] and vegetative product *mb~* words[4]] are in this group e.g.

[1]*mwaka*, year, belongs to this group;

[2]*mtoto*, child, belongs to "PEOPLE [Pp]: *Mtu-Watu*, person(s)";

[3]*mbwa*, dog, belongs to "MIX+FAUNA, VEGGIES [xFV]: *Nyanya-Nyanya*, tomato(es)";

[4]*mbaazi*, pigeon-**pea**, belongs to "MIX+FAUNA, VEGGIES [xFV]: *Nyanya-Nyanya*, tomato(es)" [but *mbaazi*, pigeon-pea **plant**, same spelling, belongs to this group]; *mbao*, plank, timber, belongs to "MIX+FAUNA, VEGGIES [xFV]: *Nyanya-Nyanya*, tomato(es)".

Reminder: nouns in the Dictionary (in Volumes 2 and 3) are listed with the noun groups they belong to as well as how their plurals are formed :-)

3: **Dafu**, unripe coconut. Plantation on Zanzibar Island, Tanzania.

Very popular with tourists - and locals - it quite often is dropped by first climbing to the top as seen above! Its milk is drunk right out of the nut, followed by scooping out its flesh! Very refreshing!

***

Flowers and fruits are found in this noun group. Also found in this group are liquids, some body parts (especially parts in pairs e.g. eyes), foreign and non-physical words.

Also found are augmentatives (bigger versions of otherwise normal size things). An augmentative is formed from the normal word by:

(1) dropping its singular prefix e.g.

kikapu, basket, becomes:
kapu, hamper

mdudu, insect, becomes:
dudu, big insect

or (2) replacing the singular prefix with **ji**- or **j**- e.g.

mtu, person, becomes:
jitu, giant

mji, town, becomes:
jiji, city

nyumba, house, becomes:
jumba, bungalow or hall

Like the "MIX+FAUNA, VEGGIES [xFV]: *Nyanya-Nyanya*, tomato(es)" group in the section below, this group too is, but to a lesser extent, a mixed bag, a catch-all group. Swahili usage sees many nouns, especially of the 'derived' types, having membership in both these classes, and sometimes even in other classes!

Singulars do not have prefixes, the plurals being formed by simply prefixing *ma*- to the singulars:

tunda, fruit
matunda, fruits

<u>Some variations to the above general rule</u>

- Often words beginning with *ja*- or *ji*- drop these before prefixing the *ma*- plural:

  jambo, issue / problem / matter
  mambo, issues / problems / matters

  jicho, eye
  macho, eyes

  jiwe, stone
  mawe, stone

- The exceptions to the above *ja*- or *ji*- rule are:

  jino, tooth
  meno, teeth

  jina, name
  majina, names

3.4 THINGS [T]: Kitu-Vitu, things(s)

4: *Kitu cha kuchezea*, literally thing to play with, meaning toy. Tanga, Tanzania.

Home-made toys are still to be seen in East Africa, this one made from discarded material.

***

Inanimate things are found in this noun group, especially man-made and of relatively smaller* size e.g.

kitabu, book
kiti, chair
kitanda, bed
chumba, room (but not *nyumba*, house, which belongs to the xFV group)

[*In fact this group's singular prefix *ki-* is used as a 'smaller' indicator – see **diminutives below.]

Also found are some body parts. All nouns in this group begin with *ki-* or *ch-*, and the vast majority of *ki-* words belong to this group.

**Also found in this group are diminutives (smaller versions of otherwise normal size) and disabilities (e.g. blind person). A diminutive is formed from the normal word by replacing its singular prefix with *ki-* e.g.

mlima, mountain, becomes: *kilima*, hill
mdudu, insect, becomes: *kidudu*, small insect
chombo, ship, becomes: *kijombo*, small ship
   [note euphonious insertion *-j-*]
mwiko, spoon, becomes: *kijiko*, teaspoon
   [*-j-* ensures no confusion with *kiko*, pipe; also see next, a homonym]
jiko, stove, becomes: *kijiko*, a small stove
   [*jiko* has no singular prefix – see the xFF group]
mjiji, town, becomes: *kiji*, village; but emphatically it is *kijiji* which is the popular version;

[More in Appendix F: Widely-used *Ki-* Prefix.]

Plurals are formed by replacing the *ki-* or *ch-* with *vi-* or *vy-* respectively:

kiti, chair
viti, chairs

chumba, room
vyumba, rooms

5: **Nyanya**, tomatoes. Darajani Market, Zanzibar, Tanzania.

Produce sections of markets in East Africa are most colourful and tour guides will typically include them in their itineraries. Being an equatorial region, a wide variety is found.

***

Animals, fish, birds, insects and vegetables are found in this noun group. [Regarding vegetables, Swahili follows the 'kitchen' definition not the botanical, the obvious example being *nyanya*, tomato, which botanically is a fruit but in the kitchen it is considered a vegetable which can be cooked with other 'real' vegetables like onions and because of that it is considered belonging to this noun group. The test that may be used in determining whether a fruit such as tomato, or for that matter a spice like clove (another fruit!) belongs here or not is: is it commonly used in cooking like other real vegetables?]

Also found are family members, body parts and most of the foreign (non-Bantu) words. Most **n-** words are in this group but a large portion of the words in this group begins with letters other than *N*.

Like the "MIX+FLOWERS, FRUITS [xFF]: *Tunda-Matunda, fruit(s)*" group above, this is, even more so, a mixed bag, catch-all group. Swahili usage sees many nouns, especially of the 'derived' types, having membership in both these classes, and sometimes even in other classes!

Words in this group have NO singular NOR plural prefixes:

nyanya, tomato
nyanya, tomatoes

U-WORDS [U]: Utenzi-Tenzi, poem(s)

Tanganyika Tanganyika

Nakupenda kwa moyo wote.

Nchi yangu Tanganyika

Jina lako ni tamu sana...

6: **Utenzi wa wimbo wa taifa**, poem/lyrics of a national song

When Tanzania used to be Tanganyika and when Tanganyika was colonial (pre-1961) this was a pseudo-anthem. Now it is a popular national song. It means:

Tanganyika Tanganyika
I love you with whole heart.
My country Tanganyika
your name is so sweet.

***

All **U-** words are found in this noun group with the exception of *ua*, flower, which belongs to "MIX+FLOWERS, FRUITS [xFF]: Tunda-Matunda, fruit(s)" [but *ua*, courtyard, IS in this group]. Except for a few **w-** words, all words in this group are **u-** words. Also found are non-plural, non-physical** and country words, and body parts.

Non-physical words can be constructed by prefixing **u- to bases of nouns, adjectives, etc e.g. from the adjectival base *zuri*, nice, we can make:

u*zuri*, beauty

In fact, such words form a large part of this group. [This usage of *u*- is akin to the -ion, -(it)y, -ing, etc used in English e.g. act: action, vital: vitality, swell: swelling, etc.]

Where plurals are in usage, the singular *u*- prefix is simply dropped in the plural. For example:

utenzi, poem
tenzi, poems

As for non-plural words, they are used in the singular form whether the use is singular or plural. For example:

uchumi, economy (of say Kenya)
uchumi, economies (of say Kenya, Uganda and Tanzania)

The plurals or non-plurals of all words are given in the Dictionary (in Volumes 2 and 3) e.g.

utenzi(u,-)   [u is dropped]
uchumi(-)   [u is NOT dropped]

How to use the above singular/plural indicators in the rounded brackets is also explained in the Dictionary in Volumes 2 and 3.

Some variations to the above general rule

- The *u*- is dropped and a prefix *n(y)*- is attached:

  uwanda, plateau, plain
  nywanda, plains [sometimes *nyanda*]

  uyoga, mushroom
  nyoga, mushrooms

- The *u*- is NOT dropped and a prefix *ny*- is attached:

  ungu, pot (native)
  nyungu, pots

  uso, face
  nyuso, faces

uma, fork
nyuma, forks

- A *w*- is dropped and a prefix *ny*- is attached:

wimbo, song
nyimbo, songs

- The *u*- is dropped and a prefix *ma*- is attached:

uvuno, harvesting
mavuno, harvest

ugomvi, quarrel
magomvi, quarrels

The above plural prefix *ma*- is the same as the plural of MIX+FLOWERS, FRUITS [xFF]. Thus, plurals such as the above two follow the rules of xFF e.g.

mavuno mazuri (not *nzuri*), nice harvests [see xFF in 4 Adjectives]
mavuno yamewekwa (not *zimewekwa*), harvests have been put away [see xFF in 5.1.1 Pronoun Prefixes]

- The *u*- is dropped and a prefix *m*- is attached:

ubali, distance
mbali, distances

- The *ul*- is dropped and a prefix *nd*- is attached:

ulimi, tongue
ndimi, tongues

- The *uw*- is dropped and a prefix *mb*- is attached:

uwinda, hunting
mbinda, huntings

Countries:

Non-African countries by definition are considered foreign. They are named with a **u**- prefix attached to a base that represents the country. For example, using the base –*ingereza* which represents English, we get:

U*ingereza*, England

Similarly:

U*faransa*, France
U*jerumani*, Germany
U*rusi*, Russia
U*china*, China

These being *U*- words they belong to U-WORDS [U]: Utenzi-Tenzi, poem(s). However, they follow the rules of MIX+FAUNA, VEGGIES [xFV]: Nyanya-Nyanya, tomato(es)!!! [Presumably, it is because normally the former group does not have any foreign words while the latter does. The latter also contains the word *nchi*, country.] For example:

*Urusi **ina** mafuta*, Russia has oil

and not *Urusi* *una* *mafuta* where *u* is what normally is prefixed for its noun group. [These prefixes are covered in section 5.1.1 Pronoun Prefixes]

[Not all country names have a *U*- prefix, the obvious example being *Marekani*, America. African countries typically also do not have a *U*- prefix viz. *Tanzania*, *Kenya*, *Afrika Kusini* (South Africa), etc these being names of 'modern' times.]

3.7 PLACE-ADVERBS [Pl]: Mahali- Mahali, place(s)

7: **Sokoni**, at the market, specifically in this case it is *gulioni*, at the open-air market. Chake Chake, Pemba Island, Tanzania.

Gulio, open-air market, is a weekly event all over Tanzania especially in small towns and villages.

***

Technically there is only one word in this group: *mahali*, place(s). However, place adverbs (e.g. at home, at work, inside something, etc) are also treated as belonging to this group. Place adverbs, which are used with prepositions 'in' or 'inside' or 'at' etc, are formed by suffixing *-ni* to a noun e.g.

kikapu, basket, results in:
kikapuni, in(side) basket

Singular and plural forms of the solitary noun of this group are the same:

mahali, place(s)

3.8 GERUNDS [G]: Kusoma- Kusoma, reading(s)

8: ***Kucheza mpira wa miguu***, playing football (soccer). Mkwakwani Stadium, Tanga, Tanzania.

Soccer is BIG in East Africa! It reaches fever pitch during regional, East African and African championships. [The above photo was a friendly match, hence the sparse crowd, with most sitting behind the goals from where this photo was taken.]

***

Gerunds (which in English are verbs converted to nouns by suffixing ~ing; for instance the verb read becomes read-ing) are found in this noun group. In Swahili, the gerund form is the same as the infinitive e.g. *kusoma* means both, to read and reading. Thus, any verb in the Dictionary (in Volumes 2 and 3) becomes a gerund by re-attaching the ***ku-***, to. [The ***ku-*** is stripped from the infinitive form of the verb when shown in the Dictionary (Volumes 2 and 3) just like "to" is in English dictionaries]. For example,

husu, concern or relate, made into a gerund is *kuhusu*, concerning

A negative version (that is, having an opposite meaning) is formed by replacing *ku-* with *kuto-* (or optionally *kutoku-*) e.g.

kusema, talking, becomes:
kutokusema, silence

kusamehe, forgiving, becomes:
kutosamehe, unforgiving

A gerund can sometimes be used as a preposition e.g. *kuhusu*, to concern or concerning, can be used as a preposition as in

habari kuhusu mchaguo, news concerning/about the election

When an intention to do the action of a verb is to be stated, the implied 'to' of the infinitive form in English translation is understood to indicate that action e.g. a newspaper headline:

Ahadi ya Serikali (Government's promise) *kupeleka* (**to** send) *hela* (money) *shuleni* (to schools)

The singular and plural forms are the same:

kusoma, reading(s)

3.9   Animates outside of PEOPLE [Pp]

For example, the following animates belong to groups other than PEOPLE [Pp]:

mbwa, dog, belongs to MIX+FAUNA, VEGGIES [xFV] as do most animals;

kijana, youth, belongs to THINGS [T];

kobe, tortoise, belongs to MIX+FLOWERS, FRUITS [xFF].

Except for how singulars and plurals are formed as explained in this chapter, all animates whether in the PEOPLE [Pp] group or not, follow the grammatical rules of the PEOPLE [Pp] group as will be seen in the examples in this book. Another exception is possessives as explained in section 8.5 Possessives for Person Nouns outside of PEOPLE [Pp]: Mtu-Watu, person(s).

3.10 Noun Summary

This is a summary of the eight noun groups showing membership, key members and key prefix characteristics.

Sing-Plural (usual)	Membership (key members in **bold**)	Singular Words Begin With
PEOPLE [Pp]: *Mtu-Watu*, person(s)		
M-Wa	**People, professions**	*M-*
VEGETATION [V]: *Mti-Miti*, tree(s)		
M-Mi	1. Primarily **trees, plants** 2. Secondly body parts, things	*M-*
MIX+FLOWERS, FRUITS [xFF]: *Tunda-Matunda, fruit(s)*		
-Ma	1. Primarily **fruits, flowers** 2. Secondly liquids, body parts, foreign and non-physical words 3. **Augmentatives**	(all letters)
THINGS [T]: *Kitu-Vitu*, things(s)		
Ki-Vi	1. Primarily inanimate **things** 2. Secondly body parts 3. **Diminutives, disabilities**	*Ki-* or *Ch-*
MIX+FAUNA, VEGGIES [xFV]: *Nyanya-Nyanya*, tomato(es)		
-	**Animals, insects, vegetables**, family members, most of the **foreign** (non-Bantu) words	(all letters; most N-words are here)

Sing-Plural (usual)	Membership (key members in bold)	Singular Words Begin With
U-WORDS [U]: *Utenzi-Tenzi*, poem(s)		
U-	**U-words** (and a few W-word) including things, body parts, and non-plural, non-physical and **country** words	*U-*, a few W- (all U-words are here*)
PLACE-ADVERBS [Pl]: *Mahali- Mahali*, place(s)		
-	Only one word: *mahali* (**place**), plus **place-adverbs** which are formed by suffixing -*ni*, in, to a noun	
GERUNDS [G]: *Kusoma- Kusoma*, reading(s)		
-	**Gerunds**	*Ku-*

Some of the above categories are presented as such in the English-Swahili Dictionary (in Volume 3) For example, body parts are listed in the "body:" grouping. More information and a list of all such categories are given in Volumes 2 and 3.

*except *ua*, flower, which being what it is belongs to the xFF group.

A note on **numbered** groupings:

Other resources elsewhere e.g. at Yale's Kamusi Project (albeit defunct for a while now) use a rule **numbering** approach to classifying singular / plural rules as compared to the group naming / descriptive approach used herein (in the first column of the table below). The group naming approach used in this textbook immediately clues you in to the singular / plural rules e.g. "THINGS [T]: *Kitu-Vitu*, things(s)" tells you the singular is *Kitu*, the plural *Vitu*, from which can be derived the singular prefix *Ki-* and the plural *Vi-*. As compared to this the numbering approach does not give any clue as to singular or plural e.g. the numbers corresponding to the THINGS [T] group are 7 and 8 which are not self-explanatory, thus you have to know what they mean and therefore it is another layer of rules to be learnt. If and when you consult any resources where rule numbering is used, the table below allows you to cross-reference rule numbers back to the group names herein. Another approach that you will encounter in some of the other resources is using the common singular-plural prefixes of the noun group to label them; these are shown in the last column of the table below. Again, in comparison to this, the approach used herein gives you these singulars-plurals in the form of iconic nouns representing them e.g. the label *Ki-Vi* in the last column of the table below is to be compared with *Kitu-Vitu*. In addition, the main content(s) of each noun group are part of its labelling as well e.g. THINGS [T] which tells you that a large portion of this group consists of things (man-made); T is a short acronym. From this point on, we will use group names exclusively with no further reference to numbers.

Group	Singular Rule#	Plural Rule#	Alt. Label
PEOPLE [Pp]: *Mtu-Watu*, person(s)	1	2	M-Wa
VEGETATION [V]: *Mti-Miti*, tree(s)	3	4	M-Mi
MIX+FLOWERS, FRUITS [xFF]: *Tunda-Matunda, fruit(s)*	5	6	Ma
THINGS [T]: *Kitu-Vitu*, things(s)	7	8	Ki-Vi
MIX+FAUNA, VEGGIES [xFV]: *Nyanya-Nyanya*, tomato(es)	9	10	N
U-WORDS [U]: *Utenzi-Tenzi*, poem(s)	11, 14	10	U
PLACE-ADVERBS [Pl]: *Mahali- Mahali*, place(s)	16, 17, 18		Pa
GERUNDS [G]: *Kusoma- Kusoma*, reading(s)	15		KU

[A comment related to this is that *Kiswahili* textbooks in Tanzania do not always discuss noun groups and their rules until later in junior high! Presumably the teacher has to orally supplement this! From my own school days, I recall the teacher indeed explaining such rules by grouping.]

3.11 Making Up Nouns
Verb to noun transformation

Using suffix *–o*:

pambana, meet (in friendship or conflict) gives us:
*pamba**no**,* encounter

chuja, filter:
chujio, filter [the *-i-* is a euphonious addition]

With foreign-origin verbs, usually an *-a* is suffixed:
ruhusu, permit:
ruhusa, permission

From nouns using prefix *mwana-* or *mw-* or *m-*

mwana-, member of:
    chama, organization: *mwanachama*, member of an organization
    nchi, country: *mwananchi*, citizen
Mwafrika, African
Mwarabu, Arab
Mwingereza, English
Mwitalia, Italian
mchungwa, orange tree [from *chungwa*, orange]
mwembe, mango tree [from *embe*, mango]

From adjectives using prefix *m-* or *u-*

nene, fat:
mnene, fat person, or as a pronoun: the fat one [similarly, pronouns from numerical adjectives are useful e.g. *moja*, one, being an adjective can give: *mmoja*, one, as a pronoun]

zuri, nice:
uzuri, beauty

But note:
ema, good:
wema, goodness i.e. quality [*uema* is spelt *wema*]

From verbs using prefix *ki-* and/or replacement suffix *–(u)o*

nywa, drink:
kinywa, mouth

chana, comb:
chanuo, comb (long-toothed)

vuka, cross:
kivuk**o**, crossing   ...[More in Appendix F: Widely-used *Ki*- Prefix.]

Professions from verbs using prefix *m*- or *ki*- and usually suffix *–(j)i* or *– (z)i*

[*m(w)*- is prefixed following PEOPLE [Pp] group rules]

winda, hunt:
mwind**aji**, hunter

chora, draw:
mchor**aji**, artist

lima, plough: **m**lim**aji**, farmer [caution: it is not derived from *mlima*, mountain] also:
mkulima, farmer, where the infinitive *ku*- is retained

pita, pass:
mpit**aji**, passerby

ongoza, lead:
kiongo**zi**, leader

ganga, mend (heal):
mgang**a**, healer

kaa, reside:
mka**aji**, resident

[More in Appendix B: Nouns/Verbs Made Up From Each Other.]

From verbs and other nouns using prefix *u*-
winda, hunt:
uwind**o**, hunting [Note the change is suffix!]

jamaa, family (thus, society):

ujamaa, socialism

Borrowed foreign words
By phonetic re-spelling and ensuring it <u>ends in a vowel</u>:
afis<u>a</u>, officer
aiskrim<u>u</u>, ice cream
bas<u>i</u>, bus
gazeti, gazette / newspaper
kway<u>a</u>, choir
polis<u>i</u>, police
swet<u>a</u>, sweater
soks<u>i</u>, socks
tenis<u>i</u>, tennis
sinema, cinema
wik<u>i</u>, week

TIPS: (1) An ending 'er' or 'or' is replaced with an 'a' e.g. director becomes *direkta,* soccer becomes *soka,* etc. (2) 'I' is the ending vowel of choice e.g. office becomes *ofisi.* (3) If the foreign word already ends in a vowel sound, that sound is retained e.g. camera becomes *kamera.* (4) Oddities: ice cream, *aiskrimu,* is an example of a 'u' ending.

These foreign words for the most part would be placed in MIX+FAUNA, VEGGIES [xFV]: *Nyanya-Nyanya,* tomato(es).

Making up nouns descriptively

Chapter 8 Possessives tackles *-a*, of, and *-enye*, having, which are very useful in making up nouns descriptively e.g.

chumba cha kulal<u>i</u>a, room of sleeping <u>in</u> = bedroom [<u>preposition</u>: tackled in 10.2.1 Embedded Prepositions]

gari la moshi, vehicle of smoke = locomotive

njia ya lami, road of tar = tarmac road

mambo ya fedha, matters of money = finance

kiti chenye magurudumu, chair having wheels = wheel-chair

*korongo **mwenye** taji*, heron having a crown = Crown Bird (Uganda's national bird)

mwenyekiti, having the chair = chair person

3.12 Practice: Nouns

Use the Swahili-English Dictionary (in Volume 2) to determine what noun group each of the nouns in the table below belongs to, and write its initials in the "Group" column and the plural of each noun under "Plural". An **example** is given for the first entry.

[The correct answers are given at the beginning of the next Practice section.]

Swahili Singular	English	Group	Swahili Plural
ajali	accident	xFV	*ajali*
asumini	jasmine		
bamia	okra		
banda	barn		
chumba	room		
chumvi	salt		
chungwa	orange		
chura	frog		
dafu	unripe coconut		
dawa	medicine		
dudu	insect (big)		
embe	mango		
eneo	area, place		

Swahili Singular	English	Group	Swahili Plural
fedha	money		
fisi	hyena		
gari	vehicle		
habari	news, info		
haragwe	bean		
idara	govt. dept.		
inzi	fly		
jua	sun		
kasuku	parrot		
kidudu	insect (small)		
kitunguu	onion		
kuimba	singing		
limau	lemon		
mahali	place		
mbamia	okra plant		
mbuga	open terrain		
mchukuzi	porter		
mdudu	insect		
neno	word		
njia	way, road		
orodha	list		

Swahili Singular	English	Group	Swahili Plural
papai	papaya, pawpaw		
pasi	clothes iron		
ramani	map		
saa	time, watch		
simba	lion		
twiga	giraffe		
ufunguo	key		
vazi	clothing		
yai	egg		
zabibu	grape		
ziwa	lake		

Using prefixes, etc given in the square brackets below write in the space provided the nouns corresponding to the given words:

chora, draw: *mchoro*, drawing [example]
kijiji, village: _____, villager [*m*-]
refu, tall: _____, height [*u*-]
shona, to sew: _____, tailor [*m*-, -*i*]
Amerika: _____, American [*Mw*-]

Convert the following foreign words into Swahili:

bicycle: *baisikeli* [example]
calendar: _____
garage: _____
mile: _____
police: _____

post office: _____
receipt: _____
torch: _____

4   Adjectives

Swahili likes to alliterate its adjectives with their nouns! We will use an adjectival base -*zuri*, nice or pretty or beautiful. Alliteration is achieved by using the same prefixes as the singular and plural ones seen above. Examples for each of the noun groups are:

PEOPLE [Pp]: *Mtu-Watu*, person(s)

> Singular [**m**ke **m**zuri, pretty wife]

> Plural [**wa**ke **wa**zuri, pretty wives]

> Special cases of <u>vowel-adjectives</u> (beginning with a vowel, shown <u>underlined</u> below): the deviations from the above rule are in **bold**. The singular prefix for such adjectives is **mw**-, plural is **we**- before **e**- or **i**-, otherwise it is the same as the normal **wa**-:

> [The only *u*- adjectives in Swahili to my knowledge are *uchi*, naked, and *urujuani*, purple, which do NOT take on any prefix, as explained in section 4.2 Foreign-origin adjectives e.g. *mtoto uchi*, naked child.]

> [*mvulana* **mw**<u>a</u>*ngalifu*, careful boy;
> *wavulana wa(<u>a</u>)ngalifu*, careful boys (-<u>a</u>- dropped from the adjective)]

> [*mvulana* **mw**<u>e</u>*ma*, good boy;
> *wavulana* **we**(<u>e</u>)*ma*, good boys (-<u>e</u>- dropped from the adjective)]

> [*mvulana* **mw**<u>i</u>*ngine*, other boy;
> *wavulana* **we**(<u>i</u>)*ngine*, other boys (-<u>i</u>- dropped from the adjective)]

> [*mvulana* **mw**<u>o</u>*vu*, wicked boy;
> *wavulana wa<u>o</u>vu*, wicked boys]

VEGETATION [V]: *Mti-Miti*, tree(s)

Singular [*mwitu mzuri*, beautiful forest]

Plural [*miitu mizuri*, beautiful forests]

Special cases of <u>vowel-adjectives</u> (beginning with a vowel, shown <u>underlined</u> below): the deviations from the above rule are in **bold**. The singular prefix for such adjectives is **mw-**, plural is **my-** before an **e-**, otherwise it is the same as the normal **mi-**:

[*mkuki **mw<u>a</u>ngavu***, shining spear;
mikuki mi<u>a</u>ngavu, shining spears]

[*mkuyu **mw<u>e</u>ma***, good sycamore / fig tree;
*mikuyu **my<u>e</u>ma***, good sycamore / fig trees]

[*mkuyu **mw<u>i</u>ngine***, other sycamore / fig tree;
mikuyu mi(<u>i</u>)ngine, other sycamore / fig trees (-<u>i</u>- dropped from the adjective)]

[*mkuyu **mw<u>o</u>roro***, soft sycamore / fig tree;
mikuyu mi<u>o</u>roro, soft sycamore / fig trees]

MIX+FLOWERS, FRUITS [xFF]: *Tunda-Matunda, fruit(s)*

Singular [*dafu zuri*, nice unripe coconut]

Plural [***ma**dafu **ma**zuri*, nice unripe coconuts]

[Reminder: all animates use the rules of the PEOPLE [Pp] group e.g. *kobe mzuri*, nice tortoise; *makobe **wa**zuri*, nice tortoises]

Special cases of <u>vowel-adjectives</u> (beginning with a vowel, shown <u>underlined</u> below): the deviations from the above rule are in **bold**. The singular prefix for such adjectives is ***j-***, plural ***me-*** before an **e-** or **i-**, otherwise it is the same as the normal ***ma-***:

[*debe **j<u>a</u>ngavu***, shining can;
madebe ma(<u>a</u>)ngavu, shining cans (-<u>a</u>- dropped from the adjective)]

[*embe jema*, good mango;
*maembe **me(e)ma***, good mangoes (-*e*- dropped from the adjective)]

[*embe jingine*, other mango – sometimes, *lingine*;
*maembe **me(i)ngine***, other mangoes (-*i*- dropped from the adjective)]

[*embe jororo*, soft mango;
maembe maororo, soft mangoes]

Oddity:

[*embe jipya*, new mango, and not *embe pya*]

THINGS [T]: *Kitu-Vitu*, things(s)

Singular [***ki**tabu **ki**zuri*, nice book]

Plural [***vi**tabu **vi**zuri*, nice books]

[Reminder: all animates use the rules of the PEOPLE [Pp] group e.g. *kifaru **m**zuri*, nice rhino; *vifaru **wa**zuri*, nice rhinos]

Special cases of <u>vowel-adjectives</u> (beginning with a vowel, shown <u>underlined</u> below): the deviations from the above rule are in **bold**. The singular prefix for adjectives beginning with *e*- is *ch*-, plural is **vy**-, and for all other vowels the prefixes are the same as the normal *ki*- and *vi*-:

[*kisu ki<u>a</u>ngavu*, shining knife;
visu vi<u>a</u>ngavu, shining knives]

[*kisu **ch**<u>e</u>ma*, good knife;
*visu **vy**<u>e</u>ma*, good knives]

[*kisu ki(<u>i</u>)ngine*, other knife (-<u>i</u>- dropped from the adjective);
visu vi(<u>i</u>)ngine, other knives (-<u>i</u>- dropped from the adjective)]

[*kisu ki<u>o</u>roro*, soft knife;
visu vi<u>o</u>roro, soft knives]

MIX+FAUNA, VEGGIES [xFV]: *Nyanya-Nyanya*, tomato(es)

Singular & Plural [*ndizi nzuri*, nice banana(s)]

[Reminder: all animates use the rules of the PEOPLE [Pp] group e.g. *mbwa mzuri*, nice dog; *mbwa wazuri*, nice dogs]

However, the above *n-* prefix CAN'T be used with MOST adjectives because, in most cases, it would be awkward to pronounce. For example, with adjective *baya*, bad, *nbaya* is unpronounceable or at most sounds like *mbaya*.

On the other hand, with certain adjectives (such as *nzuri* in the above example) it is pronounceable. Pronounceable adjectives are ones that begin with *d*, *g*, *j* or *z*. For example:

nyanya ndogo / ngumu / njazi / nzuri, small / hard / plentiful / nice tomato(es)

A nice mnemonic to remember the above four letters is (these letters are **bolded**, while the n is underlined):

Ndege **J**ozani, birds at Jozani [Jozani is a famous forest park in the middle of Zanzibar Island]

Oddities

refu, long

Swahili usage sees the leading *r-* changed to a *d-* making it acceptable to use the *n-* adjectival prefix, thus:

kamba ndefu, long rope(s)

This modification is to be compared with:

wili, two

where *wili* has its *w-* modified to a *b-*, then prefixing an *m-*, thus:

nyanya mbili, two tomatoes

mbili is a homonym of the counting word *mbili* with the difference being the former is an adjective, the latter a noun. [cf. In normal usage an adjectival prefix is attached to an unmodified *wili* e.g. *watu wawili*, two people.] Except for *mbili* none of the numbers take a prefix in this noun group e.g. *nyanya tatu*, three tomatoes, where *tatu*, three, doesn't take a prefix.

Another such adaptation is frequently using an **m-** prefix with adjectives beginning with a "**b**" or a "**p**", e.g.

*mboga **m**baya*, bad vegetable(s)

*nyumba **m**pya*, new house(s)

Other than the above, an **n-** prefix CAN'T be used. For example, *kubwa*, big, does not take an n-prefix as in:

ndizi kubwa, big banana(s)

Special cases of <u>vowel-adjectives</u> (beginning with a vowel, shown <u>underlined</u> below): the deviations from the above rule are in **bold**. The singular and plural prefix for such adjectives is **ny-**:

[*chupa **ny**<u>a</u>ngavu*, shining bottle(s)]

[*chupa **ny**<u>e</u>kundu*, red bottle(s)]

[*karafuu **ny**<u>i</u>ngine*, other clove(s)]

[*karafuu **ny**<u>o</u>roro*, soft clove(s)]

<u>Oddity</u>

[*karafuu **nj**<u>e</u>ma*, good clove(s)] not <u>*nyema*</u>

U-WORDS [U]: *Utenzi-Tenzi*, poem(s)

Singular [*ufagio **m**zuri*, nice broom]

Plural [*fagio **n**zuri*, nice brooms]

Note: This noun group uses the singular adjectival prefix **m-** of VEGETATION [V] and the plural **n-** of MIX+FAUNA, VEGGIES [xFV], as described above.

Special cases of <u>vowel-adjectives</u> (beginning with a vowel, shown <u>underlined</u> below): the deviations from the above rule are in **bold**, and again these deviations are the same as for VEGETATION [V] in the singular, and MIX+FAUNA, VEGGIES [xFV] in the plural, namely the singular prefix for such adjectives is **mw-**, the plural **ny-** (or **nj-** with *ema*):

[*ufunguo* **mw**a*ngavu*, shining key;
funguo **ny**a*ngavu*, shining keys]

[*ufunguo* **mw**e*upe*, white key;
funguo **ny**e*upe*, white keys]
[*ufunguo* **mw**e*ma*, good key;
funguo **nj**e*ma*, good keys] not _nyema_

[*ufunguo* **mw**i*ngine*, other key;
funguo **ny**i*ngine*, other keys]

[*ufunguo* **mw**o*roro*, soft key;
funguo **ny**o*roro*, soft keys]

PLACE-ADVERBS [Pl]: *Mahali- Mahali*, place(s)

Singular & Plural [*mahali* **pa**zuri, nice plac(e)s]

The **pa-** is an alliteration of **pahali**, a spelling variation of *mahali*.

Special cases of <u>vowel-adjectives</u> (beginning with a vowel, shown <u>underlined</u> below): the deviations from the above rule are in **bold**. The singular and plural prefix for such adjectives is **pe-** before an **e-** or **i-**, otherwise it is the same as the normal **pa-**:

[*mahali* pa*(a)ngavu*, shining place(s) (-a- dropped from the adjective)]

[*mahali* **pe**(e)*ma*, good place(s) (-e- dropped from the adjective)]

[*mahali* **pe**(i)*ngine*, other place(s) (-i- dropped from the adjective)]

[*mahali* pa*o*roro, soft place(s)]

GERUNDS [G]: *Kusoma- Kusoma*, reading(s)

Singular & Plural [**ku**cheza **ku**zuri, nice playing(s)]

Special cases of <u>vowel-adjectives</u> (beginning with a vowel, shown <u>underlined</u> below): the deviations from the above rule are in **bold**. The singular and plural prefix for such adjectives is **kw-** before an **e-** or **i-**, otherwise it is the same as the normal **ku-**:

[*kufanya kuangalifu*, careful doing(s)]

[*kufanya **kwe**ma*, good doing(s)]

[*kufanya **kwi**ngine*, other doing(s)]

[*kufanya kuororo*, soft doing(s)]

4.1   Summary of Vowel-adjectives

The special cases of vowel-adjectives (i.e. beginning with a vowel) are summarized below for studying and memorization:

Gp	*e/i*-adjective		*e*-adjective		other vowel-adjective		Comment
	Sing.	Plu.	Sing.	Plu.	Sing.	Plu.	
Pp		[3]*we-*			[1]*mw-*		
V				[2]*my-*	[1]*mw-*		Singular is **same** in U group
xFF		[3]*me-*			[1]*j-*		
T			[4]*ch-*	[4]*vy-*			
xFV			[5]	[5]	*ny-*	***ny-***	Plural is **same** in U group
[7]**U**				[5]	***mw-***	***ny-***	
[8]**Pl**	*pe-*	*pe-*					
[8]**G**	*kw-*	*kw-*					

[1] First three groups: only one singular prefix applies to ALL vowel-adjectives e.g. *mtu <u>mw</u>ema, mti <u>mw</u>ema, tunda <u>j</u>ema*, etc and similarly for other vowels: -*angalifu, -angavu, -ingine**, -*ovu, -ororo*. *sometimes, *lingine,* instead of *jingine* (xFF group)

This one special case of plural prefix for V applies to ONLY *e*-adjectives e.g. *miti myema*.

[3] These two plural prefixes for Pp and xFF apply to ONLY *e/i*-adjectives e.g. *wavulana wema/wengine, maembe mema/mengine*.

[4] T group: the special case is applicable to ONLY *e*-adjectives e.g. *kitu chema, vitu vyema*.

[5] *njema* is an oddity (not *nyema*).

[7] U group: borrows singular and plural prefixes from V and xFV respectively.

[8] Last two groups: these prefixes apply to ONLY *e/i*-adjectives e.g. *mahali pema/pengine, kusema kwema/kwingine*.

4.2   Foreign-origin adjectives

These do NOT take on any prefixes. For example, using the foreign-origin adjective *safi*, clean, we get:

kitabu safi, clean book [not *kisafi*]
vitabu safi, clean books [not *visafi*]

Foreign-origin words, including adjectives such as the above, are flagged "F" in the Dictionary (in Volumes 2 and 3).

Examples for each of the noun groups: [Their noun prefixes are bolded to show clearly that the nouns still have their prefixes but not the foreign adjectives]

PEOPLE [Pp]: *Mtu-Watu*, person(s)

> **mw**alimu hodari, smart teacher
> **w**alimu hodari, smart teachers

VEGETATION [V]: *Mti-Miti*, tree(s)

> **m**stari awali, initial line
> **mi**stari awali, initial lines

MIX+FLOWERS, FRUITS [xFF]: *Tunda-Matunda, fruit(s)*

> kabati kahawia, brown cupboard
> **ma**kabati kahawia, brown cupboards

THINGS [T]: *Kitu-Vitu*, things(s)

>*kitabu ghali*, expensive book
>*vitabu ghali*, expensive books

MIX+FAUNA, VEGGIES [xFV]: Nyanya-Nyanya, tomato(es)

>*nyanya rahisi*, cheap tomato
>*nyanya rahisi*, cheap tomatoes

PLACE-ADVERBS [Pl]: Mahali- Mahali, place(s)

>*mahali baridi*, cold place(s)

GERUNDS [G]: Kusoma- Kusoma, reading(s)

>*kusoma kadha*, various reading(s)

<u>Numerical Adjectives</u>

Single-digit numerical adjectives take singular / plural prefixes EXCEPT for the three foreign numbers viz. *sita*, 6, *saba*, 7, and *tisa*, 9, which DO NOT. For example:

kitabu kimoja, one book

miti mitano, five trees

BUT no prefixes in the three foreign-origin numbers:

matunda sita, six fruits

vitabu saba, seven books

miti tisa, nine trees

[Two adjectives: emphasis is on the second e.g. *kitabu kimoja kizuri* (*kizuri* emphasized); *kitabu kizuri kimoja* (*kimoja* emphasized)]

4.3   Making Up Adjectives

Swahili does not have many of the common adjectives of English. These have to be made up using the following techniques:

a) Adjective *–enye*, possessing, e.g. *watoto **wenye** afya*, children possessing health i.e. healthy children.

b) ***Bila/pasipo***, without, e.g. *mji **bila** watu*, town without people i.e. uninhabited town; *mahali **pasipo** miti*, place without trees i.e. treeless place or open terrain.

c) 'Which is (not)' relatives -*o* [this is tackled in section 10.7.3 Old -li- Present Tense of wa, be, with Relatives] e.g. *maneno yaliyo* [-*li*- is a rare present tense of *wa*, be, used with relatives] *kweli*, words which are true i.e. true words; *matunda yasiyofaa*, fruits which do not suit i.e. unsuitable fruits; *chakula kisichotosha*, food which is not sufficient i.e. insufficient food.

d) 'With(out)' objects [these are tackled in section 10.1 Embedded Object References] e.g. *magari yanayo* A. C., literally cars which have them - A. C., i.e. air-conditioned cars.

e) **Timeless** tense [this is tackled in section 5.1 Tenses] e.g. *nyanya zatosha*, tomatoes which suffice i.e. sufficient tomatoes. Note that it also equally means: tomatoes (in general) suffice, such as might be called for in a recipe.

f) Using the possessive –*a*, of [these are tackled in chapter 8 Possessives] e.g. *maji (**ya***) *moto*, literally water of heat/fire i.e. hot water (*optional, by usage); *viti **vya** kutosha*, sufficient chairs; *kusoma **kwa** mtoto*, child's reading; *miwani **ya** kusoma*, reading glasses; *hifadhi **ya** taifa*, national park; similarly, -*a kuvuta*, interesting; -*a kufuata*, next; -*a umma*, public; -*a hakika*, sure. [*The **y** in **ya** is determined by **maji**, which is the possession – see 8.1 Possessive Preposition –*a*, of.]

g) Another use of the above -*a* is with adverbs made-up using ***ki*-** [which is covered below in section 6.1 Making Up Adverbs] e.g. *macho*, eyes: -*a **kimacho***, literally of watchfully = alert. Just as in the usage of the above -*a*, here too is seen it being dropped sometimes e.g. *ajulikanwa **kitaifa***, she is known nationally (adverb) cf. *twiga ni nembo (ya) kitaifa*, the giraffe is a national (adjective) symbol. Note: *twiga ni nembo ya taifa*, can be translated as, the giraffe is a symbol of (possessive) the nation or the giraffe is a national (adjective) symbol – see example in the above bullet: *hifadhi ya taifa*.

h) Yet another use of the above -*a* is with ***dume / kike***, male / female: e.g. *ng'ombe wa **dume***, bull; *ng'ombe wa **kike***, cow. Also seen is usage of the corresponding nouns ***dume / jike*** without use of -*a*: *ng'ombe **dume** / ng'ombe **jike***.

i) Using replacement suffixes like –***fu*** or –***vu***: *angalia*, look carefully, *angali**fu***, careful; *vumilia*, tolerate, *vumili**vu***, tolerant or patient.

j) Using the negative *si* for creating an antonym: *muhimu*, important, *si muhimu*, unimportant, although *hafifu*, insignificant, may also be used. [*si* is covered in section 10.7.2 Wa, be.]

k) Comparative (...~er ...) and superlative (the ~est) adjectives are composed by using a suitable word such as **kuliko**, than / compared to e.g. *mtu huyu ni mfupi kuliko yule*, this man is short compared to him (i.e. short**er** than him); Kilimanjaro *ni mlima mrefu kuliko yote*, Kilimanjaro is the tall**est** mountain. Or, using **zaidi**, more e.g. *hiki ni kisu kikali zaidi*, this is a sharp**er** knife; *una kingine cha bei ndogo zaidi?* do you have other cheap**er**? Or, using **kabisa**, thoroughly, for a superlative e.g. *tunda hili ni tamu kabisa*, this fruit is absolutely sweet.

4.4 Practice: Adjectives

Answers to the previous practice of section 3.12 Practice: Nouns:

Swahili Singular	English	Group	Swahili Plural
ajali	accident	xFV	*ajali*
asumini	jasmine	xFF	*maasumini*
bamia	okra	xFV	(same)
banda	barn	xFF	*mabanda*
chumba	room	T	*vyumba*
chumvi	salt	xFV	(same)
chungwa	orange	xFF	*machungwa*
chura	frog	T	*vyura*
dafu	unripe coconut	xFF	*madafu*
dawa	medicine	xFF	*madawa*
dudu	insect (big)	xFF	*madudu*
embe	mango	xFF	*maembe*

Swahili Singular	English	Group	Swahili Plural
eneo	area, place	**xFF**	*maeneo*
fedha	money	**xFV**	(same)
fisi	hyena	**xFV**	(same)
gari	vehicle	**xFF**	*magari*
habari	news, info	**xFV**	(same)
haragwe	bean	**xFF**	*maharagwe*
idara	govt. dept.	**xFV**	(same)
inzi	fly	**xFF**	*mainzi*
jua	sun	**xFF**	*majua*
kasuku	parrot	**xFV**	(same)
kidudu	insect (small)	**T**	*vidudu*
kitunguu	onion	**T**	*vitunguu*
kuimba	singing	**GERUND**	(same)
limau	lemon	**xFF**	*malimau*
mahali	place	**PLACE**	(same)
mbamia	okra plant	**V**	*mibamia*
mbuga	open terrain	**xFV**	*mbuga*
mchukuzi	porter	**Pp**	*wachukuzi*
mdudu	insect	**Pp**	*wadudu*
neno	word	**xFF**	*maneno*
njia	way, road	**xFV**	(same)

Swahili Singular	English	Group	Swahili Plural
orodha	list	**xFV**	(same)
papai	papaya, pawpaw	**xFF**	*mapapai*
pasi	clothes iron	**xFV**	(same)
ramani	map	**xFV**	(same)
saa	time, watch	**xFV**	(same)
simba	lion	**xFV**	(same)
twiga	giraffe	**xFV**	(same)
ufunguo	key	**U**	*funguo*
vazi	clothing	**xFF**	*mavazi*
yai	egg	**xFF**	*mayai*
zabibu	grape	**xFF**	*mazabibu*
ziwa	lake	**xFF**	*maziwa*

chora, draw: ***mchoro***, drawing [example]
kijiji, village: ***mkijiji***, villager [*m*-]
refu, tall: ***urefu***, height [*u*-]
shona, to sew: ***mshoni***, tailor [*m*-, -*i*]
Amerika: ***Mwamerika***, American [*Mw*-]

bicycle: ***baisikeli*** [example]
calendar: ***kalenda***
garage: ***gereji***
mile: ***maili***
police: ***polisi***
post office: ***posta***
receipt: ***risiti***
torch: ***tochi***

Practice:

Knowing the groups that the nouns in the above table belong to and their adjectival prefixes learnt in this chapter, use that to fill in the blank spaces the prefixes of three adjectives (listed below) in the singular and plural adjective columns below. This is a subset of the above nouns, but they do cover all the noun groups. An **example** is given for the first entry.

[The correct answers are given at the beginning of the next Practice section.]

dogo, small
ingine, (an)other
ema, good

Singular	Sing. Adj.	Plural	Plur. Adj.
bamia	**n**dogo	bamia	**n**dogo
	nyingine		**ny**ingine
	njema		**nj**ema
chumba	__dogo	vyumba	__dogo
	__ingine		__ingine
	__ema		__ema
chungwa	__dogo	machungwa	__dogo
	__ingine		__ingine
	__ema		__ema
dawa	__dogo	madawa	__dogo
	__ingine		__ingine
	__ema		__ema
kitunguu	__dogo	vitunguu	__dogo
	__ingine		__ingine

Singular	Sing. Adj.	Plural	Plur. Adj.
	__ema		__ema
kuimba	__dogo	kuimba	__dogo
	__ingine		__ingine
	__ema		__ema
mahali	__dogo	mahali	__dogo
	__ingine		__ingine
	__ema		__ema
mbamia	__dogo	mibamia	__dogo
	__ingine		__ingine
	__ema		__ema
mdudu	__dogo	wadudu	__dogo
	__ingine		__ingine
	__ema		__ema
ramani	__dogo	ramani	__dogo
	__ingine		__ingine
	__ema		__ema
ufunguo	__dogo	funguo	__dogo
	__ingine		__ingine
	__ema		__ema

Write in the space provided below the adjectives corresponding to the given words, as per the suggestion in square brackets:

nguvu, strength: **_mwenye nguvu_**, strong [example]

akili, intelligence: _____, intelligent; [use **mwenye**, having]

akili, intelligence:_____, dumb [use **bila**, without]

rangi, colour: _____, coloured [use -**a**, of]

sumbua, to annoy: _____, annoying [use -**fu**]

potea, to lose: _____, lost [use relative -**o**; this is difficult at this stage]

Use -**a**, of, and nouns converted into adverbs using **ki-**, to make up the following adjectives: [Look up the nouns below in the Eng-Swa Dictionary in Volume 3]

-*a kitaifa*, national [example, using noun: *taifa*, nation]

-*a ki*_____, international [use the above noun in plural]

-*a ki*_____, cultural [use noun: culture]

-*a ki*_____, religious [use noun: religion]

-*a ki*_____, traditional [use noun: tradition]

-*a ki*_____, current, modern [use adverb: now]

5 Verbs

Vitenzi hupambwa sana!

Verbs are much 'decorated'!

Now that we have seen singular and plural noun and corresponding adjectival prefixes, we are ready to tackle the Swahili grand-daddy of prefixes, infixes and suffixes (attachments in general): verb construction! If attaching a prefix to a noun or an adjective is akin to say attaching a yellow sticky note, then verb construction is akin to decorating a Christmas tree! Not surprisingly then, more than half the grammar text of this book concerns verbs!

In Swahili, verb construction is different from that in English. It is constructed by loading it with many grammatical attachments. [And some advice is in order here: After learning the processes described herein, whenever a constructed verb is encountered, it is very important to de-construct it (i.e. parse it, break it down) into its component prefixes, etc and its verb base and then to understand and describe each until this process becomes second nature. And as these packed verbs roll off your tongue you will experience the sound beauty (pun intended) of Swahili.]

Verbs are conjugated in Swahili by attaching prefixes, etc to verb bases. As in English, Swahili verbs in their infinitive forms are of the format "**to** verb- base" e.g. *kutosha*, **to** suffice, where the *ku* stands for the English "**to**" and *tosha* is the verb base. We use this verb base, *tosha*, to illustrate the conjugations below. Note: verbs in the Dictionary (in Volumes 2 and 3) are given in their BASE form (similar to English dictionaries) e.g. *tosha* is listed, not *kutosha*.

The following sections describe the various Swahili prefixes, etc that get attached to this verb base:

5.1 Tenses & Pronouns

The tense prefixes that are appended to a verb base are as follows [plus examples in square brackets]:

Present tense: **na-** [**na**tosha, suffices]

Past tense: **li-** [**li**tosha, sufficed]

Future tense: **ta-** [**ta**tosha, will suffice]

Present perfect tense: **me-** [**me**tosha, has sufficed]

Timeless* tense: **a-** [**a**tosha, suffices] *Using this tense, if we say "A tomato suffices" it means it always suffices, not just now but all the time, such as say called for in a recipe.

5.1.1 Pronoun Prefixes

The equivalent of she / he / it / they is prefixed to the verb base *tosha*, suffice, after attaching the above tense prefix. These prefixes, which are specific to each of the eight noun groupings, are given in **bold** below [with examples of the present tense underlined which is independent of the noun groupings and thus is always -_na_-.]:

PEOPLE [Pp]: *Mtu-Watu*, person(s)

> **a-**, she / he. [**a**_na_tosha, she / he suffices]
>
> **wa-**, they. [**wa**_na_tosha, they suffice]
>
> The above are 3rd person conjugations. The 1st person conjugations are:
>
> **ni-**, I. [**ni**_na_tosha, I suffice]
>
> **tu-**, we. [**tu**_na_tosha, we suffice]
>
> The 2nd person conjugations are:
>
> **u-**, you (singular). [**u**_na_tosha, you suffice]

m-, you (plural). [*mnatosha*, you suffice]

VEGETATION [V]: *Mti-Miti*, tree(s)

u-, it. [*unatosha*, it suffices]

i-, they. [*inatosha*, they suffice]

MIX+FLOWERS, FRUITS [xFF]: *Tunda-Matunda, fruit(s)*

li-, it. [*linatosha*, it suffices]

ya-, they. [*yanatosha*, they suffice]

Animates, regardless of the noun groupings they belong to, use the pronoun prefixes of PEOPLE [Pp]:

a-, they. [*anatosha*, it (e.g. *kobe*, a tortoise) suffices]

wa-, they. [*wanatosha*, they (e.g. *makobe*, tortoises) suffice]

THINGS [T]: *Kitu-Vitu*, things(s)

ki-, it. [*kinatosha*, it suffices]

vi-, they. [*vinatosha*, they suffice]

Animates, regardless of the noun groupings they belong to, use the pronoun prefixes of PEOPLE [Pp]:

a-, they. [*anatosha*, it (e.g. *kiboko*, a hippo) suffices]

wa-, they. [*wanatosha*, they (e.g. *kiboko*, hippos) suffice]

MIX+FAUNA, VEGGIES [xFV]: *Nyanya-Nyanya*, tomato(es)

i-, it. [*inatosha*, it suffices]

zi-, they. [*zinatosha*, they suffice]

Animates, regardless of the noun groupings they belong to, use the pronoun prefixes of PEOPLE [Pp]:

a-, they. [*anatosha*, it (e.g. *mbwa*, a dog) suffices]

wa-, they. [*wanatosha*, they (e.g. *mbwa*, dogs) suffice]

U-WORDS [U]: *Utenzi-Tenzi*, poem(s)

> **u-**, it. [**u**<u>na</u>tosha, it suffices]

> **zi-**, they. [**zi**<u>na</u>tosha, they suffice]

PLACE-ADVERBS [Pl]: *Mahali- Mahali*, place(s)

> ***pa-**, it. [**pa**<u>na</u>tosha, it suffices]

> ***pa-**, they. [**pa**<u>na</u>tosha, they suffice]

> ***pa** refers to a definite place [e.g. **the** place]. The PLACE-ADVERBS [Pl] group has two other pronouns: **ku-** referring to an unspecified or general place [e.g. **some** place], and **m-**referring to the interior of a place [e.g. **interior** space] e.g.

> [**ku**<u>na</u>tosha, it (e.g. some place) suffices]

> [**m**<u>na</u>tosha, it (e.g. interior space) suffices]

GERUNDS [G]: *Kusoma- Kusoma*, reading(s)

> **ku-**, it. [**ku**<u>na</u>tosha, it suffices]

> **ku-**, they. [**ku**<u>na</u>tosha, they suffice]

Other tenses

The other tenses are also conjugated in the same way as the above present tense [examples in square brackets]:

PEOPLE [Pp]: *Mtu-Watu*, person(s)

> Using pronouns: **a-**, she / he. **wa-**, they.

> [**a***tosha, he / she suffices] <u>Timeless</u> tense
> 　　*One of the two "*a*" in a-<u>a</u>tosha is dropped.

> Also, newspaper headlines typically use this tense e.g. *rais <u>a</u>sema uchumi unaendelea vizuri*, the president say<u>s</u> the economy is progressing well.

[*ali̱tosha*, she / he sufficed] Past tense

[*ata̱tosha*, she / he will suffice] Future tense

[*ame̱tosha*, she / he has sufficed] Present Perfect tense

[*w*a̱tosha*, they suffice] Timeless tense
> *One of the two "*a*" in *wa-a̱tosha* is dropped.

[*wali̱tosha*, they sufficed] Past tense

[*wata̱tosha*, they sufficed] Future tense

[*wame̱tosha*, they have sufficed] Present Perfect tense

The above are 3rd person conjugations. The 1st person conjugations are:

Using pronouns: *ni-*, I. *tu-*, we.

[*n*a̱tosha*, I suffice] Timeless tense

> *The -*i*- in *ni-a̱tosha* is euphoniously dropped.

[*nili̱tosha*, I sufficed] Past tense

> Swahili conversational usage frequently sees *na-* being used instead of the above *ni-* e.g. *nalitosha*.

[*nita̱tosha*, I will suffice] Future tense

[*nime̱tosha*, I have sufficed] Present Perfect tense

[*tw*a̱tosha*, we suffice] **Timeless** tense

> *The *tua̱*- sound is spelt *twa̱*-.

[*tuli̱tosha*, we sufficed] Past tense

[*tuta̱tosha*, we will suffice] Future tense

[*tume̱tosha*, we have sufficed] Present Perfect tense

The 2nd person conjugations are:

Using pronouns: *u-*, you (singular). *m-*, you (plural).

[*w***a*tosha, you suffice] <u>Timeless</u> tense

　　　*The *ua*- sound is spelt *wa*-.

[*u*litosha, you sufficed] <u>Past</u> tense

[*u*tatosha, you will suffice] <u>Future</u> tense

[*u*metosha, you have sufficed] <u>Present Perfect</u> tense

[*mw***a*tosha, you suffice] <u>Timeless</u> tense

　　　*The -w- is euphoniously added.

[*m*litosha, you sufficed] <u>Past</u> tense

[*m*tatosha, you will suffice] <u>Future</u> tense

[*m*metosha, you have sufficed] <u>Present Perfect</u> tense

VEGETATION [V]: *Mti-Miti*, tree(s)

Using pronouns: *u-*, it. *i-*, they.

[*mmea w***a*ota, a plant grows] <u>Timeless</u> tense

　　　*The *ua*- sound is spelt *wa*-.

[*mmea u*liota, the plant grew] <u>Past</u> tense

[*mmea u*taota, the plant will grow] <u>Future</u> tense

[*mmea u*meota, the plant has grown] <u>Present Perfect</u> tense

[*mimea y***a*ota, plants grow] <u>Timeless</u> tense

　　　*The *ia*- sound is spelt *ya*-.

[*mimea i*liota, the plants grew] <u>Past</u> tense

[*mimea i*taota, the plant will grow] <u>Future</u> tense

[*mimea i*meota, the plants have grown] <u>Present Perfect</u> tense

MIX+FLOWERS, FRUITS [xFF]: *Tunda-Matunda, fruit(s)*

Using pronouns: *li-*, it. *ya-*, they.

[*ua l*aota*, a flower grows] <u>Timeless</u> tense

> *The *–i-* in *li-aota* is euphoniously dropped.

[*ua liliota*, a flower grew] <u>Past</u> tense

[*ua litaota*, a flower will grow] <u>Future</u> tense

[*ua limeota*, a flower has grown] <u>Present Perfect</u> tense

[*maua y*aota*, flowers grow] <u>Timeless</u> tense
> *One of the two "*a*" in *ya-atosha* is dropped.

[*maua yaliota*, flowers grew] <u>Past</u> tense

[*maua yataota*, flowers will grow] <u>Future</u> tense

[*maua yameota*, flowers have grown] <u>Present Perfect</u> tense

THINGS [T]: *Kitu-Vitu*, things(s)

Using pronouns: *ki-*, it. *vi-*, they.

[*kiatu ki*chakaa*, a shoe wears out] <u>Timeless</u> tense

> *The *–a-* in *ki-achakaa* is euphoniously dropped.

> [Note: if *-i-* was dropped, as is done elsewhere, the resulting *kachakaa* would be ambiguous as the *ka-* could be interpreted as a consecutive tense – see section 10.6 Immediate 2nd Verbs.]

> Usually though, *ch-*, it, is used e.g.

> [*kisu chakata*, the knife cuts]

[*kiatu kilichakaa*, a shoe wore out] <u>Past</u> tense

[*kiatu kitachakaa*, a shoe will wear out] <u>Future</u> tense

[*kiatu kimechakaa*, a shoe has worn out] <u>Present Perfect</u> tense

[*viatu v*achakaa*, shoes wear out] <u>Timeless</u> tense

*The –*i*- in *vi-achakaa* is euphoniously dropped.

Usually though, *vy*-, they, is used e.g.

[*visu vyakata*, the knives cut]

[*viatu vilichakaa*, shoes wore out] Past tense

[*viatu vitachakaa*, shoes will wear out] Future tense

[*viatu vimechakaa*, shoes have worn out] Present Perfect tense

MIX+FAUNA, VEGGIES [xFV]: *Nyanya-Nyanya*, tomato(es)

Using pronouns: *i*-, it. *zi*-, they.

[*mboga y*aota*, a vegetable grows] Timeless tense

*The *ia*- sound is spelt *ya*-.

[*mboga iliota*, a vegetable grew] Past tense

[*mboga itaota*, a vegetable will grow] Future tense

[*mboga imeota*, a vegetable has grown] Present Perfect tense

[*mboga z*aota*, vegetables grow] Timeless tense

*The –*i*- in *zi-aota* is euphoniously dropped.

[*mboga ziliota*, vegetables grew] Past tense

[*mboga zitaota*, vegetables will grow] Future tense

[*mboga zimeota*, vegetables have grown] Present Perfect tense

U-WORDS [U]: *Utenzi-Tenzi*, poem(s)

Using pronouns: *u*-, it. *zi*-, they.

[*ukuta w*alinda*, a wall protects] Timeless tense

*The *ua*- sound is spelt *wa*-.

[*ukuta ulilinda*, the wall protected] Past tense

[*ukuta utalinda*, the wall will protect] Future tense

[*ukuta u̲melinda*, the wall has protected] <u>Present Perfect</u> tense

[*kuta z*a̲linda*, walls protect] <u>Timeless</u> tense

>*The *-i-* in *zi-a̲linda* is euphoniously dropped.

[*kuta zil̲ilinda*, the walls protected] <u>Past</u> tense

[*kuta zit̲alinda*, the walls will protect] <u>Future</u> tense

[*kuta zim̲elinda*, the walls have protected] <u>Present Perfect</u> tense

PLACE-ADVERBS [Pl]: *Mahali- Mahali*, place(s)

Using pronouns: **pa**-, it, **pa**-, they, singular and plural being the same. Reminder: This noun group has two other pronouns: **ku**- (referring to an indefinite place as compared to **pa**- referring to a definite place) and **m**- (referring to the interior space). Also to be mindful of is that place-adverb suffix -**ni** can mean "at" / "in(side)" / etc. The place used in the example below, *nyumbani*, usually means "at home" or "indoors" but could be used to specifically refer to the interior space of a house in which case the pronoun **m**- is used.

[*nyumbani p*a̲pendeza*, indoors pleases] <u>Timeless</u> tense
>*One of the two "*a*" in *pa-a̲pendeza* is dropped.

[*nyumbani pal̲ipendeza*, indoors pleased] <u>Past</u> tense

[*nyumbani pat̲apendeza*, indoors will please] <u>Future</u> tense

[*nyumbani pam̲ependeza*, indoors has pleased] <u>Present Perfect</u> tense

GERUNDS [G]: *Kusoma- Kusoma*, reading(s)

Using pronouns: **ku**-, it, **ku**-, they, singular and plural being same.

[*kusema kw*a̲wasiliana*, speaking communicates] <u>Timeless</u> tense

>*The **ku̲**- sound is spelt **kwa̲**-.

[*kusema kul̲iwasiliana*, speaking communicated] <u>Past</u> tense [*kusema **ku**tawasiliana*, speaking will communicate] <u>Future</u> tense

[*kusema **ku**mewasiliana*, speaking has communicated] <u>Present Perfect</u> tense

5.1.2 Standalone Pronouns for Animates

Swahili also has standalone pronouns for animates, similar to the ones found in English, which can optionally *also* be used, redundantly, with the above pronoun prefixes. These are:

Yeye, she / he / it [the "it" in English would be referring to an animal which in Swahilii can belong to not only the PEOPLE [Pp] group but more commonly to MIX+FAUNA, VEGGIES [xFV] as well as other groups.]

Wao, they

Examples [in square brackets] in the present tense:

[***Yeye** anatosha*, she / he / it suffices]

[***Wao** wanatosha*, they suffice]

BUT note that the pronoun prefixes ***a-*** and ***wa-*** are usually still used even though the standalone pronouns make them redundant. Conversationally they are often dropped. In here we will not drop them for illustrative purposes.

People have additional pronouns, the 1st and 2nd person pronouns (the above are 3rd person pronouns) and they have their respective pronoun prefixes. These are [with examples in square brackets of the present tense]:

PEOPLE [Pp]: *Mtu-Watu*, person(s)

> ***Mimi***, I, the 1st person singular pronoun, with pronoun prefix *ni-*, previously given above.
> [***Mimi** ninatosha*, I suffice]

Wewe, you, the 2nd person singular pronoun, with pronoun prefix *u-*.
[*Wewe* unatosha, you suffice]

Sisi, we, the 1st person plural pronoun, with pronoun prefix *tu-*.
[*Sisi* tunatosha, we suffice]

Ninyi, you, the 2nd person plural pronoun, with pronoun prefix *m-*.
[*Ninyi* mnatosha, you suffice]

Again, note that the pronoun prefixes *ni-*, *u-*, *tu-* and *mn-* are used even though the standalone pronouns make them redundant.

Standalone demonstrative pronouns (e.g. for things) are tackled in section 7.4 Standalone Demonstrative Pronouns.

5.2   Practice: Verbs in Present Tense

Answers to the previous practice of section 4.4 Practice: Adjectives:

Singular	Sing. Adj.	Plural	Plur. Adj.
bamia	<u>nd</u>ogo	bamia	(same)
	<u>ny</u>ingine		(same)
	<u>nj</u>ema		(same)
chumba	<u>ki</u>dogo	vyumba	<u>vi</u>dogo
	<u>kin</u>gine		<u>vin</u>gine
	<u>ch</u>ema		<u>vy</u>ema
chungwa	dogo	machungwa	<u>ma</u>dogo
	<u>j</u>ingine		<u>me</u>(i)ngine
	<u>j</u>ema		<u>me</u>ma
dawa	dogo	madawa	<u>ma</u>dogo

Singular	Sing. Adj.	Plural	Plur. Adj.
	*j*ingine		*me(i)*ngine
	*j*ema		*m*ema
kitunguu	*ki*dogo	vitunguu	*vi*dogo
	*ki*ngine		*vi*ngine
	*ch*ema		*vy*ema
kuimba	*ku*dogo	kuimba	(same)
	*kw*ingine		(same)
	*kw*ema		(same)
mahali	*pa*dogo	mahali	(same)
	*pe(i)*ngine		(same)
	*p*ema		(same)
mbamia	*m*dogo	mibamia	*mi*dogo
	*mw*ingine		*mi*ngine
	*mw*ema		*my*ema
mdudu	*m*dogo	wadudu	*wa*dogo
	*mw*ingine		*we(i)*ngine
	*mw*ema		*w*ema
ramani	*n*dogo	ramani	(same)
	*ny*ingine		(same)
	*nj*ema		(same)
ufunguo	*m*dogo	funguo	*n*dogo
	*mw*ingine		*ny*ingine

Singular	Sing. Adj.	Plural	Plur. Adj.
	**mw**ema		_**nj**ema_

nguvu, strength: _**mwenye** nguvu_, strong [example]
akili, intelligence: _**mwenye** akili, intelligent;_ [use _**mwenye**_]
akili, intelligence: _**bila** akili, dumb_ [use _**bila**_]
rangi, colour: _- **a** rangi, coloured_ [use -_**a**_]
sumbua, to annoy: _sumbu**fu**, annoying_ [use -_**fu**_]
potea, to lose: _-li-**o**potea, lost_ [use relative -_**o**_; this is difficult at this stage]
-_a ki**taifa**_, national [this is an example; _taifa_, nation]
-_a ki**mataifa**_, international [use the above noun in plural]
-_a ki**utamaduni**_, cultural
-_a ki**dini**_, religious
-_a ki**jadi**_, traditional
-_a ki**sasa**_, current, modern

Practice:

Fill in the blank spaces the prefixes to two numeric adjectives (listed below) in the adjective column below. Fill in the blank spaces the pronoun and present tense prefixes of the verb (listed below). An **example** is provided for the first entry.

[The correct answers are given at the beginning of the next Practice section.]

moja, one
tano, five
kutosha, to suffice
e.g. singular: _kiti **ki**moja **kina**tosha_, plural: _viti **vi**tano **vina**tosha_

Noun	Adjective	Verb
bamia	__moja	_**ina**tosha_
bamia	__tano	__tosha
chumba	__moja	__tosha

Noun	Adjective	Verb
vyumba	__tano	__tosha
chungwa	__moja	__tosha
machungwa	__tano	__tosha
kuimba	__moja	__tosha
kuimba	__tano	__tosha
mahali	__moja	__tosha
mahali	__tano	__tosha
mbamia	__moja	__tosha
mibamia	__tano	__tosha
mdudu	__moja	__tosha
wadudu	__tano	__tosha
ufunguo	__moja	__tosha
funguo	__tano	__tosha

5.3   Practice: Verbs in Other Tenses

Answers to the previous practice of section 5.2 Practice: Verbs in Present Tense:

Noun	Adjective	Verb
bamia	moja	**ina**tosha
bamia	tano	**zina**tosha
chumba	**ki**moja	**kina**tosha

Noun	Adjective	Verb
vyumba	**vi**tano	**vina**tosha
chungwa	moja	**lina**tosha
machungwa	**ma**tano	**yana**tosha
kuimba	**ku**moja	**kuna**tosha
kuimba	**ku**tano	**kuna**tosha
mahali	**pa**moja	**pana**tosha
mahali	**pa**tano	**pana**tosha
mbamia	**m**moja	**una**tosha
mibamia	**mi**tano	**ina**tosha
mdudu	**m**moja	**ana**tosha
wadudu	**wa**tano	**wana**tosha
ufunguo	**m**moja	**una**tosha
funguo	tano	**zina**tosha

Practice:

Instead of the present tense infix in the above, fill in the blank spaces the tense infix as indicated below in square brackets. An **example** is given for the first entry.

[The correct answers are given at the beginning of the next Practice section.]

Noun	Adjective	Verb
bamia	moja	*ita*tosha [future]

Noun	Adjective	Verb
bamia	tano	zi_tosha [future]
chumba	kimoja	ki_tosha [past]
vyumba	vitano	vi_tosha [past]
chungwa	moja	li_tosha [present perfect]
machungwa	matano	ya_tosha [present perfect]
kuimba	kumoja	ku_tosha [future]
kuimba	kutano	ku_tosha [future]
mahali	pamoja	pa_tosha [past]
mahali	patano	pa_tosha [past]
mbamia	mmoja	u_tosha [present perfect]
mibamia	mitano	i_tosha [present perfect]
mdudu	mmoja	a_tosha [past]
wadudu	watano	wa_tosha [past]

Noun	Adjective	Verb
ufunguo	mmoja	u_tosha [future]
funguo	tano	zi_tosha [future]
ua	moja	l_tosha [timeless]
maua	matano	y_tosha [timeless]

5.4 Negatives

To form the negative of a verb, the conjugated verb is prefixed with **ha-**, plus the following changes:

- in the negative **present** tense, the tense prefix -na- shown in the positive examples above is DROPPED and the final 'a' of a verb is changed to 'i'; this negative is also the **same for** the negative of the **timeless** tense; [foreign verbs mostly do not end in 'a', thus their final vowels are not changed e.g. *faulu*, succeed, in the negative present or timeless tense is *hafaulu*, he does not succeed]
- in the negative **past** tense, the tense infix is -**ku**- instead of the -li- shown in the positive examples above;
- in the negative **present perfect** tense, the tense infix is -**ja**- instead of the -me- shown in the positive examples above.

For example:

PEOPLE [Pp]: *Mtu-Watu*, person(s)

> [**hatoshi***, she / he does not suffice] Present & Timeless
> *One of the two 'a' in *ha-atoshi* is euphoniously dropped

[*hawatoshi*, they suffice] Present & Timeless

[*hakutosha**, she / he did not suffice] Past
*One of the two '*a*' in *ha-akutosha* is euphoniously dropped

[*hawakutosha*, they did not suffice] Past

[*hatatosha**, she / he will not suffice] Future
*One of the two '*a*' in *ha-atatosha* is euphoniously dropped

[*hawatatosha*, they will not suffice] Future

[*hajatosha**, she / he has not yet sufficed] Present Perfect
*One of the two '*a*' in *ha-ajatosha* is euphoniously dropped

[*hawajatosha*, they have not yet sufficed] Present Perfect

Note: This PEOPLE [Pp] group's 1st and 2nd person singular have negative prefixes which are DIFFERENT from the above *ha-* prefixes. These are **si-** and **hu-**, respectively, as follows:

[*sitoshi*, I don't suffice] Present & Timeless

[*sikutosha*, I didn't suffice] Past

[*sitatosha*, I won't suffice] Future

[*sijatosha*, I have not yet sufficed] Present Perfect

[*hutoshi*, you don't suffice] Present & Timeless

[*hukutosha*, you didn't suffice] Past

[*hutatosha*, you won't suffice] Future

[*hujatosha*, you have not yet sufficed] Present Perfect

The 1st and 2nd person plurals follow the normal **ha-** rule viz.

[*hatutoshi*, we don't suffice] Present & Timeless

[*hatukutosha*, we didn't suffice] Past

[*hatutatosha*, we won't suffice] Future

[*hatujatosha*, we haven't yet sufficed] Present Perfect

[*hamtoshi*, you don't suffice] Present & Timeless

[*hamkutosha*, you didn't suffice] Past

[*hamtatosha*, you won't suffice] Future

[*hamjatosha*, you haven't yet sufficed] Present Perfect

VEGETATION [V]: *Mti-Miti*, tree(s)

[*hautoshi*, it does not suffice] Present & Timeless

[*haukutosha*, it did not suffice] Past

[*hautatosha*, it will not suffice] Future

[*haujatosha*, it has not yet sufficed] Present Perfect

[*haitoshi*, they do not suffice] Present & Timeless

[*haikutosha*, they did not suffice] Past

[*haitatosha*, they will not suffice] Future

[*haijatosha*, they have not yet sufficed] Present Perfect

MIX+FLOWERS, FRUITS [xFF]: *Tunda-Matunda*, fruit(s)

[*halitoshi*, it does not suffice] Present & Timeless

[*halikutosha*, it did not suffice] Past

[*halitatosha*, it will not suffice] Future

[*halijatosha*, it has not yet sufficed] Present Perfect

[*hayatoshi*, they do not suffice] Present & Timeless

[*hayakutosha*, they did not suffice] Past

[*hayatatosha*, they will not suffice] Future

[*hayajatosha*, they have not yet sufficed] Present Perfect

THINGS [T]: *Kitu-Vitu*, things(s)

[*hakitoshi*, it does not suffice] Present & Timeless

[*hakikutosha*, it did not suffice] Past

[*hakitatosha*, it will not suffice] Future

[*hakijatosha*, it has not yet sufficed] Present Perfect

[*havitoshi*, they do not suffice] Present & Timeless

[*havikutosha*, they did not suffice] Past

[*havitatosha*, they will not suffice] Future

[*havijatosha*, they have not yet sufficed] Present Perfect

MIX+FAUNA, VEGGIES [xFV]: Nyanya-Nyanya, tomato(es)

[*haitoshi*, it does not suffice] Present & Timeless

[*haikutosha*, it did not suffice] Past

[*haitatosha*, it will not suffice] Future

[*haijatosha*, it has not yet sufficed] Present Perfect

[*hazitoshi*, they do not suffice] Present & Timeless

[*hazikutosha*, they did not suffice] Past

[*hazitatosha*, they will not suffice] Future

[*hazijatosha*, they have not yet sufficed] Present Perfect

U-WORDS [U]: Utenzi-Tenzi, poem(s)

[*hautoshi*, it does not suffice] Present & Timeless

[*haukutosha*, it did not suffice] Past

[*hautatosha*, it will not suffice] Future

[*haujatosha*, it has not yet sufficed] Present Perfect

[*hazitoshi*, they do not suffice] Present & Timeless

[*hazikutosha*, they did not suffice] Past

[*hazitatosha*, they will not suffice] Future

[*hazijatosha*, they have not yet sufficed] Present Perfect

PLACE-ADVERBS [Pl]: Mahali- Mahali, place(s)

[*hapatoshi*, it/they does/do not suffice] Present & Timeless

[*hapakutosha*, it/they did not suffice] Past

[*hapatatosha*, it/they will not suffice] Future

[*hapajatosha*, it/they has/have not yet sufficed] Present Perfect

-*pa*- refers to a specific place, -*ku*- to an indefinite place and -*m*- to an interior space (-*ku*- and -*m*- are not shown above but are easily used by replacing -*pa*- with them)

GERUNDS [G]: Kusoma- Kusoma, reading(s)

[*hakutoshi*, it/they does/do not suffice] Present & Timeless

[*hakukutosha*, it/they did not suffice] Past

[*hakutatosha*, it/they will not suffice] Future

[*hakujatosha*, it/they has/have not yet sufficed] Present Perfect

5.5   Practice: Verbs in Negative Sense

Answers to the previous practice of section 5.3 Practice: Verbs in Other Tenses:

Noun	Adjective	Verb
bamia	moja	*ita̱tosha* [future]
bamia	tano	*zita̱tosha* [future]
chumba	kimoja	*kili̱tosha* [past]

Noun	Adjective	Verb
vyumba	vitano	vi*li*tosha [past]
chungwa	moja	li**me**tosha [present perfect]
machungwa	matano	ya**me**tosha [present perfect]
kuimba	kumoja	ku**ta**tosha [future]
kuimba	kutano	ku**ta**tosha [future]
mahali	pamoja	pa*li*tosha [past]
mahali	patano	pa*li*tosha [past]
mbamia	mmoja	u**me**tosha [present perfect]
mibamia	mitano	i**me**tosha [present perfect]
mdudu	mmoja	a*li*tosha [past]
wadudu	watano	wa*li*tosha [past]
ufunguo	mmoja	u**ta**tosha [future]
funguo	tano	zi**ta**tosha [future]

Noun	Adjective	Verb
ua	moja	l**a**tosha [timeless]
maua	matano	y**a**tosha [timeless]

Practice:

For the same set of sentences previously used change them to their negative senses by filling in the blank spaces. An **example** is given for the first entry.

[The correct answers are given at the beginning of the next Practice section.]

Noun	Adjective	Verb (negative)
bamia	moja	**haita**tosha [future]
bamia	tano	____tosha [future]
chumba	kimoja	____tosha [past]
vyumba	vitano	____tosha [past]
chungwa	moja	____tosha [present perfect]
machungwa	matano	____tosha [present perfect]
kuimba	kumoja	____tosha [future]

Noun	Adjective	Verb (negative)
kuimba	kutano	____tosha [future]
mahali	pamoja	____tosha [past]
mahali	patano	____tosha [past]
mbamia	mmoja	____tosha [present perfect]
mibamia	mitano	____tosha [present perfect]
mdudu	mmoja	____tosha [past]
wadudu	watano	____tosha [past]
ufunguo	mmoja	____tosha [future]
funguo	tano	____tosha [future]
ua	moja	____toshi [present, timeless]
maua	matano	____toshi [present, timeless]

5.6   Hu- Routine Conjugation

To state a routine action Swahili has a very simple construction as follows:

hu- + verb-base

for ALL noun-groups and for ALL tenses, that is no prefixes nor pronouns nor tense infixes need be attached! For example, using the verbs

pita, pass
oga, bathe

hupita kila siku, I / we / it / they / etc [will] [have] pass[ed] by everyday
But to be explicit:
*magari **hu**pita kila siku*, cars [will] [have] pass[ed] by everyday

huoga kila siku, I / we / it / they / etc [will] [have] bathe[d] everyday
But to be explicit:
*sisi **hu**oga kila siku*, we [will] [have] bathe[d] everyday

Negatives:

The negatives of this conjugation is the same as the negative timeless which is the same as the negative present (section 5.4 Negatives) e.g.

halipiti kila siku, it does not pass every day
haogi kila siku, he does not bathe every day

5.7   Practice: Verbs in Timeless & Routine Tenses

Answers to the previous practice of section 5.5 Practice: Verbs in Negative Sense:

Noun	Adjective	Verb
bamia	moja	**haita**tosha [negative future]
bamia	tano	**hazita**tosha [negative future]
chumba	kimoja	**hakiku**tosha [past]

Noun	Adjective	Verb
vyumba	vitano	**haviku**tosha [past]
chungwa	moja	**halija**tosha [present perfect]
machungwa	matano	**hayaja**tosha [present perfect]
kuimba	kumoja	**hakuta**tosha [future]
kuimba	kutano	**hakuta**tosha [future]
mahali	pamoja	**hapaku**tosha [past]
mahali	patano	**hapaku**tosha [past]
mbamia	mmoja	**hauja**tosha [present perfect]
mibamia	mitano	**haija**tosha [present perfect]
mdudu	mmoja	**haku**tosha [past]
wadudu	watano	**hawaku**tosha [past]
ufunguo	mmoja	**hauta**tosha [future]
funguo	tano	**hazita**tosha [future]

Noun	Adjective	Verb
ua	moja	**hali**toshi [present, timeless]
maua	matano	**haya**toshi [present, timeless]

Practice:

Now for an easy* practice: Fill in the following: [An **example** is provided for the first one]

*Easy because it does not require a tense infix, just one prefix which is your only quest here :-)

[The correct answers are given at the beginning of the next Practice section.]

Chungwa **_la_**tosha, an orange always suffices [timeless]

Machungwa ___tosha, oranges always suffice [timeless]

Mahali ___tosha, the places have always been sufficient [timeless]

Chumba ___tosha, the room was always sufficient [routine past]

Vyumba ___tosha, rooms will always be sufficient [routine future]

Mahali ___tosha, the places will always be sufficient [routine future]

5.8   Verb Transformations

In Swahili, active verbs can be transformed into related verbs as explained in the table below. [It should be noted though that there are verbs that are say of a Stative type but for which there are no related Active types from which they would have been transformed e.g. *choka*, be tired, is a Stative verb with no corresponding Active form. Also, a verb ending in say *-ka* (see Stative verb in the table below) does not necessarily mean it is a Stative verb e.g. *peleka*, send, is an Active not Stative verb.]

Active verb	This is where the subject is the verb-actor acting on an implicit or explicit object, or on the subject itself. When an object is mentioned it makes the verb transitive, otherwise it is intransitive. This is the most basic form of a verb which is transformed into different types as explained below.
E.g. *penda*, like. *Mwanamke anapenda nguo*, the woman likes clothes.	
E.g. *funga*, close. *Mlinzi anafunga mlango*, the watchman is closing the door.	
Passive verb **[-w-]**	With this type of verb there is a role reversal between the subject and object of an active verb: what was the object of the active verb becomes the verb-actor and its verb-action is 'action**ed**' on the subject of the active verb.
E.g. *pendwa*, be lik**ed**. *Mwanamke anapendwa na wote*, the woman is lik**ed** by all.	
E.g. *fungwa*, be clos**ed**. *Mlango unafungwa na mlinzi*, the door is being clos**ed** by the watchman. *Mlango imefungwa na mlinzi*, the door has been clos**ed** by the watchman. *Mlango ulifungwa na mlinzi*, the door was clos**ed** by the watchman. A slight variation: from **fungia*, tie up/with, we get *fungiwa*, be tied e.g. *mwizi anafungiwa na askari*, the thief is being ti**ed** up (i.e. handcuff**ed**) by the policeman. [*This is a verb with a preposition -*i*-	

embedded in it, which is dealt with in section 10.2.1 Embedded Prepositions.]

Occasionally, -*man*- is used (instead of the -*w*- in the above examples) e.g. *unga*, join. *Mfupa uliovunjika umeungamana*, the broken bone has set. [Note: a euphonious -*a*- has been inserted.]

Stative verb [-*k*-]	This type of verb describes a state / condition / relation such as by words ending in ~able / ~ing / ~ful / ~ent as in the examples below. But in certain usage it bears a grammatical resemblance to the Passive verb with the key difference being stative verbs do not give the cause of the condition, as seen in an example below*.

E.g. *pendeka*, be likable. *Mwanamke anapendeka*, the woman is likable. [Note: a euphonious -*e*- has been inserted.]

E.g. *fungika*, be closable. *Mlango unafungika*, the door is closable. [Note: a euphonious -*i*- has been inserted.] If a tense other than the present is used e.g. present perfect -*me*- the meaning is as follows: *Mlango umefungika*, the door has become clos**ed**, which grammatically resembles a Passive type but where it does not resemble it is that the <u>cause</u> of the resultant state is not given which a passive verb does (*Mlango umefungwa na mlinzi*, the door was clos**ed** <u>by the watchman</u>). A past tense example: *Mlango ulifungika*, the door became clos**ed**. The above present tense example can also be translated in the same way e.g. *mlango unafungika*, the door is being clos**ed**.

Sometimes a <u>euphonious</u> -*an*- is inserted in addition to the one added above (-*e*-) e.g. *weza*, be able to: *Kurudi kesho kunawezekana?* To return tomorrow is doable/possible?

Causal verb [-*sh*- or -*z*-]	Here the subject <u>causes</u> the object to verb-act e.g. they are causing the tree to fall, that is they are felling the tree, which involves usage of words like "cause", "make", "let", "asked", etc.

E.g. *pendeza*, make likable. *Nguo zinampend<u>e</u>za mwanamke*, clothes make the woman attractive. [Note: a euphonious -<u>e</u>- has been inserted. Also -*m*- is a 3rd person singular object reference, to be dealt with in section 10.1 Embedded Object References.]

E.g. *fung<u>i</u>za*, make shut. *Upepo unaufung<u>i</u>za mlango*, the wind is making the door shut. [Note: a euphonious -<u>i</u>- has been inserted.]

E.g. *angua*, drop*: angusha*, fell. *Mlimaji aliangusha miti*, the farmer felled the trees.

A Causative verb can be made Causative-Passive by appending -**w** to the -*sh* e.g. Causative: *mlimaji anaangusha mti*, the farmer is felling the tree; Causative-Passive: *mti inaangushw**a** na mlimaji*, the tree is being felled by the farmer.

Reflexive verb [-*ji*-]	This involves the idea of ~self e.g. she teaches herself.

E.g. ***jipenda***, like oneself. *Mwanamke anajipenda*, the woman likes herself.

E.g. ***jifunga***, shut itself. *Mlango inajifunga*, the door shuts by itself.

Reciprocal verb [-*na*-]	This involves the idea of "one another" e.g. they teach each other.

E.g. *pendana*, like each other. *Mwanamke na mwanamume wanapendana*, the woman and the man like each other.

Antonym verb [-*u*-]	This type of verb has a meaning opposite to an active verb.

E.g. *funga*, close, *fungua*, open. *Mlinzi alifungua mlango*, the watchman opened the door.

Synonym verb **[-u-]**	This type of verb has the same meaning as an active verb!

E.g. *kama* or *kamua*, squeeze. *Msichana anakam(u)a ng'ombe*, the girl is milking the cow.

Interrogative verb **[-je, -pi]**	This type of verb converts an active verb to an interrogative "How" or "What".

E.g. *pendaje?*, like how? *Anapendaje?* How does she like (it)?

E.g. *fungaje?*, shut how? *Alifungaje?* How did he shut (it)?

E.g. *wezapi?*, be able to how? *Atawezapi?* How will he be able to?

E.g. *amejibuje?* What is his reply?

E.g. *nifanyeje?* What shall I do?

Note: foreign verbs which mostly do not end in -*a* are first made to be so before transforming e.g. *jibu,* reply: *kujibiana,* reply each other; an -*i*- is euphoniously added).

Tip: When analyzing a constructed verb, check if it ends in -*wa, -ka, -sha, -za, -je, -pi,* in which case it could be a transformed verb and, therefore, its entry in any dictionary will be found without the -*w-, -k-, -sh-, -z-, -je, -pi* (and without any attached prefix, infixes) e.g. *ashindwa,* where, by removing -*w-* (and the pronoun prefix *a-*), we end up with *shinda* which is found in the dictionary, meaning 'win or defeat', ergo *shindwa* would mean 'defeated'!

5.9   Practice: Verb Transformations

Answers to the previous practice of section 5.7 Practice: Verbs in Timeless & Routine Tenses:

Chungwa latosha, an orange always suffices [timeless]

*Machungwa **ya**tosha*, oranges always suffice [timeless]

*Mahali **pa**tosha*, the places have always been sufficient [timeless]

*Chumba **hu**tosha*, the room was always sufficient [routine]

*Vyumba **hu**tosha*, rooms will always be sufficient [routine]

*Mahali **hu**tosha*, the places will always be sufficient [routine]

Practice:

Fill in the blank spaces in the Transformed Verb column the transformation indicated in the Type of Transformation column below. An **example** is provided for the first entry.

[The correct answers are given at the beginning of the next Practice section.]

Noun or Pronoun	Transformed Verb	Type of Transformation
--	***Ulijua_je_?*** [jua, know] ["How did you know?"]	Interrogative
--	***Asema___?*** [sema, say] ["What does he say?"]	Interrogative
Msichana, the girl	***ana__funza*** [funza, teach] ["is learning/teaching herself"]	Reflexive
Kikombe, the cup	***kimevunj___a*** [vunja, break] ["it has become broken"]	Stative
Mtoto, the child	***aliangu___a*** [angua, drop] ["he fell"]	Stative
Kitabu, the book	***hakisome___i*** [soma, read]	Stative

Noun or Pronoun	Transformed Verb	Type of Transformation
	["it is not readable"]	
Njia, the road	**huend__a** [*enda*, go] ["it is driveable"]	Stative
Nyama, meat	**hupati__a** [*pata*, get] ["it is available"]	Stative
Mwalimu, the teacher	**aliniona__** [*ona*, see] ["he met me"]	Reciprocal
Mtu, the man	**atawa__a** [*waka*, blaze] ["he will set ablaze"; this is a little tricky]	Causative
Mtumishi, the servant	**anakunj__a** [*kunja*, fold] ["he is unfolding"]	Antonym
Mwizi, the thief	**alinyak__a** [*nyaka*, grab] ["he grabbed"]	Synonym
Mizigo, the luggage	**inachuku__a** [*chukua*, carry] ["they are being carried"]	Passive
Vitu, things	**vinavunj__a** [*vunja*, break] ["they are being broken"]	Passive

5.10 Imperatives

Imperative is the command form of a verb, addressed to a 2nd person, singular or plural. The transformation of the infinitive form of a verb (which in English has a 'to' in front of it, and in Swahili, a *ku-* prefix) to its infinitive form is the same in Swahili as in English, that is, the 'to' or *ku-* is dropped e.g. infinitive *kuchukua*, to carry, becomes imperative:

chukua, carry (addressed to a 2nd person singular)

It is a homonym of the verb base, only the moods are different. This form is for addressing a single person. For multiple people (2nd person plural), the ending of the verb *–a* is changed to an *-e*, which makes it a subjunctive form dealt with in section 10.5 Subjunctives, and a *–ni* is suffixed, which is a shortened form of the 2nd person plural standalone pronoun *ninyi*, you, dealt with in section 5.1.2 Standalone Pronouns for Animates e.g.

*chuku**eni***, carry (addressed to 2nd person plural)

But foreign verbs typically do not end in *–a* (a few do), in which case there is no change in its ending vowel and the suffix *–ni* is simply added to it e.g.

jaribu, try, becomes *jaribu**ni***

If an object is prefixed (covered below in section 10.1 Embedded Object References), the verb's ending *-a* is changed to *-e* e.g.

*ki**chuku**e* *kisu*, carry it the knife

where *ki-* is a direct object referring to *kisu*.

If the object inserted is an indirect object, a **prepositional** insert is required as per the rule below in section 10.2.1 Embedded Preposition e.g.

*ni**lete**e* *kisu*, bring **to** me the knife

where *ni-*, me, is the *indirect* object, the *-e-*, **to**, is the **prepositional** insert. Note that the direct object *ki-* (for *kisu*) is not used with a prepositioned verb.

If an object is inserted into foreign verbs, there is no change like the above '*a*' to '*e*' e.g. *jibu*, reply, with an object prefix is

*m**jibu*, answer him
*ni**jibu*, answer me

Similarly, for *fikiri*, think, *samehe*, forgive, *kubali*, agree, *dhani*, think, etc.

Negatives

Negation is achieved using the subjunctive form which is covered below in section 10.5 Subjunctives.

Oddities:

> *ka*, sit, imperative: *keti*, sit
>
> *ja*, come, imperative: *njo[o]*, come
>
> *kwenda*, go, imperative: *nenda*, go
>
> *leta*, bring, imperative: *lete*, bring.
>
> *pongeza*, congratulate, imperative: *hongera*, congratulations.

5.11 Practice: Imperatives

Answers to the previous practice of section 5.9 Practice: Verb Transformations:

Noun or Pronoun	Expression	Type of Transformation
--	*Ulijuaje?* [*jua*, know] ["How did you know?"]	Interrogative
--	*Asemaje?* [*sema*, say] ["What does he say?"]	Interrogative
Msichana, the girl	*anajifunza* [*funza*, teach] ["she is learning/teaching herself"]	Reflexive
Kikombe, the cup	*kimevunjika* [*vunja*, break] ["it has become broken"]	Stative

Noun or Pronoun	Expression	Type of Transformation
Mtoto, the child	**alianguka** [*angua*, drop] ["he fell"]	Stative
Kitabu, the book	**hakisomeki** [*soma*, read] ["it is not readable"]	Stative
Njia, the road	**huendeka** [*enda*, go] ["it is driveable"]	Stative
Nyama, meat	**hupatikana** [*pata*, get] ["it is available"]	Stative
Mwalimu, the teacher	**alinionana** [*ona*, see] ["he met me"]	Reciprocal
Mtu, the man	**atawasha** [*waka*, blaze] ["he will set ablaze"]	Causative
Mtumishi, the servant	**anakunjua** [*kunja*, fold] ["he is unfolding"]	Antonym
Mwizi, the thief	**alinyakua** [*nyaka*, grab] ["he grabbed"]	Synonym
Mizigo, the luggage	**inachukuliwa** [*chukua*, carry] ["they are being carried"]	Passive
Vitu, things	**vinavunjwa** [*vunja*, break] ["they are being broken"]	Passive

Practice:

Fill in the blank spaces in the Imperative column as per the English translations given in square brackets. An **example** is provided for the first entry.

[The correct answers are given at the beginning of the next Practice section.]

Verb	Imperative
amsha, awaken	<u>*Amsha*</u> *bwana* Abdallah ["Awaken Mr. Abdallah"]
fikiri, think	_____*i_ jinsi ya kufanya kazi* [*fanya*, do; *kazi*, work; the *-i-* preposition has been inserted for you as we have yet to cover it but it still is a bit tough as this stage – give it a try] ["Think of how to do the work"]
anza, begin	_____ *kusoma* ["Begin to read"]
kaa, sit	_____ ["Sit"]

5.12 Making Up Verbs

Logically, the verb-to-noun process above in section 3.12 Making Up Nouns and the verb-to-adjective process above in section 4.3 "Making Up Adjectives" can be applied in reverse to produce verbs e.g.

chimbo, pit: *chimba*, dig

baraka*, blessing: *bariki*, bless [Barack Obama's first name is derived from this! Note: native (Bantu) verbs end in -*a* but this being of foreign origin it ends in -*i*. But then see the next example!]

bahati, luck: *bahatisha*, guess [This uses Verb Transformation to make it a <u>causative</u> verb as explained in section 5.8 Verb Transformations.]

In addition to the above reverse processing, we have two-word constructions as follows:

ku(ji)ona usingizi, 'see (oneself)' sleep i.e. to feel sleepy

ku(ji)sikia vizuri, 'hear (oneself)' good i.e. to feel good

penda zaidi, prefer

piga, hit, +..., e.g. *piga shauri*, decide; *piga picha*, snap photo - more on *piga* and other wide-use verbs in Appendix C: Wide-use Verbs.

Using **katika**, in, e.g.

yumo katika matatizo, he is facing problems

5.13 Practice: Making Up Verbs

Answers to the previous practice of section 5.11 Practice: Imperatives:

Verb	Imperative
amsha, awaken	**_Amsha_** *bwana* Abdallah ["Awaken Mr. Abdallah"]
fikiri, think	**_Fikiria_** *jinsi ya kufanya kazi* [*fanya*, do; *kazi*, work; the -*i*- preposition has been inserted for you as we have yet to cover it but it still is a bit tough as this stage – give it a try] ["Think of how to do the work"]
anza, begin	**_anza_** *kusoma* ["Begin to read"]
kaa, sit	**_keti_**

	["Sit"]

Practice:

Fill in the blank spaces in the New Use column as per the English translations given in double quotes in square brackets. An **example** is provided for the first entry.

[The correct answers are given at the beginning of the next Practice section.]

Using	New Use
sikia, hear or *ona*, see	**Ninasikia** or **ninaona** *harufu* [*harufu*, smell] ["I smell"]
piga, hit	_____ *chafya* [*chafya*, sneeze] ["He is sneezing"]
chanuo, long-toothed comb	_____ *nywele* [*nywele*, hair] ["Comb hair (imperative)"]
tamaa, greed	_____ *sana* [*sana*, very much; you may want to seek the answer in the Swahili-English Dictionary (Volume 2)] ["He covets very much"]
fupi, short	_____ [use causative verb transformation] ["Shorten" (imperative)]

6 Adverbs

Adverbs <u>describe</u> how / where / when / etc a verb-action executes e.g. the moon is shining <u>nicely</u>. Basically there is nothing to it in Swahili: there are no prefixes to attach, they are used as found in the Dictionary (in Volumes 2 and 3).

There is also a generic adverb derived from adjective *zuri*, nice, by attaching **vi-** which is a prefix for the plurals of THINGS [T] used in a generic sense here e.g.

*mwezi unawasha **vi**zuri*, the moon is shining nicely

Locational adverbs: recall that the noun group PLACE-ADVERBS [Pl] includes adverbs formed by suffixing **-ni** e.g.

mna nguo sandukuni, there are clothes in the suitcase [*mna* is covered in section 10.9 Pana/Kuna/Mna, There is/are.]

Demonstratives (see below, chapter 7 Demonstratives) can be used as locational adverbs. These are:

hapa, here (specifically)
huku, here (generally)
humu, in here
pale, there (specifically)
kule, there (generally)
mle, in there

Examples:

kuja hapa, come here

nenda pale, go there

mna vitu humu, there are things in here

6.1 Making Up Adverbs

Ki- = -ly e.g.

kiutamaduni, culturally, from *utamaduni*, culture
kitoto, childishly, from *mtoto*, child
kifundi, expertly, from *mfundi*, artisan
kifupi, briefly, from *fupi*, short [an adjective cf. nouns above]
And, as a **simile**:
kiMuhammadAli, like/à la Muhammad Ali, or Muhammad Ali style
[More in Appendix F: Widely-used *Ki-* Prefix.]

Kwa, at / by / etc, e.g.
nitakuja kwa miguu, I will come on foot

An adjective can sometimes be used as an adverb. For example, adjective *sawa*, correct e.g.
hili ni* jibu sawa, this is the correct (adjective) answer
        *ni, is, is covered in section 10.7.2 Wa, be
jibu sawa, reply correctly (adverb)

Conversely, an adverb can sometimes be used as an adjective. For example,
adverb *chini*, down e.g.
weka chini, put (it) down (adverb)

yeye ni mtu mchini, he is a low / humble (adjective) person

Chini is also used as noun! For example,

hii ni chini, this is the downstairs; the preferred usage though is:

yeye ni mtu wa chini [see section 4.3 Making Up Adjectives]

6.2 Practice: Adverbs

Answers to the previous practice of section 5.13 Practice: Making Up Verbs:

Using	New Use
sikia, hear or *ona*, see	**Nasikia** or **Naona** *harufu* [*harufu*, smell] ["I smell"]
piga, hit	**Anapiga** *chafya* [*chafya*, sneeze] ["He is sneezing"]
chanuo, long-toothed comb	**Chana** *nywele* [*nywele*, hair] ["Comb hair (imperative)"]
tamaa, greed	**Anatamani** *sana* [*sana*, very much] ["He covets very much"]
fupi, short	**Fupisha** [use causative verb transformation] ["Shorten / Summarize" (imperative)]

Practice:

Fill in the blanks below to match the underlined word in the English translation. An **example** is provided for the first entry.

[The correct answers are given at the beginning of the next Practice section.]

*Vyombo vimeoshwa **kabisa***, the utensils have been <u>thoroughly</u> washed.

Kuna soko _____, there is a market <u>downtown</u>. _____ *hupatikana mazao mbalimbali*, <u>in there</u> a variety of produce is obtainable.

Anafanya kazi _____ *na* _____, he works <u>expertly</u> and <u>with effort</u>.

Kaka alifika _____, the elder brother arrived <u>yesterday</u>.

7 Demonstratives

Demonstratives are 'pointers' which point to items e.g. **this** (closer) or **that** (farther) thing.

7.1 Demonstrative Adjectives (closer)

The closer/nearby demonstratives "this" and "these" are constructed as follows:

h+<u>matching-vowel</u>+**pronoun-prefix**

where <u>matching-vowel</u> is a vowel same as that in the **pronoun-prefix** e.g. in the VEGETATION [V] group the **pronoun prefixes** are *u*- (singular) and *i*- (plural) from which we get the demonstratives *h*+<u>u</u>+*u* (this), *h*+<u>i</u>+*i* (these). Examples: [<u>descriptive</u> adjective precedes e.g. *mti <u>mrefu</u> huu*, this tall tree]

PEOPLE [Pp]: *Mtu-Watu*, person(s)

[*mtu h<u>u</u>**yu****, this person]

*this is an exception to the rule which would have resulted in *h*+<u>a</u>+*a*, but the use of a -**yu**- is quite common with the 3rd person singular

[*watu h<u>a</u>**wa***, these persons]

VEGETATION [V]: *Mti-Miti*, tree(s)

[*mti h<u>u</u>**u***, this tree]

[*miti h<u>i</u>**i***, these trees]

MIX+FLOWERS, FRUITS [xFF]: *Tunda-Matunda, fruit(s)*

[*tunda h<u>i</u>**li***, this fruit]

[*matunda h<u>a</u>**ya***, these fruits]

[Reminder: all animates use the rules of the PEOPLE [Pp] group e.g. *kobe huyu*, this tortoise; *makobe hawa*, these tortoises]

THINGS [T]: *Kitu-Vitu*, things(s)

[*kitu hiki*, this thing]

[*vitu hivi*, these things]

[Reminder: all animates use the rules of the PEOPLE [Pp] group e.g. *kifaru huyu*, this rhino; *vifaru hawa*, these rhinos]

MIX+FAUNA, VEGGIES [xFV]: *Nyanya-Nyanya*, tomato(es)

[*nyanya hii*, this tomato]

[*nyanya hizi*, these tomatoes]

[Reminder: all animates use the rules of the PEOPLE [Pp] group e.g. *mbwa huyu*, this dog; *mbwa hawa*, these dogs]

U-WORDS [U]: *Utenzi-Tenzi*, poem(s)

[*utenzi huu*, this poem]

[*tenzi hizi*, these poems]

PLACE-ADVERBS [Pl]: *Mahali- Mahali*, place(s)

[*mahali hapa*, this/these place(s)]

This noun group has two other forms: *huku* denoting a non-specific place, and *humu* denoting inside a place e.g. *mahali huku*, this/these place(s) speaking generally, *mahali humu*, this/these place(s) inside. Place words belonging outside of this noun group use the demonstratives of their own OR this group e.g. *dunia hii* or *dunia huku*, this world.

GERUNDS [G]: *Kusoma- Kusoma*, reading(s)

[*kusoma huku*, this/these reading(s)]

7.2   Demonstrative Adjectives (farther)

The farther demonstratives "that" and "those" are constructed in a simpler way than the above, as follows:

pronoun-prefix+*le* e.g.

ule, that, *ile*, those, in the VEGETATION [V] group,

lile, that, *yale*, those, in the MIX+FLOWERS, FRUITS [xFF] group.

[<u>descriptive</u> adjective precedes e.g. *mti <u>mrefu</u> ule*, that tall tree]

PEOPLE [Pp]: *Mtu-Watu*, person(s)

> [*mtu yule**, that person]

> *this is an exception to the rule which normally would have resulted in *a+le*, but the use of a *-yu-* is quite common with the 3rd person singular

> [*watu wale*, those persons]

VEGETATION [V]: *Mti-Miti*, tree(s)

> [*mti ule*, that tree]

> [*miti ile*, those trees]

MIX+FLOWERS, FRUITS [xFF]: *Tunda-Matunda, fruit(s)*

> [*tunda lile*, that fruit]

> [*matunda yale*, those fruits]

> [Reminder: all animates use the rules of the PEOPLE [Pp] group e.g. *kobe yule*, that tortoise; *makobe wale*, those tortoises]

THINGS [T]: *Kitu-Vitu*, things(s)

> [*kitu kile*, that thing]

> [*vitu vile*, those things]

> [Reminder: all animates use the rules of the PEOPLE [Pp] group e.g. *kifaru yule*, that rhino; *vifaru wale*, those rhinos]

MIX+FAUNA, VEGGIES [xFV]: *Nyanya-Nyanya*, tomato(es)

> [*nyanya ile*, that tomato]

> [*nyanya zile*, those tomatoes]

> [Reminder: all animates use the rules of the PEOPLE [Pp] group e.g. *mbwa yule*, that dog; *mbwa wale*, those dogs]

U-WORDS [U]: *Utenzi-Tenzi*, poem(s)

> [*utenzi ule*, that poem]

> [*tenzi zile*, those poems]

PLACE-ADVERBS [Pl]: *Mahali- Mahali*, place(s)

> [*mahali pale*, that/those place(s)]

This noun group has two other forms: *kule* denoting a non-specific place, and *mle* denoting inside a place e.g. *mahali kule*, that/those place(s) speaking generally, *mahali mle*, that/those place(s) inside.

GERUNDS [G]: *Kusoma- Kusoma*, reading(s)

> [*kusoma kule*, that/those reading(s)]

7.3 Specific Demonstrative (closer)

When "this" or "these" specifically refer to something such as a previously mentioned subject, the last letter is changed to *–o* e.g.

huu becomes *huo*, *hii* becomes *hiyo* in VEGETATION [V]
hili becomes *hilo*, *haya* becomes *hayo* in MIX+FLOWERS, FRUITS [xFF], etc.

Note the syllable change in THINGS [T]:

hiki becomes *hicho*, *hivi* becomes *hivyo*.

Examples for all noun groups:

[The examples in each of the noun groups below are given in two lines: first the regular demonstrative, second the specific demonstrative (referring to something previously mentioned). Both lines translate the same in English but when written the demonstratives can be differentiated by using either the normal or an alternative type style e.g. this person versus **this** person in the first example below.]

PEOPLE [Pp]

> [*mtu huyu*; *watu hawa*: this / these person(s)]
> [*mtu huyo*; *watu hao*: **this** / **these** person(s)]
> > [Notice '*hawo*' is spelt '*hao*'.]

VEGETATION [V]

> [*mti huu*; *miti hii*; this / these tree(s)]
> [*mti huo*; *miti hiyo*; **this** / **these** tree(s)]
> > [Notice '*hio*' is spelt '*hiyo*'.]

MIX+FLOWERS, FRUITS [xFF]

> [*tunda hili*; *matunda haya*; this / these fruit(s)]
> [*tunda hilo*; *matunda hayo*; **this** / **these** fruit(s)]

> [Reminder: all animates use the rules of the PEOPLE [Pp] group e.g. *kobe huyo*, this tortoise; *makobe hao*, these tortoises]

THINGS [T]

> [*kitabu hiki*; *vitabu hivi*: this / these book(s)]
> [*kitabu hicho*; *vitabu hivyo*: **this** / **these** book(s)]

> [Reminder: all animates use the rules of the PEOPLE [Pp] group e.g. *kifaru huyo*, this rhino; *vifaru hao*, these rhinos]

MIX+FAUNA, VEGGIES [xFV]

> [*nyanya hii*; *nyanya hizi*: this / these tomato(es)]
> [*nyanya hiyo*; *nyanya hizo*: **this** / **these** tomato(es)]
> > [Notice '*hio*' is spelt '*hiyo*'.]

[Reminder: all animates use the rules of the PEOPLE [Pp] group
e.g. *mbwa huyo*, this dog; *mbwa hao*, these dogs]

U-WORDS [U]

[*utenzi huu*; *tenzi hizi*: this / these poem(s)]
[*utenzi huo*; *tenzi hizo*: **this / these** poem(s)]

PLACE-ADVERBS [Pl]

[*mahali hapa* [*or *huku, humu*]: this / these place(s)]
[*mahali hapo* [*or *huko, humo*]: **this / these** place(s)]
*These refer to, respectively, a non-specific place (this may seem illogical since -*o* refers to something specifically mentioned before but that specific reference may be to a general place say a desert in general, thus e.g. *bila maji unaweza kufa mahali huko*, without water you can die in **this** place, referring to a desert in general) and the interior of a place. By usage, *huko* has come to meaning "some place over there somewhere" or simply "there".

GERUNDS [G]

[*kusoma huku*: this / these reading(s)]
[*kusoma huko*: **this / these** reading(s)]

7.4   Standalone Demonstrative Pronouns

The above demonstrative adjectives can be used as standalone pronouns, as in the following few examples (in timeless tense), shown only for a few of the noun groups since these pronouns are identical to their corresponding demonstrative adjectives and are easily (very mechanically) used:

[The pronouns are **bolded** but if the nouns enclosed in brackets () are used then these pronouns revert to their demonstrative sense, in both English and Swahili. Note: *ni*, is, and *si,* is not, used in these examples are covered in section 10.7.2 Wa, be]

PEOPLE [Pp]: *Mtu-Watu*, person(s)

[(*Mtu*) **huyu** *ni/si Ali*, this (person) is/is not Ali]

[(*Mtu*) **yule** *ni/si Ali*, that (person) is/is not Ali]

[(*Watu*) **hawa** *ni/si wapishi*, these (persons) are/are not cooks]

[(*Watu*) **wale** *ni/si wapishi*, those (persons) are/are not cooks]

VEGETATION [V]: *Mti-Miti*, tree(s)

[(*Mti*) **huu** *ni/si mzuri*, this (tree) is/is not nice]

[(*Mti*) **ule** *ni/si mzuri*, that (tree) is/is not nice]

[(*Miti*) **hii** *ni/si mizuri*, these (trees) are/are not nice]

[(*Miti*) **ile** *ni/si mizuri*, those (trees) are/are not nice]

PLACE-ADVERBS [Pl]

[(*Mahali*) **hapa** *ni/si pazuri*, this (place) is/is not nice]

[(*Mahali*) **pale** *ni/si pazuri*, that (place) is/is not nice]

[Plural is same as above.]

This noun group has two other forms: **huku** / **kule**, here / there denoting a non-specific place, and **humu** / **mle**, in here / there, denoting inside a place e.g. *huku*, this/these (place(s)) (speaking generally), *humu*, inside this/these (place(s)). By changing the last letter of the above pronouns to **–o** they then refer to something previously mentioned e.g. *huu ni soko la samaki; hum**o** hupatikana aina nyingi za samaki*, this is a fish market; in there many kinds of fish are obtainable.

Swahili usage often drops the *ni* e.g.

kile kizuri = kile ni kizuri, that is nice

7.5   Emphatic Demonstratives

Emphasis is achieved by <u>doubling a demonstrative adjective</u> e.g. to confirm something far:

Kitu <u>kilekile</u>, <u>that very</u> thing

The near case is emphasized by <u>doubling a subject pronoun</u> and prefixing it to the demonstrative pronoun e.g.

<u>*Kikihiki*</u>, <u>just</u> this

7.6   Summary: Demonstrative Adjectives, Pronouns, Adverbs

These are best summarized by examples, as follows:

[Note: *ni*, is, used in these examples is covered in section 10.7.2 Wa, be]

<u>Adjectives</u>

Kitu <u>hiki</u> ni kiti, <u>this</u> thing is a chair.

Kitu <u>kile</u> ni kiti, <u>that</u> thing is a chair.

<u>Pronouns</u>

<u>*Hiki*</u> *ni kiti*, <u>this</u> is a chair.

<u>*Kile*</u> *ni kiti*, <u>that</u> is a chair.

<u>Adverbs (locational)</u>

<u>*Huku*</u> *ni kiti*, <u>here</u> is a chair. [also: hapa, humu]

<u>*Kule*</u> *ni kiti*, <u>there</u> is a chair [also: pale, mle]

8   Possessives

As in English, Swahili also has two ways of forming possessives e.g. the house **of** the lady (i.e. the lady's house), or **her** house. How these are formed in Swahili is covered in the sections below:

8.1   Possessive Preposition –a, of

The Swahili possessive word *–a*, of, is used, as in English, as follows:

possession possession-prefix-*a* possessor e.g.

mazao ya shamba, produce of the farming plot

Note that the "*y*" above is a <u>possession</u>-prefix and not a possessor-prefix and so is determined by the <u>possession</u> (*mazao*). Below are the prefixes (in bold) for all the groups.

Actually, these prefixes are derivable from pronoun prefixes by dropping the vowel and if the pronoun prefix was a vowel it is replaced thus: *a-* and *u-* become *w-*, *i-* becomes *y-*. The exceptions are the prefix *ch-/vy-* of "THINGS [T]: *Kitu-Vitu*, things(s)" and the prefix *kw-* of GERUNDS [G]: *Kusoma- Kusoma*, reading(s). Having said that, you might find it better to just memorize these prefixes instead of trying to derive them in the head.

Each pair of examples is singular and plural respectively:

PEOPLE [Pp]: *Mtu-Watu*, person(s)

      [*Mtoto* **wa** *mwalimu*, teacher's child]

      [*Watoto* **wa** *mwalimu*, teacher's children]

VEGETATION [V]: *Mti-Miti*, tree(s)

      [*Mti* **wa** *mwalimu*, teacher's tree]

      [*Miti* **ya** *mwalimu*, teacher's trees]

MIX+FLOWERS, FRUITS [xFF]: *Tunda-Matunda, fruit(s)*

[*Tunda la mwalimu*, teacher's fruit]

[*Matunda ya mwalimu*, teacher's fruits]

THINGS [T]: *Kitu-Vitu*, things(s)

[*Kiti cha mwalimu*, teacher's chair]

[*Viti vya mwalimu*, teacher's chairs]

MIX+FAUNA, VEGGIES [xFV]: *Nyanya-Nyanya*, tomato(es)

[*Nyanya ya mwalimu*, teacher's tomato]

[*Nyanya za mwalimu*, teacher's tomatoes]

U-WORDS [U]: *Utenzi-Tenzi*, poem(s)

[*Utenzi wa mwalimu*, teacher's poem]

[*Tenzi za mwalimu*, teacher's poems]

PLACE-ADVERBS [Pl]: *Mahali- Mahali*, place(s)

[*Mahali *pa mwalimu*, teacher's place(s)]

"PLACE-ADVERBS [Pl]: *Mahali- Mahali*, place(s)" has two other prefixes: *kw-* referring to a place in general, and *mw-* referring to the inside of a place e.g. *mahali kwa wanyama wa pori*, wild animals' land (but not stated exactly where or which); *ndani mwa nyumba*, inside of house.

GERUNDS [G]: *Kusoma- Kusoma*, reading(s)

[*Kusoma kwa mwalimu*, teacher's reading(s)]

8.2 Possessor Adjective –ake, her, his, its; -ao, their

The 3rd person possessor adjectives –*ake*, his/her/its, -*ao*, their, are used, as in English but in reverse order, as follows:

possession possession-prefix-*ake* e.g.

*mazao **yake***, his/her or its (e.g. a plantation's) produce
*mazao **yao***, their produce

Note that it is a possession-prefix i.e. the prefix (*y-* in the above example) is determined by the possession (*mazao*). The previous possession prefixes (section 8.1 Possessive Preposition *–a*, of) are used here (instead of the usual underlined adjectival prefixes, underlined below for comparison):

[**other** adjectives follow the possessor adjective e.g. *mti wake **mrefu***, his tall tree]

PEOPLE [Pp]: *Mtu-Watu*, person(s)

> [*Mtoto **wake***, her/his/its child]
> [*Mtoto **wao***, their child]
>
> [*Watoto **wake***, her/his/its children]
> [*Watoto **wao***, their children]
>
> This is to be compared with how adjectives are normally prefixed:
>
> *mtoto mdogo*, small child
>
> Putting the above together, we can see the difference side-by-side:
>
> *mtoto **wake** mdogo*, her/his/its small child

VEGETATION [V]: *Mti-Miti*, tree(s)

> [*Mti **wake***, her/his/its tree]
> [*Mti **wao***, their tree]
>
> [*Miti **yake***, her/his/its trees]
> [*Miti **yao***, their trees]

MIX+FLOWERS, FRUITS [xFF]: *Tunda-Matunda, fruit(s)*

> [*Tunda **lake***, her/his/its fruit]
> [*Tunda **lao***, their fruit]
>
> [*Matunda **yake***, her/his/its fruits]
> [*Matunda **yao***, their fruits]

THINGS [T]: *Kitu-Vitu*, things(s)

>[*Kiti chake*, her/his/its chair]
>[*Kiti chao*, their chair]

>[*Viti vyake*, her/his/its chairs]
>[*Viti vyao*, their chairs]

MIX+FAUNA, VEGGIES [xFV]: *Nyanya-Nyanya*, tomato(es)

>[*Nyanya yake*, her/his/its tomato]
>[*Nyanya yao*, their tomato]

>[*Nyanya zake*, her/his/its tomatoes]
>[*Nyanya zao*, their tomatoes]

U-WORDS [U]: *Utenzi-Tenzi*, poem(s)

>[*Utenzi wake*, her/his/its poem]
>[*Utenzi wao*, their poem]

>[*Tenzi zake*, her/his/its poems]
>[*Tenzi zao*, their poems]

PLACE-ADVERBS [Pl]: *Mahali- Mahali*, place(s)

>[*Mahali *pake*, her/his/its place(s)]

>[*Mahali *pao*, their place(s)]

>*PLACE-ADVERBS [Pl] group also has, in addition to *p-*, two other prefixes: *kw-* and *mw-* e.g. *mahali kwake*, her/his/its place(s), *nyumbani mwake*, inside her/his/its home(s).

GERUNDS [G]: *Kusoma- Kusoma*, reading(s)

>[*Kusoma kwake*, her/his reading(s)]

>[*Kusoma kwao*, their reading(s)]

A common usage is placing the relevant noun after any of the above examples to specify whom or what is the possession about e.g.

Mtoto wake mwalimu, his child - teacher's

This is to be compared with section 8.1 Possessive Preposition –a, of:

Mtoto wa mwalimu, teacher's child

8.3   1st / 2nd / 3rd Possessor Adjectives

Only the 3rd person possessor adjectives *–ake* (his/her/its) and *-ao* (their) were shown above. Below is the complete set of possessor suffixes for all persons:

1st Person: Singular *–angu*, Plural *–etu*

2nd Person: Singular *–ako*, Plural *–enu*

3rd Person: Singular *–ake*, Plural *–ao***

Reminder: the possession prefixes conform to the possession and thus are the same for all three singular persons or all three plural persons e.g.

*mti **wangu/wako/wake**, my/your/her/his tree
*miti **yetu/yenu/yao**, our/your/their trees

**Note: *wao* also happens to be the 3rd person plural pronoun 'they' [section 5.1.2 Standalone Pronouns for Animates] e.g.

<u>wao</u> *ni watoto **wao**, <u>they</u> are **their** children!

Compare:
<u>huu</u> *ni mti **wao**, <u>this</u> is **their** tree
<u>hii</u> *ni miti **yao**, <u>these</u> are **their** trees

[Note: *ni*, is, used in these examples is covered in section 10.7.2 Wa, be]

Kwangu, kwako, kwake, kwetu, kwenu and ***kwao*** are frequently used with *-a*, of, to denote: of mine, of yours, etc as in the following examples:

*vitu **vya** **kwangu***, things of mine (or, of my own)
*tunda **la** **kwangu***, fruit of mine (or, of my own)
*nguo **za** **kwako***, clothes of yours (or, of your own)

These adjectives are also used as prepositioned personal objects:
[prepositions are covered in section 10.2 Prepositions]

*ataleta vitu **kw**angu*, he will bring things **to** me [literally, to my (place)]

*masomo yalikuwa magumu **kw**ake*, the studies were hard **for** him

For <u>emphasis</u> a personal pronoun (*mimi*, I, *yeye*, he, in the above cases) can be added e.g.

... ***kw**angu <u>mimi</u>,* **to** <u>me</u>

... ***kw**ake <u>yeye</u>,* **for** <u>him</u>

8.4   Truncated Possessor Suffixes

The suffixes covered above can optionally be truncated by dropping the letters in brackets () below and then suffixing them to the possessions as shown in these examples:

<u>1st Person Singular *–angu*</u>

*mwana (wa)ngu > mwan**angu**,* my child

<u>2nd Person Singular *–ako*</u>

*mume (wak)o > mume**o**,* your husband

*jina l(ak)o > jina**lo**,* your name

*mwana (wak)o > mwana**o**,* your child

<u>3rd Person Singular *–ake*</u>

*mke w(ak)e > mke**we**,* his wife

baba y(ak)e > baba**ye**,* his/her father [*yake not *wake* – see section 8.5 Possessives for Person Nouns outside of PEOPLE [Pp]: Mtu-Watu, person(s)]

*mwenzi w(ak)e > mwenzi**(w)e**,* his/her companion

<u>1st Person Plural *–etu*</u>

*wenz(i) (w)etu > wenz**etu**,* our colleagues

<u>2nd Person Plural –*enu*</u>

*wenz(i) (w)enu > wenz**enu***, your colleagues

<u>3rd Person Plural –*ao*</u>

baba (za)o > bab**ao***, their father [*zao not *wao* – see section 8.5 Possessives for Person Nouns outside of PEOPLE [Pp]: Mtu-Watu, person(s)]

*wenz(i) (w)ao > wenz**ao***, their companions

*baadhi y(a) (w)ao > baadhi y**ao***, some of them

*mwan(a) (w)ao > mwan**ao***, their child [Note: *mwanao* can mean their or your child, as seen above!]

*mengine y(a)o > mengine**yo***, their other such (e.g. *chungwa, ndizi, embe na mengineyo*, orange, banana, mango and their other such)

8.5   Possessives for Person Nouns outside of PEOPLE [Pp]: Mtu-Watu, person(s)

As previously explained in section 3.9 Animates outside of PEOPLE [Pp], all such animates follow the grammatical rules of PEOPLE [Pp]: *Mtu-Watu*, person(s) e.g.

*rafiki **wa**zuri **wa**wili **wa**nakuja*, two nice friends are coming

But there is a 'twist' to this general rule: <u>person nouns</u> that belong to the MIX+FAUNA, VEGGIES [xFV] group as *rafiki* above does, use possessive prefixes of the xFV group, namely **y**- and **z**- (singular and plural respectively) e.g.

[*rafiki **y**a mwalimu*, teacher's friend, or *rafiki **y**ake*, his friend] – NOT, as would be logical, *rafiki wa mwalimu*, nor, *rafiki wake*.

[*rafiki **z**a mwalimu*, teacher's friends, or *rafiki **z**ake*, his friends] – NOT *rafiki wa mwalimu*, nor, *rafiki wake*.

As compared to this, animals in the xFV group follow the general rule for animates, that is they follow Pp rules e.g.

> [*mbwa wa mwalimu*, teacher's dog, or *mbwa wake*, his dog]
> [*mbwa wa mwalimu*, teacher's dogs, or *mbwa wake*, his dogs]

Similarly, for animals in other groups:

THINGS [T]: *Kitu-Vitu*, things(s)THINGS [T]: *Kitu-Vitu*, things(s)

> [*kiboko wa mwalimu*, teacher's hippo, or *kiboko wake*, his hippo]
> [*viboko wa mwalimu*, teacher's hippos, or *viboko wake*, his hippos]

MIX+FLOWERS, FRUITS [xFF]: *Tunda-Matunda, fruit(s)*

> [*kobe wa mwalimu*, teacher's tortoise, or *kobe wake*, his tortoise]
> [*makobe wa mwalimu*, teacher's tortoises, or *makobe wake*, his tortoises]

Is there a rhyme or reason for this? A plausible explanation is that almost all person words of the xFV group are familial relations [*baba*, father, *mama*, mother, etc] as compared to those of the Pp group which are of all kinds including a lot of professions. Perhaps then, as a sign of distinction we get:

> [*mama yangu*, my mother] using xFV possession prefix
> versus:
> [*mlinzi wangu*, my watchman] using Pp possession prefix

How hard and fast are such 'twists'? Being a result of usage over time, and usage being fluid, watch out for deviations. But also watch out for improper use or simply carelessness in usage which is to be found from time to time.

Sometimes you hear another 'twist':

> [*ng'ombe zetu*, our cows] which uses a xFV possession prefix
> instead of the 'standard':
> [*ng'ombe wetu*, our cow(s)] using Pp possession prefix

Presumably the former is used because it specifies plurality whereas the latter can be interpreted as singular or plural!

8.6 Possessive Pronouns

The above possessive adjectives can be used as standalone **possessive pronouns**, as follows :

[Note: *ni*, is, used in these examples is covered in section 10.7.2 Wa, be]

*Kitu hiki ni **changu***, this thing is **mine**

Compare the above example with the previous approach:

Hiki ni kitu changu, this is <u>my</u> thing

where <u>my</u> is a possessive <u>adjective</u> as used previously while **mine** in the example here is a possessive **pronoun**.

8.7 All/whole, any, possessing, ~self [-ote, -o –ote, -enye, -enyewe]

The previous **possession** prefixes (section 8.1 Possessive Preposition *–a*, of) are used here for the adjectives listed in this section's title. These are used instead of the usual <u>adjectival prefixes</u> (underlined below for comparison). For example:

MIX+FLOWERS, FRUITS [xFF]: *Tunda-Matunda, fruit(s)*

> *tunda **l**ote*, whole fruit
>
> *tunda **l**o **l**ote*, any fruit
>
> *matunda **y**ote*, all fruits
>
> *matunda **y**o **y**ote*, any fruits
>
> This is to be compared with how adjectives are normally prefixed:
>
> *matunda <u>ma</u>zuri*, nice fruits
>
> Putting the above together, we can see the difference side-by-side:
>
> *matunda <u>ma</u>zuri **y**ote*, all nice fruits

More examples:

[Note: *ni*, is, used in these examples is covered in section 10.7.2 Wa, be]

Singular [*tunda kubwa lenye mbegu*, a big fruit having seeds; *tunda lenyewe ni tamu/chungu*, the fruit itself is sweet/bitter]

Plural [*matunda makubwa yenye mbegu*, big fruits having seeds; *matunda yenyewe ni tamu/machungu*, the fruits themselves are sweet/bitter; *tamu* being of foreign origin does NOT take a prefix]

Other noun group examples:

PEOPLE [Pp]: *Mtu-Watu*, person(s)

Singulars use **mw***-, plurals **w**-: [*true to its 'shifty personality' the 3rd person singular does NOT use its possession prefix w- but its adjectival prefix for vowel adjectives **mw**-, and the other singular persons 1st and 2nd follow suit.]

mimi **mw**enyewe, I myself [1st person singular]

wewe **mw**enyewe, you yourself [2nd person singular]

yeye **mw**enyewe, she / he her/himself [3rd person singular]

sisi **w**enyewe, we ourselves [1st person plural]

ninyi **w**enyewe, you yourselves [2ne person plural]

wao **w**enyewe, they themselves [3rd person plural]

Note these variations:

mtu **mw**enye afya, healthy person, but also *mtu yenye afya*, the **ye**- also being used in *mtu ye yote*, any person [3rd person singular]

sisi **w**ote, we all, but also *sisi sote* [1st person plural]

ninyi **w**ote, you all, but also *ninyi nyote* [2nd person plural]

ninyi **w**enye afya, you of health, but also *ninyi nyenye afya* [2nd person plural]

More examples:

sisi **wo wote**, any of us [1st person plural]

sisi **w**enye afya, we of health [1st person plural]

watu **wote**, all persons [3rd person plural]

watu **wo wote**, any of the persons [3rd person plural]

watu **w**enye afya, people of health [3rd person plural]

VEGETATION [V]: *Mti-Miti*, tree(s)

Mti m̲zuri **wote**, whole nice tree.

Mti m̲zuri **wo wote**, any nice tree.

Mti **w**enye *matunda*, tree with fruits.

Miti m̲izuri **y**ote, all nice trees.

Miti m̲izuri **yo** *yote*, any nice trees.

Miti **y**enye *matunda*, trees with fruits.

THINGS [T]: *Kitu-Vitu*, things(s)

Kitu k̲izuri **ch**ote, whole nice thing.

Kitu k̲izuri **cho ch**ote, any nice thing.

Kitu **ch**enye *thamani*, thing of value.

Vitu v̲izuri **vy**ote, all nice things.

Vitu v̲izuri **vyo** *vyote*, any nice things.

Vitu **vy**enye *thamani*, things of value.

The notion of 'thing' as something generic is used to express "whatever":

chochote or **vyovy**ote, whatever

MIX+FAUNA, VEGGIES [xFV]: *Nyanya-Nyanya*, tomato(es)

> *Nyanya n̲zuri y̲ote*, whole nice tomato.
>
> *Nyanya n̲zuri y̲o y̲ote*, any nice tomato.
>
> *Nyanya y̲enye mbegu*, tomato having seeds.
>
> *Nyanya n̲zuri z̲ote*, all nice tomatoes.
>
> *Nyanya n̲zuri z̲o z̲ote*, any nice tomatoes.
>
> *Nyanya z̲enye mbegu*, tomatoes having seeds.

U-WORDS [U]: *Utenzi-Tenzi*, poem(s)

> *Utenzi m̲zuri w̲ote*, whole nice poem.
>
> *Utenzi m̲zuri w̲o w̲ote*, any nice poem.
>
> *Utenzi w̲enye thamani*, poem of value.
>
> *Tenzi n̲zuri z̲ote*, all nice poems.
>
> *Tenzi n̲zuri z̲o z̲ote*, any nice poems.
>
> *Tenzi z̲enye thamani*, poems of value.

PLACE-ADVERBS [Pl]: *Mahali- Mahali*, place(s)

> *Mahali p̲azuri p̲ote*, whole nice place.
>
> *Mahali p̲azuri p̲o p̲ote*, any nice place.
>
> [*po pote* is also adverb 'anywhere' e.g.
> *unaweza kukaa po pote*, you can sit anywhere
> It can be also be used to construct adverb 'wherever' using
> relative -***po***-, where (covered in section 10.3 Relative Pronouns):
> *po pote ali**po**kwenda*, wherever he went
> cf. whenever / anywhere in section 10.4 Conditionals under
> "WHEN"]
>
> [More in Appendix G: -po- infix / suffix.]
>
> *Mahali p̲enye thamani*, place of value.

Mahali pazuri pote, all nice places.

Mahali pazuri po pote, any nice places.

Mahali penye thamani, places of value.

GERUNDS [G]: *Kusoma- Kusoma*, reading(s)

Kusoma kuzuri kwote, whole nice reading.

Kusoma kuzuri kwo kwote, any nice reading.

Kusoma kwenye maana, meaningful reading.

Kusoma kuzuri kwote, all nice readings.

Kusoma kuzuri kwo kwote, any nice readings.

Kusoma kwenye maana, meaningful readings.

A note about *enyewe*

There are three very similar-looking uses:

1. **Adjective** *enyewe*, ~self e.g. *mtu mwenyewe ni mrefu*, the person himself is tall, as described in this section above.
2. **Noun** *mwenyewe*, owner (see the Swahili-English Dictionary, in Volume 2) e.g. *mwenyewe ni mrefu*, the owner is tall.
3. But *enyewe*, ~self, can also be used a **pronoun** e.g. *mwenyewe ni mrefu*, himself is tall*. [Swahili and English usage defers here. In English this phrase* would be frowned up, the preferred usage being: he himself is tall, where pronoun 'himself' is used to emphasize the pronoun 'he'. But 'himself' as a standalone pronoun is seen in Swahili as in this example.]

The adjective is easy enough to distinguish as it is always associated with a noun or pronoun, *mtu* in the above case (1). It is with its use as a noun or a pronoun the difficulty arises. *Mwenyewe ni mrefu* can mean:

The owner is tall
OR:
Himself is tall

Thus, we have to look to the context for clarification! As if this is not confusing enough, there is another word for owner with a similar spelling: *mwenyeji!*

8.8   Practice: Demonstratives, Possessives

Answers to the previous practice of section 6.2 Practice: Adverbs:

*Vyombo vimeoshwa **kabisa**,* the utensils have been <u>thoroughly</u> washed.

*Kuna soko **mjini**,* there is a market <u>downtown</u>. ***Mle** hupatikana mazao mbalimbali,* <u>in there</u> a variety of produce is obtainable.

*Anafanya kazi **kifundi** na **kwa bidii**,* he works <u>expertly</u> and <u>with effort</u>.

*Kaka alifika **jana**,* the elder brother arrived <u>yesterday</u>.

<u>Practice:</u>

Fill in the blanks below to match the underlined word in the English translation. An **example** is provided for the first entry.

[The correct answers are given at the beginning of the next Practice section. Note: *ni,* is, used in these examples is covered in section 10.7.2 Wa, be]

***Hiki** ni kitabu **changu**,* <u>this</u> is <u>my</u> book. *Kitabu* _____ *kina hadithi,* <u>this</u> (specific) book has stories. *Lakini vitabu* _____ *vina picha* _____ *kupaka rangi,* but <u>those</u> books have pictures <u>of</u> colouring. *Je, unapenda gani?** Well, which do you like? _____, <u>just this</u>. *Tena* _____ *ni vitabu vya aina nyingine,* also <u>over there</u> are books of other kinds. [**Not yet tackled: section 9 Interrogatives.]

Vitabu _____ *watoto ni* _____ *mwandishi Mabruki,* books <u>of</u> children are <u>his</u>, the writer Mabruki. *Hata watoto___ wasoma vitabu* _____, even <u>his</u> (own) children read <u>his</u> books. *Hata paka* _____ *na mbwa* _____ *hupenda kusikia watoto wakisoma kwa sauti,* even <u>his</u> cats and <u>his</u> dog like to listen to the children reading aloud. *Na yule Mabruki husema na* _____ *kwa furaha "Vitabu* _____ _____!",* and he Mabruki says to <u>himself</u> with joy "Books <u>of</u> <u>my own</u>!". *Tena vitabu* _____ _____*vina picha nyingi,* also <u>all</u> his books have many pictures.

9 Interrogatives

Kuwa au kutokuwa: To be or not to be,
hilo ndilo swali: that is the question.

na Bwana Atingisha-mkuki

by Sir Shakes-spear ;-)

Interrogatives are NOT different from their corresponding statements in Swahili. For example, the statement "You are going to school" is converted to its question form (in English: Are you going to school?) by just adding a **question mark** to the end of the statement: "You are going to school**?**" and, when saying it, by raising the last word's tone. For example:

Unakwenda shuleni, you are going to school.
[*Je,*]* *Unakwenda shuleni?* Are you going to school? *[*Je* alerts the listener that what follows is a question!]

Swahili also has the following common interrogative adjectives (which are labelled "iadj" in the Dictionary in Volumes 2 and 3), some of which are prefixed (shown with a hyphen in front) with a relevant <u>pronoun prefix</u>:

-pi, which e.g.

> *Mwezi upi?* Which month?
> *Miezi ipi?* Which months?
> *Papi?* Which [place(s)]? [place(s) is/are implied]
> *Vipi?* How? [by usage]
>
> *Mtu yupi?* Which person? [*yu-* is used instead of *a-*; this type of change is often the case with 3rd person singular]

-ngapi, how many e.g.

> *Mahali pangapi?* How many places?

wapi, where (no prefix) e.g.

> *Mfuko uko **wapi**?* Where is the bag? *Uko hapa*, it is here.
> *Mifuko iko **wapi**?* Where are the bags? *Iko hapa*, they are here.

nini, what (no prefix) e.g.

> *Mahali **nini**?* What place?

kwa nini, why (no prefix) e.g.

> ***Kwa nini** aliondoka?* Why did he leave?

mbona, why (no prefix) e.g.

> ***Mbona** anafanya hivi?* Why is he doing thus?

nani, who, what, what sort (no prefix) e.g.

> *Mahali **nani**?* What sort of place?
> *Jina lako **nani**?* What is your name?

lini, when (no prefix) e.g.

> *Alikuja **lini**?* when did she come?

gani, what, which (no prefix) e.g.

> *Unataka aina **gani**?* What type do you want?

hodi, anybody home? [A response: *karibu*, come in]

Some of these interrogative adjectives are usable as interrogative pronouns e.g. *kitu kipi?* which thing? (*-pi* used as adjective) versus *kipi kimetosha?* which sufficed? (*-pi* used as pronoun)

Two common response words for yes/no type questions are:

ndiyo, yes

hapana or *siyo*, no

Practice: Interrogatives

Answers to the previous practice of section 8.8 Practice: Demonstratives, Possessives:

Hiki ni kitabu ***changu****,* this is my book. *Kitabu **hicho** kina hadithi,* this (specific) book has stories. *Lakini vitabu **vile** vina picha **za** kupaka rangi,* but those books have pictures of colouring. *Je, unapenda gani?** Well, which do you like? ***Kikihiki****,* just this. *Tena **kule** ni vitabu vya aina nyingine,* also over there are books of other kinds. [*Not yet tackled: section 9 Interrogatives.]

*Vitabu **vya** watoto ni **vyake** mwandishi* Mabruki, books of children are his, the writer Mabruki. *Hata watoto**we** wasoma vitabu **vyake****,* even his (own) children read his books. *Hata paka **zake** na mbwa **wake** hupenda kusikia watoto wakisoma kwa sauti,* even his cats and his dog like to listen to the children reading aloud. *Na yule* Mabruki *husema na **mwenyewe** kwa furaha "Vitabu **vya** **kwangu****!",* and he Mabruki says to himself with joy "Books of my own!". *Tena vitabu **vyake** **vyote** vina picha nyingi,* also all his books have many pictures.

Practice:

Fill in the blanks below to match the underlined word in the English translation. An **example** is provided for the first entry.

[The correct answers are given at the beginning of the next Practice section.]

*Maua **yapi** unayapenda?* Which flowers do you like?
Mtatembelea _____ ? Which place(s) will you visit?
Umeleta visu _____ ? How many knives have you brought?
Mtoto yuko _____ ? Where is the child?
Kitabu _____ ? What book?
_____ *ulinunua hiki?* Why did you buy this?
Mti _____ ? What sort of tree?
Aliwasili _____ ? How did she arrive?
Alikuja _____ ? When did she come?
Utakuja kwa basi _____ ? You will come by what bus?

10 More on Verbs

Bado hujaona marembo yote ya kitenzi!

You haven't yet seen all the 'decorations' of a verb!

10.1 Embedded Object References

Objects in English are written as separate words whereas Swahili, in addition to using separate object words, also uses object references which are *embedded* in verbs; there is no equivalent to the latter in English e.g. "I told you" in English, versus in Swahili:

niliambia wewe, I told you [using a separate object word *wewe*, you]
*nili**ku**ambia*, I told you [using an embedded object reference -**ku**-, you]

Only one object reference can be embedded e.g. [another verb is introduced here: *ona*, see]

*nili**pa**ona yeye*, I saw him **there**

where -**pa**-, there, is embedded. OR, we can say:

*nili**mw**ona pale*, I saw **him** there

where -**mw**-, him, is embedded.

If the verb is prepositioned (see section 10.2.1 Embedded Prepositions) then its related indirect object has to be present e.g. using the verb *letea*, bring to, which is <u>prepositioned</u> from *leta*, bring, by insertion of the <u>e</u>:

ananilet<u>e</u>a, he is bringing <u>to</u> **me**

[Or, using *kwangu* we could say: *analeta kwangu,* he is bringing to me. *Kwangu* is explained in section 8.3 1st / 2nd / 3rd Possessor Adjectives.]

These object references are the same as the pronoun prefixes given in section 5.1.1 Pronoun Prefixes, except for the PEOPLE [Pp] group which is dealt with in section 10.1.1 Object References for PEOPLES: *Mtu-Watu*, person(s). The object references for the other groups are as follows:

The 1st person singular pronoun of the PEOPLE [Pp] group, *mimi*, I, can be optionally used in front of all these examples.

Each of these examples translates the same:

I see it (singular) or I see them (plural)

where, it/them refers to an object(s) of that group e.g. the VEGETATION [V] example could be referring to tree(s). Note: The standalone object can be explicitly used instead of an embedded reference to it, but for clarity or emphasis BOTH are used e.g.

mimi ninaona mti, I see the tree
mimi ninauona mti, I see it, the tree

VEGETATION [V]: *Mti-Miti*, tree(s)

> **u** [*ninauona*] Present
>
> **i** [*ninaiona*] Present

MIX+FLOWERS, FRUITS [xFF]: *Tunda-Matunda, fruit(s)*

> **li** [*ninaliona*] Present
> cf. *nililiona*, I saw it (past tense) where the first -*li*- is the past tense infix, the second -**li**- is the embedded object. The order of insertion is discussed in chapter 11 ANATOMY OF VERBS which also has a handy mnemonic for recalling the insertion order :-)
>
> **ya** [*ninayaona*] Present

THINGS [T]: *Kitu-Vitu*, things(s)

> **ki** [*ninakiona*] Present
>
> **vi** [*ninaviona*] Present

MIX+FAUNA, VEGGIES [xFV]: *Nyanya-Nyanya*, tomato(es)

> *i* [*ninaiona*] Present

> *zi* [*ninaziona*] Present

U-WORDS [U]: *Utenzi-Tenzi*, poem(s)

> *u* [*ninauona*] Present

> *zi* [*ninaziona*] Present

PLACE-ADVERBS [Pl]: *Mahali- Mahali*, place(s)

> *pa** [*ninapaona*] Present

> *pa** [*ninapaona*] Present

> [More in Appendix G: -po- infix / suffix.]

**pa* refers to a definite place. The "PLACE-ADVERBS [Pl]: *Mahali- Mahali*, place(s)" group has two other object references: *ku* referring to an unspecified place, and *mu* referring to the interior of a place e.g. *ninakuona, ninamuona*.

GERUNDS [G]: *Kusoma- Kusoma*, reading(s)

> *ku* [*ninakuona*] Present

> *ku* [*ninakuona*] Present

Object references are embedded in the same way for all the other tenses.

10.1.1 Object References for PEOPLES: Mtu-Watu, person(s)

Again, using the 1st person singular pronoun of the PEOPLE [Pp] group, *mimi* (which is optional) as the subject, the object references for 1st, 2nd and 3rd persons of this group are shown below. [Compare these object references to the corresponding pronoun prefixes in sections 5.1.1 Pronoun Prefixes and 5.1.2 "Standalone Pronouns for ". The pronoun prefix is not always the same as its corresponding object reference e.g. the 2nd person singular pronoun prefix is *u-* whereas the object is *-ku-*.]

Another verb is introduced here:

-penda, love

Each of the examples translates as: I love me/you/him/her/us/them.

PEOPLE [Pp]: *Mtu-Watu*, person(s)

> **ni** 1st person singular (me) [*ninanipenda*, I love myself] Present
> **ku** 2nd person singular (you) [*ninakupenda*, I love you (singular)] Present
> **m(w)*** 3rd person singular (she/he) [*ninampenda*, I love her / him] Present
> *3rd person singular object reference **mw-** is used with a verb base that begins with a vowel e.g. (*Mimi*) *ninamwona*, I see him.
> **tu** 1st person plural (us) [*ninatupenda*, I love us] Present
> **wa** 2nd person plural (you) [*ninawapenda*, I love you (plural)] Present
> **wa** 3rd person plural (they) [*ninawapenda*, I love them] Present

Note:

(1) *wa* is the object reference for both 2nd and 3rd person plural.
(2) *ku* is the object reference for 2nd person singular, for the indefinite version of the PLACE-ADVERBS [PI] group and for the GERUNDS [G] group e.g.
Ninakuona, I see you / it (indefinite place, or a gerund such as writing)

Reminder: all animates outside the PEOPLE [Pp] group use its rules:

> **mw** [*ninamwona kifaru*, I see it, the rhino] Present
> **wa** [*ninawaona vifaru*, I see them, the rhinos] Present

For emphasis / clarity, the corresponding **standalone pronoun** can follow the above verbs, just as do the nouns *kifaru / vifaru* above, e.g.

> *Ninawaona ninyi*, I am seeing you, **you** (plural), often for second person plural the two words being compressed into one:
> *Ninawaon<u>e</u>ni* [the verb ending is euphoniously changed to -<u>e</u>]

10.1.2 Practice: Embedded Object References

Answers to the previous practice of section 9.1 Practice: Interrogatives:

*Maua **yapi** unayapenda?* <u>Which</u> flowers do you like?

*Mtatembelea **papi**?* <u>Which place(s)</u> will you visit?

*Umeleta visu **vingapi**?* <u>How many</u> knives have you brought?

*Mtoto yuko **wapi**?* <u>Where</u> is the child?

*Kitabu **nini**?* <u>What</u> book?

*Kwa **nini** ulinunua hiki?* <u>Why</u> did you buy this?

*Mti **nani**?* [or, *Mti **wa aina gani**?*] <u>What sort</u> of tree?

*Aliwasili **vipi**?* <u>How</u> did she arrive?

*Alikuja **lini**?* <u>When</u> did she come?

*Utakuja kwa basi **gani**?* You will come by <u>what</u> bus?

<u>Practice:</u>

Fill in the blanks below to match the underlined word in the English translation. An **example** is provided for the first entry.

[The correct answers are given at the beginning of the next Practice section.]

Nina̠iona miti shambani, vilevile na̠uona ule mnazi mrefu, I see <u>them</u>, the trees, in the plantation, also I see <u>it</u>, that tall palm tree.

Uli__kuta rafiki yangu jana lakini bado huja__ona ndugu zangu, you met <u>him</u>, my friend, yesterday but you have not yet met <u>them</u>, my brothers.

Hana__ vitabu vyangu leo lakini jana alikuwa na__, he does not have <u>them</u>, my books, today but yesterday he had <u>them</u>. [The *-na* in *Hana* meaning "have" is covered in section 10.7.5 Wa na, have. The two answers here are difficult at this stage but are explained in section 10.7.5.1 Exception: embedded object SUFFIXED to na.] *Una__taka kimojawapo?* Do you want <u>it</u>, one of them?

10.2 Prepositions

10.2.1 Embedded Prepositions

Prepositions in English are written as separate words whereas Swahili has both prepositional words as well as prepositional inserts (*-e/i-*) which are *embedded* in verbs; there is no equivalent to the latter in English e.g. the verb "get for" in English, versus in Swahili:

Pata, get, becomes *patia*, get for

This one letter *-i-* (or *-e-*) stands for ANY preposition: at, for, in, etc!

<u>More examples:</u>

Leta, bring, becomes *letea*, bring to.

Kata, cut, becomes *katia*, cut with.

Piga, strike, becomes *pigia*, strike at.

Pika, cook, becomes *pikia*, cook for.

Lima, cultivate, becomes *limia*, cultivate for.

Lala, sleep, becomes *lalia*, sleep in.

The <u>indirect object</u> that a preposition refers to can itself be an object reference inserted immediately preceding the preposition-modified verb base e.g.

Ana<u>tu</u>pikia [*chakula* – optional], he/she is cooking [food] **for** <u>us</u>

Ana<u>ni</u>limia [*shamba* – optional], he/she is cultivating [the farming plot] **for** <u>me</u>

When to use a preposition in English is not consistent (nor which preposition to use), the most common example being the British usage: "throw it out **of** the window" where a preposition **of** is used and the American equivalent "throw it out the window" where **NO** preposition is used. In addition to this, whether a preposition is used in English or Swahili is not the same. This is illustrated in the table below by showing cases where a preposition is or is not used in Swahili and English side-by-side:

No preposition	Prepositioned
anarudi Mombasa *alipiga picha (ya[1]) simba*	he is returning **to** Mombasa he took a photo **of** the lion
the students are revising the lessons	*wanafunzi wanarudia[2] masomo*
fikiri maneno haya, think these words	*fikiria maneno haya*, think **about** these words
[1]If *ya* is used, it would be identical to English. [2]Note the change in meaning of the prepositioned *rudia*, repeat / revise.	

The moral of the story with prepositions in Swahili is that English rules do not necessarily apply, thus Swahili rules have to be learnt from usage. However, if you do throw in a preposition where it is not required it is not the end of the world, just like the Americanese "off of" where the second "of" is not usually necessary and yet the rest of the English world tolerates it ;-)

Special Cases

Two-vowel verbs: e.g. *tia*, put. Instead of inserting the preposition *–i/e-* just by itself and thereby ending up with three consecutive vowels (awkward to pronounce), a euphonious filler "*l*" is first prefixed to the preposition. Thus, we get:

tia, put: *tilia*, put into

tembea, walk: *tembelea*, walk to (i.e. to visit)

nunua, buy: *nunulia*, buy for

Foreign verbs not ending with an -*a* e.g. *jibu*, reply: the ending is simply first changed to an -*a* before inserting the preposition *–i/e*. Thus, we get:

jibu, reply: *jibia*, reply to.

10.2.2 Standalone Prepositions

Instead of embedding a preposition, one can use a underline standalone preposition just like in English. For example: [the embedded preposition in the **comparison** in square brackets is **bolded**]

niliambia na yeye, or *naye*, I said to him/her [cf. *nilimwambia*]

For other prepostions see the "prep" entries in the Adjective, Adverbs section of the English-Swahili Dictionary (in Volume 3).

10.2.3 Practice: Prepositions

Answers to the previous practice of section 10.1.2 Practice: Embedded Object References:

Ninaiona miti shambani, vilevile nauona ule mnazi mrefu, I see them, the trees, in the plantation, also I see it, that tall palm.

Ulimkuta rafiki yangu jana lakini bado hujawaona ndugu zangu, you met him, my friend, yesterday but you have not yet met them, my brothers.

Hanavyo vitabu vyangu leo lakini jana alikuwa navyo, he does not have them, my books, today but yesterday he had them. *Unakitaka kimojawapo?* Do you want it, one of them?

Practice:

Fill in the blanks below to match the underlined word in the English translation. An **example** is provided for the first entry.

[The correct answers are given at the beginning of the next Practice section.]

Huogea sabuni, I bathe with soap

Walifurah__a ushindi, they rejoiced in the victory

Tenzi za kuvut__a, poems of pulling towards = appealing poems

Alinij__a kusema pole, she came to me to say sorry (in consolation)

10.3 Relative Pronouns

The main thing to notice about these pronouns is its use of syllables ending in "-o", which is to be compared with the English prefix "wh" of the relative pronouns "who(m)", "which", "where".

Swahili relative pronouns are of the form:

-?o-

where the ? is substituted with a noun group letter (or left blank) as follows:

Noun Group	Singular	Plural
PEOPLE [Pp]*	-ye-***	-o-
VEGETATION [V]	-o-	-yo-
MIX+FLOWERS, FRUITS [xFF]	-lo-	-yo-
THINGS [T]	-cho-	-vyo-
MIX+FAUNA, VEGGIES [xFV]	-yo-	-zo-
U-WORDS [U]	-o-	-zo-
PLACE-ADVERBS [Pl]**	-po-	-po-
	-ko-	-ko-
	-mo-	-mo-
GERUNDS [G]	-ko-	-ko-

*The singular and plural are applicable to all persons: 1st, 2nd and 3rd
**-po- refers to a specific place, -ko- to a place in general, -mo- to the inside of a place
***a –ye- is used, as it sometimes is done with the other 3rd person singular situations

The relative pronoun along with a relative-tense-infix (this tense infix is used only with relative construction) are inserted into the construction of a verb as follows:

pronoun-prefix+relative-tense-infix+*ʔo*+verb-base.

The tense infixes for relative construction are as follows:

Present: *–na-* being the same as in normal construction

Past: *–li-* being the same as in normal construction

Future: *-taka-* instead of the *–ta-* in normal construction

Present Perfect: *–me-* as in normal construction, or using the Past tense infix-*li-*

Timeless: the relative infix *ʔo* is <u>suffixed</u> instead being infixed e.g. *matokeo yafuata<u>yo</u>*, results which follow

Examples: [These examples are not full sentences e.g. the first example is only the beginning of a sentence which could be completed in any number of ways such as:

Mtu anaye tosha... ni yule, person who suffices... is that one.]

PEOPLE [Pp]: *Mtu-Watu*, person(s)

[*Mtu anayetosha*, person who suffices] Present

[*Mtu aliyetosha*, person who sufficed, or has sufficed] Past, or Present Perfect

[*Mtu atakayetosha*, person who will suffice] Future

[*Mtu atoshaye*, person who suffices] Timeless

[*Watu wanaotosha*, persons who suffice] Present

[*Watu waliotosha*, persons who sufficed, or have sufficed] Past, or Present Perfect

[*Watu watakaotosha*, persons who will suffice] Future

[*Watu watoshao*, persons who suffice] Timeless

The PEOPLE [Pp] group also has 1st and 2nd persons whose singular and plural relative pronouns are the same as the above singular and plural e.g.

[*Mimi ninayetosha*, I who suffice] Present

[*Sisi tunaotosha*, we who suffice] Present

[*Wewe unayetosha*, you who suffices] Present

[*Ninyi mnaotosha*, you who suffice] Present

VEGETATION [V]: *Mti-Miti*, tree(s)

[*Mti unaotosha*, tree which suffices] Present

[*Mti uliotosha*, tree which sufficed, or has sufficed] Past, or Present Perfect

[*Mti utakaotosha*, tree which will suffice] Future

[*Mti utoshao*, tree which suffices] Timeless

[*Miti inayotosha*, trees which suffice] Present

[*Miti iliyotosha*, trees which sufficed, or have sufficed] Past, or Present Perfect

[*Miti itakayotosha*, trees which will suffice] Future

[*Miti itoshayo*, trees which suffice] Timeless

MIX+FLOWERS, FRUITS [xFF]: *Tunda-Matunda, fruit(s)*

[*Tunda linalotosha*, fruit which suffices] Present

[*Tunda lililotosha*, fruit which sufficed, or has sufficed] Past, or Present Perfect

[*Tunda litakalotosha*, fruit which suffices] Future

[*Tunda litoshalo*, fruit which suffices] Timeless

[*Matunda yanayotosha*, fruits which suffice] Present

[*Matunda yaliyotosha*, fruits which sufficed, or have sufficed] Past, or Present Perfect

[*Matunda yatakayotosha*, fruits which will suffice] Future

[*Matunda yatoshayo*, fruits which suffice] Timeless

Reminder: all animates outside the PEOPLE [Pp] group use its rules, for example, in the present tense:

> [*Kobe anayetosha*, tortoise which suffices] Present

> [*Makobe wanaotosha*, tortoises which suffice] Present

THINGS [T]: *Kitu-Vitu*, things(s)

[*Kitu kinachotosha*, thing which suffices] Present

[*Kitu kilichotosha*, thing which sufficed, or has sufficed] Past, or Present Perfect

[*Kitu kitakachotosha*, thing which will suffice] Future

[*Kitu kitoshacho*, thing which suffices] Timeless

[*Vitu vinavyotosha*, things which suffice] Present

[*Vitu vilivyotosha*, things which sufficed, or have sufficed] Past, or Present Perfect

[*Vitu vitakavyotosha*, things which will suffice] Future

[*Vitu vitoshavyo*, things which suffice] Timeless

Reminder: all animates outside the PEOPLE [Pp] group use its rules, for example, in the present tense:

[*Kifaru anayetosha*, rhino who suffices] Present

[*Vifaru wanaotosha*, rhinos which suffice] Present

MIX+FAUNA, VEGGIES [xFV]: *Nyanya-Nyanya*, tomato(es)

[*Nyanya inayotosha*, tomato which suffices] Present

[*Nyanya iliyotosha*, tomato which sufficed, or has sufficed] Past, or Present Perfect

[*Nyanya itakayotosha*, tomato which will suffice] Future

[*Nyanya itoshayo*, tomato which suffices] Timeless

[*Nyanya zinazotosha*, tomatoes which suffice] Present

[*Nyanya zilizotosha*, tomatoes which sufficed, or have sufficed] Past, or Present Perfect

[*Nyanya zitakazotosha*, tomatoes which will suffice] Future

[*Nyanya zitoshazo*, tomatoes which suffice] Timeless

Reminder: all animates outside the PEOPLE [Pp] group use its rules, for example, in the present tense:

[*Mbwa anayetosha*, dog who suffices] Present

[*Mbwa wanaotosha*, dogs which suffice] Present

U-WORDS [U]: *Utenzi-Tenzi*, poem(s)

[*Utenzi unaotosha*, poem which suffices] Present

[*Utenzi uliotosha*, poem which sufficed, or has sufficed] Past, or Present Perfect

[*Utenzi utakaotosha*, poem which will suffice] Future

[*Utenzi utoshao*, poem which suffices] Timeless

[*Tenzi zinazotosha*, poems which suffice] Present

[*Tenzi zilizotosha*, poems which sufficed, or have sufficed] Past, or Present Perfect

[*Tenzi zitakazotosha*, poems which will suffice] Future

[*Tenzi zitoshazo*, poems which suffice] Timeless

PLACE-ADVERBS [Pl]: *Mahali- Mahali*, place(s)

[*Mahali panapotosha*, place(s) which suffice(s)] Present

[*Mahali pali**po**tosha*, place(s) which sufficed, or has/have sufficed] Past, or Present Perfect

[*Mahali pataka**po**tosha*, place(s) which will suffice] Future

[*Mahali patosha**po***, place(s) which suffice(s)] Timeless

[More in Appendix G: -po- infix / suffix.]

***-po**- refers to a definite place. There are two other relative infixes in this noun group: -ko referring to an indefinite place, and -mo referring to the interior of a place e.g.

[*Mahali kuna**ko**tosha*, place(s) which suffice(s)] Present

[*Mahali kutosha**ko***, place(s) which suffice(s)] Timeless

[*Nyumbani mna**mo**tosha*, house interior(s) which suffice(s)] Present

[*Nyumbani mnatosha**mo***, house interior(s) which suffice(s)] Timeless

Plurals are the same as their singulars!

GERUNDS [G]: *Kusoma- Kusoma*, reading(s)

[*Kusoma kuna**ko**tosha*, reading(s) which suffice(s)] Present

[*Kusoma kuli**ko**tosha*, reading(s) which sufficed, or has / have sufficed] Past, or Present Perfect

[*Kusoma kutaka**ko**tosha*, reading(s) which will suffice] Future

[*Kusoma kutosha**ko***, reading(s) which suffice(s)] Timeless

Plurals are the same as their singulars!

Truncations: The above tense and relative pronoun infixes are sometimes seen to be contracted, especially in literary writing e.g. in the above example of *Matunda yaliyotosha*, fruits which sufficed, the past tense infix -li- and the relative infix -yo- are contracted so that -liyo- becomes -**lo**-, thus: *Matunda ya**lo**tosha*, fruits which sufficed!

As Object

The above examples all showed relative pronouns as **subjects**, generally of the form:

Someone/something **who/which** suffices.

Relative pronouns can also be used as **objects**, generally of the form:

Someone/something **whom/which/where** the subject acts on e.g.

kitu ulichokileta kinatosha, the thing **which** <u>you</u> brought (it) suffices

Pronoun prefix <u>u</u>-, you, is the subject in the above example whereas relative pronoun infix -**cho**-, which, is the object. [Note the use of embedded object reference –*ki*-, it; this is Swahili usage not English. See section 10.1 Embedded Object References.] Compare this to the relative pronoun's use as a subject:

kitu <u>ki</u>licholetwa na wewe kinatosha, the thing **which** was brought by you suffices

Pronoun prefix <u>ki</u>- and the relative pronoun infix -**cho**- are subject pronouns. [Note the use of the passive form of the verb *leta*, bring, namely *letwa*, be brought, made so with the insertion of -*w*-. See section 5.8 Verb Transformations.]

And now a side-by-side example:

msichana aliyenipenda, the <u>girl</u> **who** liked me [relative <u>subject</u>]
msichana niliyempenda, the <u>girl</u> **whom** I liked (her) [relative <u>object</u>]

Another way to analyze this is to break the above sentences into two: (1) using a relative only, (2) using an object only e.g.

msichana aliyenipenda, the <u>girl</u> **who** liked me [relative <u>subject</u>]:
   (1) *msichana aliyependa*, the girl <u>who</u> liked [<u>relative</u>]
   (2) *msichana alinipenda*, the girl liked <u>me</u> [<u>object</u>]
thus you can see the composite sentence and its components :-)

Note: For noun group PLACE-ADVERBS [Pl] the relative object is **which** OR **where**, generally of the form:

Somewhere, **which** the subject refers to, suffices

OR

Somewhere, **where** the subject went to, suffices

For example:

*mahali ali**ko**kupenda panatosha*, the place **which** she liked (it) suffices

OR

*mahali ali**ko**kwenda panatosha*, the place **where** she went to (it) suffices

Note the use of embedded place object reference *–ku–* as well as its transformation to *–kw–* in front of vowel *e*. However, *–kw–* is also the infinitive prefix "to" for *enda*, come, thus its dual interpretation and yet the English translation is the same in either case (because it's only in Swahili – not in English - an object infix exists and which is typically used after its relative, as in this case).

10.3.1 Relative Subject-Object Summary

The table below shows various combinations of relative subjects and objects which can be compared and contrasted in one place here.

Relative subject verb infix is underlined and cross-referenced by superscripts to its corresponding word in the sentence.

Relative object verb infix is bolded and underlined and cross-referenced by superscripts to its corresponding word in the sentence.

Verb's **object** infix and the word it refers to in the sentence are both bolded.

Verb's subject is easily identified by the pronoun prefix in the verb e.g.

#1 the "*a*" prefix in the verb means "he or she", in this example being *mtu*, person, which also happens to be the relative subject *ye*[1], who[1], which is cross-referenced by superscript[1] to its corresponding word *mtu*[1], person[1].

#	Subj. or **Obj.**	Verb	Subj. or **Obj.**	.....
1	*mtu[1]*	*aliye[1]kileta*	**kitu**	*ni Ali*
	the person[1]	who[1] brought **it**	the **thing**	is Ali
2	**mtu[2]**	*waliye[2]msalimu*	**watu*	*ni Ali*
	the **person[2]**	**whom[2]** they greeted **him**	the people	is Ali
3	*kitu[3]*	*nilicho[3]kileta*	**mimi*	*ni kizuri*
	the **thing[3]**	**which[3]** I brought **it**	I	is nice
4	*kitu[4]*	*kilicho[4]letwa*		*ni kizuri*
	the thing[4]	**which[4]** was brought		is nice
5	*gari[5]*	*lililo[5]ichukuwa*	**mizigo**	*limefika*
	the vehicle[5]	**which[5]** took **them**	the **luggage**	has arrived
6	**askari** *walifuata* **maneno[6]**	*aliyo[6]waagiza*	**akida*	
	soldiers obeyed **words[6]**	**which[6]** he ordered **them**	the officer	
7	**duka[7]**	*niliko[7]kwenda*		*limefungwa*
	the **shop[7]**	**where[7]** I went		is closed
8	*kitu[7]*	*nilicho[7]kuwa nacho*		*kimepotea*
	the **thing[7]**	**which[7]** I had		is lost

*Note: these words in this penultimate column are subjects of the verb in the "Verb" column, whereas the subjects of the last column are the objects of the verb in the "Verb" column! Read the English translations to see this. The reverse is the case for the other words in the penultimate column (except for #4 and #6 where either the penultimate or the last column is empty). Again read their English translations to see this.

#2, #3, #7, #8: The verb's relative infix and its object reference BOTH refer to the ONE thing in the column to its left. In the other examples, the relative and the object reference refer to DIFFERENT things. [cf. #4 has only a relative, no embedded object reference.] Note: #8 has the relative embedded with verb *wa*, be, while the object is suffixed to *na*, with - *wa na*, be with, meaning 'have'.

Negatives

These are very easy to construct: a *–si-* tense infix is used for ALL tenses, for example:

miti isiyotosha, trees which are not, or will not be, or have not been, or were not sufficient!

kitabu kisichokuwa na picha, a book which does not have, or will not have, or has not had, or did not have pictures

But to be specific as to tense the alternative relative is used (next below).

Alternative Relative

Instead of the above construct, a construction identical to the way "who" and "which" are used in English, can be constructed as follows:

amba+?o

For example, instead of:

kitu kinachotosha, the thing which suffices, we can write:

kitu ambacho kinatosha, wherein the above -**cho**- is moved out of the verb and suffixed to *amba-* which is inserted between the noun and the verb, both translating the same viz. the thing which suffices.

Other examples:

watu ambao hawajalima, people who have not yet cultivated
[cf. negative using embedded relative: *watu wasiolima*]

mtoto ambaye alichoka, child who was tired

miti ambayo haikutosha, trees which were not sufficient
[cf. negative using embedded relative: *miti isiotosha*]

It can also serve as an object same as with the embedded references (see As Object above) e.g.

(1) An example we learnt above: [embedded references]
kitu ulichokileta kinatosha, the thing **which** you brought (it) suffices
(2) Using *amba-* :
*kitu amba**cho** ulikileta kinatosha*, the thing **which** you brought (it) suffices: again, the *-cho-* is moved out of the verb and suffixed to *ambacho*. The object *-ki-* is often also dropped from the verb.

Another example, with a passive verb:

mtu ambaye watoto walichukuliwa naye ni dereva yetu, the man who the children were taken by is our driver

Generic "...how..." / "...as ~ (as) ..."

-vyo- which is the plural relative infix for THINGS [T], is frequently used along with *jinsi*, how, or *kama*, like, or *namna*, like, or *vile*, in that manner, to express "...how..." e.g.

*nieleze **jinsi** ulivyokwenda*, tell me **how** you went
*fanya **kama** nilivyokwambia jana*, do like **how** I told you yesterday
namna ilivyojengwa ni vizuri sana, **how** (or, the way) it has been built is very nice
*fedha ni maisha, **vile** anavyofikiri yeye*, money is life, that's **how** he thinks

Jinsi / kama / namna may not always be present [but implied, as below]:

sijui [jinsi] alivyofanya kazi hii, I don't know **how** he did this work
andika [kama] asemavyo, write **how** she tells you
mtoto huyu hufanya [kama] apendavyo, this child does **how** he pleases
kesho nitafanya [kama] ni*pendavyo, tomorrow I will do **how** I like

*Strictly speaking, being a timeless tense, it should be *napendavyo*, which itself is a modification of *ni-a-penda* where the *-i-* is euphoniously dropped as explained in section 5.1.1 Pronoun Prefixes whereas in this usage* it is the *-a-* which is dropped! Note: instead of using the verb *penda*, like, the verb *taka*, want, can be used:

kesho nitafanya nitakavyo, tomorrow I will do **how** I want

-vyo is also used with *kadiri*, extent, as well as with any of the above terms, to express "to the extent (of)..." e.g.

kadiri tujuavyo kuna magomvi tele duniani, to the extent [or as] we know conflicts abound in the world
kadiri awezavyo, to the extent of her ability

and by extension with *ndivyo...-vyo-*, thus:
kadiri alivyoendelea kusoma ndivyo alivyokuwa hodari, to the extent [or as] she continued to study she thus became smart

Generic "matter" or "thing" reference

The MIX+FLOWERS, FRUITS [xFF] singular relative pronoun *–lo-* may be implicitly taken to refer to one of its nouns *jambo*, matter, or *neno*, word, etc which can in turn be interpreted to refer to any generic matter or thing. For example:

sitaki [jambo] alilofanya jana, I do not want **what** [matter/thing] he did yesterday
sijui afanyalo, I do not know **what** [matter/thing] he does

Similarly, the THINGS [T] singular relative pronoun *–cho-* may be implicitly taken to refer to one of its nouns *kitu*, thing. For example:

[kitu] alichohitaji ni shahada, **what** [thing] he needed was a diploma

10.3.2 Summary of Relative Suffixes

These are the cases of relative -*o* pronouns that are **suffixed** in constructed verbs. We saw an example of this above (timeless tense, first row below) as compared to the more common infix position discussed above in section 10.3 Relative Pronouns. The other instances of this are covered in sections referenced in the last column:

Type of usage	Which verbs?	Examples	Section reference
Timeless Relative	with ALL verbs	*magari yatoshayo*, cars which suffice; *mkeo upendaye*, your wife whom you like -ve: *yasitoshayo usipendaye*	section 10.3 Relative Pronouns
Present Relative	with ALL verbs, when using an old -*li*- tense, especially with: *wa*, be	*magari yaliyo hapa*, cars which are here, or: *magari yaliyomo uani*, cars which are in the yard, or: *magari yalipo*, the cars where they are -ve: *yasiyo yasiyomo yasipo*	section 10.7.3 Old -li- Present Tense of wa, be, with Relatives
Relative as an Object	with *wa na*, have	e.g. *magari yanayo*, cars having it, or: *magari tuliyonayo*, the cars which we have (them); using -*li*- tense – see above -ve: *yasiyo na tusiyo na*	section 10.7.5.1 Exception: embedded object SUFFIXED to na

Type of usage	Which verbs?	Examples	Section reference
"...is/are" + Place	--	e.g. *magari <u>ya</u>po hapa*, the cars are here <u>-ve</u>: *hayapo*	section 10.8 – po/ko/mo, ...is/are
*ndi- emphasis	--	e.g. *ndi<u>yo</u> magari yake*, they <u>indeed are</u> her cars <u>-ve</u>: *siyo*	more under the *ndi-* entry in the Swahili-English Dictionary in Volume 2)

*This last case is included here because of the resemblance of its suffix to a relative, but it is NOT a relative, it is an abbreviated demonstrative of the specific variety e.g. the *ndiyo* above is derived from *ni hayo*, they are these.

10.3.3 Practice: Relative Pronouns

Answers to the previous practice of section 9.1 Practice: Prepositions:

Huog<u>e</u>a sabuni, I bathe <u>with</u> soap

Walifurah<u>i</u>a ushindi, they rejoiced <u>in</u> the victory

Tenzi za kuvut<u>i</u>a, poems of pulling <u>towards</u> = appealing poems

Alinij<u>i</u>a kusema pole, she came <u>to</u> me to say sorry (in consolation)

<u>Practice:</u>

Fill in the blanks below to match the underlined word in the English translation. An **example** is provided for the first entry. The various prefixes in the verbs have been separated by hyphens for you to analyze :-)

[The correct answers are given at the beginning of the next Practice section. Note: *ni*, is, used in these examples is covered in section 10.7.2 Wa, be]

Mti u-li-<u>o</u>-anguka ulikuwa mkuukuu, the tree <u>which</u> fell was aged. OR, *mti amba<u>o</u> ulianguka ulikuwa mkuukuu.*

Tenzi ni-taka-___-ku-somea ni za kwangu, the poems <u>which</u> I will read to you are of my own. OR, *tenzi amba___ nitakusomea ni za kwangu*.

Ndani ya mahali ni-li-___-zi-ficha fedha ni siri, in the place inside <u>which</u> I hid it, the money, is secret. OR, *mahali amba___ nilizificha fedha ni siri*.

Matunda ya___iva nimeyaacha mtini, the fruits <u>which have not</u> ripened I have left them on the tree.

Mfanyakazi ameandika hesabu kama ni-li-___-___-eleza, the employee (literally doer-of-work) wrote the accounts <u>how</u> I explained it <u>to him</u>.

Hatujui jinsi a-taka-___-fika hapa, we don't know <u>how</u> he will arrive here.

Asema___? <u>What</u> says he?

___mesikiwa kwamba njia zitafunguliwa kesho, <u>it</u> has been heard that the roads will be opened tomorrow.

10.4 Conditionals

Conditional statements are of two parts. The first part is the condition and second part is a statement based on the condition. There are a number of different condition types:

<u>IF</u>:

Infix **–ki-**, if, is used in verb construction for making the condition. For example:

nikitaka nitakuambia, **if** I want I will tell you

akiwa nyumbani nitamwona, **if** she is at home I will see her

tukicheza hivyo tutashinda, **if** we play like this we will win

kikianguka *kikombe kitavunjika, **if** it, the cup, falls it will break

yakichanua *maua yatapendeza, **if** they, the flowers, bloom they will be attractive

[*This placement of a noun <u>after</u> the verb is quite common.]

But, compare:

*nyanya i**kiwa** mbivu tutaitumia*, **if** the tomato is ripe we will use it

and:

*i**kiwa** ni pamoja na*, (a phrase meaning) including, in which *ikiwa*, it being, uses -*ki*- as a <u>continuous</u> tense (as explained in section 10.6 Immediate 2nd Verbs)

ikiwa is also a standalone conditional 'if' – see Standalone "IF" words below

The <u>negative</u> version is constructed with **–*sipo*-**:

***usipo**amka sasa hivi utachelewa*, **if** you do **not** get up right now you will be late

***usipo**kula sasa utaona njaa baadaye*, **if** you do **not** eat now you will be hungry later [The infinitive *ku*- of the verb *la*, eat, is retained. See section 10.7 Exceptions: Single Syllable Verbs.]

If the second part of an "IF" conditional statement concerns what **could** have happened, infix **–*nge*-** is used in **BOTH** parts to express this, instead of -***ki***-. For example:

*ni**nge**jua unakuja ni**nge**pika chakula*, **if** I knew you were coming I **would** have cooked food

If only a second part is stated it translates as follows e.g.

*li**nge**kuwa jambo*, it **would have been** a problem, with an implicit first part

*walitumaini kwamba a**nge**wapata msaada*, they hoped that he **would** help them

*niliwasema kwamba ni**nge**watembelea, basi niko hapa*, I told you / them that I would visit you / them, well then here I am

The above -***nge***- is in the present moment. For something in the past, –***ngali***- (*nge+li*) is used e.g.

ningalijua unakuja ningalipika chakula, **if** I **had** known you were coming I **would have** cooked food

The <u>negative</u> is formed by inserting infix *–si-* e.g.

nisingejua unakuja nisingeweza kupika chakula, **if** I did **not** know you were coming I would **not** have been able to cook food

nisingalikuwa mgonjwa ningalikuja nawe, **if** I **had not** been sick I **would** have come with you

Standalone "IF" words exist: ***ikiwa, iwapo, kama*** e.g.

ikiwa *itanyesha tutakaa nyumbani*, **if** it will rain we will stay home

A <u>negative</u> is formed by verb negation in the usual way, for example:

*ikiwa **ha**itanyesha tutatembelea rafiki*, **if** it will **not** rain we will visit friends

<u>REGARDING</u>:

A gerund (in Swahili being the same form as the infinitive) is used to make this condition in which "<u>regarding</u>" is implied. For example:

kufika hajafika, <u>regarding</u> arriving he has not yet arrived

<u>WHEN</u>:

Infix *–po-*, when, is used in verb construction for making the condition. For example:

*nili**po**kuwa mchanga niliogelea kila siku*, **when** I was young I swam everyday

If the tense is future *taka* is used since *–po-* being a relative it follows relative rules [see section 10.3 Relative Pronouns]:

*nitaka**po**fika nitakupiga simu*, **when** I arrive I will phone you
kila *nitaka**po**kuja nitakaa*, **whenever** I will come I will stay

If the tense is timeless, the *-po* is suffixed:

kila aja**po** *kwetu hunywa chai*, **whenever** he comes to our place he has tea

*nienda**po** ko kote huendesha baisikeli*, **when** I go anywhere I ride a bicycle

> [More in Appendix G: -po- infix / suffix.]

The -***nge***-, would, previously covered above, can be used with this –***po***-, when, construction e.g.

*utakapotembelea Unguja unge**penda kufanya nini?*** **when** you visit Zanzibar you **would** want to do what?

The <u>negative</u> is formed in the same way as the negative of "IF" given above: -***sipo***- e.g.

*ni**sipo**kuwa mzee ningeogelea kila siku*, **if** I **wasn't** old I would swim everyday

<u>WHEN</u>:

-***kisha***, then, prefixed with a pronoun is used as a 'when' to express the first part (condition). For example:

*a**kisha** maliza kazi aende nyumbani*, **when** he finishes work he may go home

10.5 Subjunctives

We now deal with the troublesome subjunctive tense, separately from the other easier-to-understand tenses dealt with above in chapter 5 Verbs.

A subjunctive has no inherent indication of time, unlike say the present or the past tense. It is meant to describe something that *may* become an actuality or is just imagined or desired as such. As compared to this, 'normal' sentences are statements or questions intended for elaborating some actuality. Also to be compared are imperatives which are commands. A common word used in subjunctives is "were" e.g. were you a bird you could fly; I wish I were you (or in literary lingo, would that I were you). Besides "were", which comes from the verb "to be", other verbs can be used in the subjunctive mood e.g. parents always suggesting their children work smarter. Work is being suggested here so it is in the subjunctive mood, even though in form it appears to be the present tense of the verb "to work". The past subjunctive is similar e.g. if I had worked smarter I would have been ahead today. The use of "if" is also a clue that this is a subjunctive mood.

The subjunctive in Swahili is formed by attaching a pronoun prefix to the verb base and whose ending vowel -a is changed to -e e.g. *fanya*, do, whose subjunctive is:

afanye, that he do

the *a*- prefix being the pronoun for the 3rd person singular. Most foreign verbs do not end in –*a*, in which case there is no –*a* to change and the pronoun prefix is simply attached to verb base e.g. *jaribu*, try, becomes:

ajaribu, that he try

Using *kazi*, work:

afanye kazi is literally translated as "that he do work"

Being in subjunctive mood, it represents something that is not yet an actuality and that it is *intended* that he work and so an implicit translation would be *afanye kazi*, [I suggest] that he work.

Other examples: [Negation using –*si*- infix]

asifanye kazi, [I suggest] that he not work

chakula kisipate baridi, [I want] that the food not get cold

ununue mboga, [I wish] that you buy vegetables, and in the negative: *usinunue mboga*, [I wish] that you not buy vegetables

The last example above is to be compared with the imperative mood (covered in section 5.10 Imperatives):

nunua mboga, buy vegetables

Whereas the subjunctive has an explicit pronoun *u-*, you, the above imperative implies it, and in addition both the positive and especially the negative subjunctives can be interpreted as 'nicer' versions of imperatives. [More below under "Explicit Imperatives".]

An example with both the <u>imperative</u> and the subjunctive:

<u>soma</u> *kwa bidii* [*ili*] *ufanikie mtihani*, study with effort so that you pass the exam

Note *ili*, so that, is optional. [In place of the subjunctive *ufanikie*, the infinitive *kufanikia* can be used as per section 10.6 Immediate 2nd Verbs.]

Often you will encounter in Swahili, for example, the <u>implied</u> "[I suggest]" or "[I wish]" is made explicit:

<u>ninataka</u> *afanye kazi*, <u>I wish</u> that he work

where again the indirect instruction to the 3rd party "that he work" is in the subjunctive mood, *afanye*.

Cautionary note: personal pronoun prefixes ***ni-***, I, *tu-*, we, and *wa-*, they, look the same as their corresponding object references -***ni-***, me, -*tu-*, us, and -*wa-*, them, therefore subjunctives formed with these look similar to the corresponding *object form* of the imperative e.g.

ni*pige simu*, phone me
[being an imperative the ***ni-***, me, is an **object**!]

OR

*leta namba **ni****pige simu*, bring the number that I make a phone call
[being a subjunctive the ***ni-***, I, is a personal **pronoun**!]

In question form, the subjunctive translates as 'may subject verb ...?' e.g.

afanye kazi hii? May he do this work?
watu waamke? May the people wake up?

Explicit Imperatives:

The imperatives covered in section 5.10 Imperatives did not attach a pronoun prefix for the 2nd person singular to which the imperative was addressed – it was implicit. To make it explicit the subjunctive form is used e.g. *ngoja*, wait; *ngoja* is an imperative with an implicit *u-*, you, whereas the subjunctive *ungoje*, is a subjunctive used as an imperative with an explicit *u-*. BUT, as stated in section 5.10 Imperatives, a command to a group of people attaches a *-ni* suffix to the subjunctive e.g. attaching suffix *-ni* we get *chukueni* (from *chukua*, take) which is a command to a group of persons. Comparing the two subjunctive command forms:

2nd person singular: *ungoje*, wait [uses *u-*, you, pronoun prefix]
2nd person plural: *ngojeni*, wait [uses *-ni* suffix, a short form of *ninyi*, you]

Negative imperative always uses <u>negative</u> subjunctive e.g.

usingoje, don't wait (to a 2nd person singular)
msingoje, don't wait (to 2nd person plural)
asingoje, don't let him wait (indirect instruction for a 3rd person singular)
wasingoje, don't let them wait (indirect instruction for 3rd person plural)

Whenever it is a two-part construction, the first being your desire or a command, the second part is always subjunctive. For example:

nenda ununue mboga, go buy vegetables

where the first part *nenda* is an imperative and the second part *ununue* is subjunctive. If there is a third instruction being addressed to all parties, the 2nd person plural pronoun *m-*, you, dealt with in section 5.1.1 Pronoun Prefixes, is used e.g.

nenda[1] uwambie[2] rafiki zako[3] mzichume[4] nyanya, go[1] tell[2] your friends[3] that you (all) pick[4] the tomatoes, where:

[1]is addressed to the first party
[2]is addressed to the first party, for conveying it to a second party[3]
[4]is addressed to both the first and second parties

More **imperative**, subjunctive examples:

njoo usome, come read
nipe kitabu nisome, give me the book that I may read
njoo usikilize, come listen
mwambie mtoto asome, tell him / her, the child, that he / she read

nenda u<u>ka</u>chume maua, go pick flowers [to 2nd person singular]
nendeni m<u>ka</u>nunue, go buy [2nd person plural]

> Swahili usage often sees the use of -<u>ka</u>- which indicates a consecutive action [covered below in section 10.6 Immediate 2nd Verbs]. Conversationally the *u-* or *m-* pronoun in the second verb is dropped: **nenda** <u>ka</u>chume or **nendeni** kanunue, and sometimes the first part is also omitted (which then is implied): *kachume* or *kanunue*, which in this stand alone form looks like a 'primary' instruction to a 2nd person but it isn't, it is a 'secondary' subjunctive with an implicit imperative before it (**nenda** or **nendeni**). Had it been the primary, it would have had to be the imperative *chuma* or *nunue<u>ni</u>* (the <u>ni</u> suffix is 2nd person plural pronoun).

sitaki ukisome, I do not wish you read it, where -*ki*-, it, is an object reference to say a book

10.5.1 Imperative vs. Subjunctive Summary

Note: The 'true' **Imperative** (see column labelled as such) is used ONLY for the 2nd person singular positive. For all others, the **Subjunctive** is used as an imperative.

	Imperative*		Subjunctive** as an imperative	
	Positive	Negative	Positive	Negative
To 2nd person singular	*chukua,* carry	(see subjunctive)	*uchukue,* you carry	*usichukue,* do not carry
	kichukue, carry it (with		*ukichukue,* you carry it (with	*usichukue kitu,* do not carry a thing

	embedded object *ki-*)		embedded object *ki-*)	(an embedded object *ki-* is typically not used)
To 2nd person plural	(see subjunctive)	(see subjunctive)	*chukueni*, you carry	*msichukue*, do not carry
			kichukueni, you carry it (with object *ki-*)	*msichukue kitu*, do not carry a thing (an embedded object *ki-* is typically not used)

Subjunctive** as a verb in a sentence (i.e. not as an imperative)		
To 2nd person singular	*ninataka uchukue vitu vyangu*, I wish that you carry my things	*ninataka usichukue vitu vyangu*, I wish that you not carry my things
To 2nd person plural	*ninataka mchukue vitu vyangu*, I wish that you carry my things	*sitaki mchukue vitu vyangu*, I wish that you not carry my things

*Imperative NEVER has a personal pronoun prefix, the 2nd person singular is implied. It can take an OBJECT PREFIX as shown above.

**Subjunctive ALWAYS has a personal pronoun prefix or suffix. It can take an OBJECT PREFIX or INFIX as shown above.

10.5.2 Practice: Subjunctives, Conditionals

Answers to the previous practice of section 10.3.3 Practice: Relative Pronouns:

Mti u-li-o-anguka ulikuwa mkuukuu, the tree <u>which</u> fell was aged. OR, *mti amba**o** ulianguka ulikuwa mkuukuu.*

*Tenzi ni-taka-**zo**-ku-somea ni za kwangu*, the poems <u>which</u> I will read to you are of my own. OR, *tenzi amba**zo** nitakusomea ni za kwangu.*

*Ndani ya mahali ni-li-**mo**-zi-ficha fedha ni siri*, inside the place where I hid it, the money, is secret. OR, *mahali amba**mo** nilizificha fedha ni siri.*

*Matunda ya**siyo**iva nimeyaacha mtini*, the fruits <u>which have not</u> ripened I have left them on the tree.

*Mfanyakazi ameandika hesabu kama nili**vyo**mweleza*, the employee (literally doer-of-work) wrote the accounts <u>how</u> I explained it to him.

*Hatujui jinsi ataka**vyo**fika hapa*, we don't know <u>how</u> he will arrive here.

*Asema**lo**? <u>What</u> says he?*

<u>I</u>mesikiwa kwamba njia zitafunguliwa kesho, <u>it</u> has been heard that the roads will be opened tomorrow.

Practice:

Fill in the blanks below to complete the subjunctive form of the verb underlined in the English translation. An **example** is provided for the first entry.

[The correct answers are given at the beginning of the next Practice section.]

*Mamangu apendelea niw**e** daktari*, my mother prefers I <u>become</u> a doctor.

Nenda ukilet__ chakula kutoka jikoni, go <u>bring</u> it, the food, from the kitchen.

Angalia chakula ki__chomek__, keep an eye on the food that it does <u>not</u> <u>burn</u>.

Mwambi__ mwanafunzi aj__ hapa, <u>tell</u> the student to <u>come</u> here.

10.6 Immediate 2nd Verbs

For a second action which follows the first, that is, a **consecutive** action, -*ka*- [e.g. *katosha*, suffice(d)] is used instead of the required tense infix (which is inserted only in the first verb). The -*ka*-, as well as the other prefixes in here, are constant for all tenses. If the second action is **continuous** (in progress), -*ki*- is used. For a second action verb which is also in the same time frame as the first verb and thus a **concurrent** action, the infinitive: *ku*- [e.g. *kutosha*, to suffice] is used, preceded by a *na*, and. But if this is an **intended** action, *na* is not used.

To summarize:

2nd Verb	Use (for all tenses)	Example
Consecutive	**ka-*	*alifika akapumzika*, he arrived **then/and** he rested *nawaacha watoto nikaenda kazini*, I drop the children **then/and** I go to work
Continuous	***ki-*	*alikuja akikimbia*, he came runn**ing** *huendesha gari kukiangalia mahali pote*, we drive cars, carefully look**ing** all around [Note use of *ku*- prefix — see *ku*- below.]
Concurrent	*na ku-*	*alisoma **na ku**andika*, he read **and** wrote [Note: there is no pronoun before *ku*-]
Intended	*ku-*	*alikuja **ku**pumzika*, he came **to** rest *aje **ku**la*, that he come to dine [Note: there is no pronoun before *ku*-]

*Swahili usage finds *ka*- being used in narratives as a past tense infix:

*aka*ondoka, she left, or conversationally without the *a*- pronoun, *ka*ondoka. [cf. the normal *aliondoka*.]

The underlying sense of narratives is 'this happened, then that happened', and so on, and thus of a series of consecutive actions. Another example:

akawa alisomea chuo kikuu, she **was** studying at university

akawa hodari kwa masomo, she **became** smart in studies

ikawa alikuwa daktari, it **was** (it came to be) she became a doctor. [The generic *i-*, it, in *ikawa* is covered in section 10.11 Ya-/i-, It is....]

**Swahili usage finds *ki-* also being used as follows:

jozi ni vitu viwili vikiwa pamoja, a pair is two things **being** together

watu ishirini watashiriki katika Michezo ya Afrika, akiwemo Mweri kutoka na shule yetu, 20 people will participate in the African Games, **including** Mweri from our school [note: *akiwemo* instead of *akiwamo* is by usage, see section 10.8 –po/ko/mo, ...is/are...]

ni is the first verb, *wa* the second. [Note: *ni*, is, used in these examples is covered in section 10.7.2 Wa, be]

Negatives:

The negatives are the same as the negative subjunctive [section 10.5 Subjunctives under Negation] e.g.

alifika asipumzike, he arrived, he did not rest

alikuja asikimbie, he came not running

Usage when the first verb is *wa*, be: the second verb can make use of the usual tense infixes instead of the ones in the above table e.g.

alikuwa anazichukua, OR: *alikuwa alizichukua*, he was carrying them [cf. *alikuwa akizichukua*]

10.7 Exceptions: Single Syllable Verbs

As seen at the beginning of chapter 5 Verbs, the **ku-**, to, of an infinitive verb is dropped in verb construction. The exception to this is the handful of single syllable verb bases found in Swahili:

fa, die
ja, come
la, eat
nya, excrete
nywa, drink
pa, give
the above being the common* ones, plus a couple of uncommon ones:
cha, dawn,
pwa, ebb & dry,
in which the **ku-** is RETAINED for all tenses EXCEPT for the TIMELESS:
[**wa*, be, is THE most common single syllable verb base but it is dealt with separately in section 10.7.2 Wa, be, and its related extension in section 10.7.5 Wa na, have.]

[*anakula*, he / she is eating] Present tense
[*ala**, he / she eats] Timeless tense *As is often the case with 3rd person singular an alternative form *yu*- is sometimes used instead of *a*-, i.e. *yuala*.
[*alikula*, he / she ate] Past tense
[*atakula*, he / she will eat] Future tense
[*amekula*, he / she has eaten] Present Perfect tense

In addition to these single syllable verb bases, Swahili usage has treated two other verbs in the same way: *enda*, go, *isha*, finish, e.g.

[*anakw*enda*, he / she is going] Present
*Note: Swahili spelling has changed the written form of *-kue*- to *-kwe*- but the pronunciation is the same.
[*anakwisha*, he / she is finishing] Present
but note the contraction often seen with the present perfect:
[*amekwisha*, he / she has finished] Present Perfect, contracted to:
[*amesha*]

Note: when used with another verb it <u>emphasises</u> the completion of the action e.g.

*ame**kw**isha ondoka*, he / she has <u>already</u> left

which is seen contracted to:

*ame**sh**aondoka*, he / she has <u>already</u> left]

<u>An Exception to the above Exceptions!</u> *pa*, give:

The verb *pa*, give, is always used with an object, embedded or standalone e.g.

anani̱pa, he / she is giving me

ki̱pe, give it

Mungu apa mvua, God gives rain

   lakini hapi kwa mvua tu, but does not give by rain only

Effectively then, the infinitive *-ku-* of *pa* is not used, and it is as if it were not single-syllable.

<u>More Exceptions to the above Exceptions:</u>

The general rule is that the *ku-* of the infinitive is retained <u>except</u> for the timeless tense as stated above. In addition to this exception, there are a number of other <u>exceptions</u> where it is NOT RETAINED as compared to other situations where it IS RETAINED. This table shows the cases where the **ku-** is retained or not, along with examples:

Ku- is Retained?	Section
	Examples
	5.4 Negatives
No	Present: *hali*, he / she is not eating Present: *sili*, I am not eating
	Present Perfect: *hajala*, she has not yet eaten Present Perfect: *sijala*, I have not yet eaten
	Timeless: *hali*, he / she does not eat e.g. meat Timeless: *sili*, I do not eat e.g. meat
	Past: *ha**ku**la*, she did not eat Past: *si**ku**la*, I did not eat This <u>ku</u> is the tense infix, NOT the *ku* of the infinitive *kula!*

Ku- is Retained?	Section
	Examples
Yes	Future: *hata__ku__la*, she will not eat Future: *sita__ku__la*, I will not eat The __ku__ here IS the infinitive prefix of *kula*!
	5.6 Hu- Routine Conjugation
No	*sisi* **hula** *matunda kila siku*, we eat /ate / will eat / have eaten fruits every day **hu**- with verb **wa**, be, can be used to indicate "every time, or all the time, or constantly, or customarily": **huwa** *tunacheza*, all the time we [will] [have] play[ed]
	The negative routine = negative present / timeless, as given under the Negatives row above.
	5.10 Imperatives
Yes	*ku*la, eat
No	negative: *usile*, do not eat
	when an object is inserted e.g. *ki__e__ chakula*, eat the food where the __ki__- object refers to *chakula*, giving us: eat it, the food
	10.1 Embedded Object References

No	*simba ana__m__la*, lion is eating <u>it</u> - Present tense
	simba ha__m__li, lion is not eating it - Present -ve tense
	      m is the <u>object</u> reference for a prey
	nili__ki__la, I ate it (the food) - Past tense
	      ki is the <u>object</u> reference for the food
	ata__ni__pa matunda, she will give me fruits - Future tense
	      ni is the <u>object</u> reference for me
	wame__vi__nywa vinywaji, they have drunk beverages - Future tense
	      vi is the <u>object</u> reference for beverages

	10.3 Relative Pronouns
Yes	All tenses except timeless: *mgeni anaye__ku__nywa*, guest who is drinking *watu wanao__kw__enda*, people who are going *atakaye__ku__ja*, he who will come

Ku- is Retained?	Section
	Examples
	Negative: *asiyekula*, he who doesn't/didn't/won't eat
No	Timeless tense: *alaye nyama*, he who eats meat
	Negative: *asilaye nyama*, he who doesn't eat meat
	10.4 Conditionals
Yes	negative: *asipokuwa nyumbani nitamngojea*, if she is not at home I will wait for her
No	*akija nitafurahi*, if he comes I will be happy
	10.5 Subjunctives
No	*ale*, that he eat
	negative: *asile*, that he not eat
	10.6 Immediate 2nd Verbs
No	*huamka nikanywa maji*, I wake up and drink water
	negative: *huamka nisinywe maji*, I wake up and don't drink water

10.7.1 Practice: Verbs – Single Syllable & Immediate 2nd

Answers to the previous practice of section 10.3.3 Practice: Relative Pronouns:

Mamangu apendelea niwe daktari, my mother prefers I become a doctor.

Nenda ukilete chakula kutoka jikoni, go bring it, the food, from the kitchen.

Angalia chakula kisichomeke, keep an eye on the food that it does not burn.

Mwambie mwanafunzi aje hapa, tell the student to come here.

Practice:

Fill in the blank spaces as indicated below in square brackets in the verb columns. An **example** is given for the first entry.

fa, die
ja, come
la, eat
nywa, drink
pa, give
cha, dawn
wa, be

Plus a few new verbs used below:

amka, awake
kimbia, run
karibisha, welcome

[The correct answers are given at the beginning of the next Practice section.]

Verb	2nd Verb [type]
*nita**kula*** [I will eat]	--
si_____ [I am not eating]	--
hatu_____ [we are not eating]	--
tuli_____ [we came]	--
hatuku_____ [we did not come]	--

Verb	2nd Verb [type]
hata_____ [he will not come]	--
ame_____ [he has come]	--
haja_____ [he has not come yet]	--
ali**amka** [she woke up,]	a **ka** la [consecutive: she ate]
wana_____ [they are coming]	wa__kimbia [continuous: running]
a_____ [he eats]	___ ___nywa [concurrent: and drinks]
ali_____ [she came]	__tukaribisha [intention: to welcome us]

Wa, be, is conjugated in the same way as other verbs (see section 5.1 Tenses) EXCEPT:

(1) As given in section 10.7 Exceptions: Single Syllable Verbs, the **ku-** of its infinitive form is RETAINED for positives. For example:

PEOPLE [Pp]: *Mtu-Watu*, person(s)

a-, she / he [*anakuwa*, she / he is being / becoming] Present tense

a-, she / he [**hawi**, she / he is not being / becoming] Present tense negative

wa-, they [*wanakuwa*, they are being / becoming]
Present tense

wa-, they [*hawawi*, they are not being / becoming]
Present tense negative

(2) The Timeless Conjugation is made in a very simple way:

The verb is conjugated as "*ni*" for ALL noun groups, and is typically followed by a descriptive word or phrase or noun. In the negative it is "*si*". For example:

PEOPLE [Pp]: *Mtu-Watu*, person(s)

[*mpishi **ni** muhimu hotelini*, a cook is important in a hotel]

As is often the case with 3rd person singular an alternative form **yu** is sometimes used instead of **ni** e.g. *mpishi **yu** ...* It is also sometimes used for 2nd person singular e.g. *wewe **yu** mzuri*, you are fine

[*mpishi **si** muhimu dukani*, a cook is not important in a shop]

[*wapishi **ni** muhimu mahotelini*, cooks are important in hotels]

[*wapishi **si** muhimu madukani*, cooks are not important in shops]

VEGETATION [V]: *Mti-Miti*, tree(s)

[*mwaridi **ni** mmea mzuri*, a rose bush is a pretty plant]

Sometimes, instead of **ni** the singular pronoun for this noun group **u** is used in singular e.g. *mwaridi **u** mmea mzuri*, I in plural e.g. *miwaridi **i** mimea mizuri*. Such alternatives to **ni** in other noun groups have to be watched for e.g.

xFF: **li** e.g. *kabati **li** zuri*, the cupboard is nice;

ya e.g. *makasha **ya** tayari*, the cupboard is ready

[*mbuyu **si** mti mzuri*, a baobab is not a pretty tree]

[*miwaridi **ni** mimea mizuri*, rose bushes are pretty plants]

[*mibuyu **si** miti mizuri*, baobabs are not pretty trees]

10.7.3 Old -*li*- Present Tense of *wa*, be, with Relatives

Relatives [section 10.3 Relative Pronouns] when used with the verb *wa*, be, make use of an old form of the present tense, -**li**-, and shift the relative pronoun to the end (like with the timeless tense) e.g.

maneno yaliyo kweli, words (they) which are true i.e. true words

Note that the verb *wa* itself is not used, it is implied.

If the word following this construction is a place adverb a -*po/ko/mo* construction [section 10.8 –po/ko/mo, …is/are] is added e.g.

mtu aliye, the person who is… [construction introduced above]
+ *mtu yupo pale*, the person is there [section 10.8]
= *mtu aliyepo pale…*, the person who is there… [*yu*- is redundant]

Similarly, *kijiji cha* Tangata *kilicho*, the village of Tangata which is…
+ *kijiji cha* Tangata *kipo karibu na Tanga*, the village of Tangata is near Tanga
= *kijiji cha* Tangata *kilichopo karibu na* Tanga…, the village of Tangata which is near Tanga…

If the phrase is terminal (as compared to the above incomplete ones, indicated by the ellipses …) then the relative pronoun e.g. -*cho*- is dropped (and which is implied):

anakwenda Tangata *kilipo*, he is going where Tangata is

This present tense -*li*- is to be compared with the past tense -*li*- e.g.

maneno yaliyokuwa kweli, words (they) which were true [the verb *wa* IS present here, which clues you in to -*li*- being a past tense here]

[More in Appendix G: -po- infix / suffix.]

Although the -*li*- present tense is typically used with *wa*, it is also seen used with passive verbs as a present perfect, as shown bolded below:

chakula kilichoachwa ndani ya sufuria, the food which has been **left** in the pot

10.7.4 Practice: Verb *wa*, be(come)"

Answers to the previous practice of section 10.7.1 Practice: Verbs – Single Syllable & Immediate 2nd:

Verb	2nd Verb [type]
*nita**kula*** [I will eat]	--
*si**li*** [I am not eating]	--
*hatu**li*** [we are not eating]	--
*tuli**kuja*** [we came]	--
*hatuku**ja*** [we did not come]	--
*hata**kuja*** [he will not come]	--
*ame**kuja*** [he has come]	--
*haja**ja*** [he has not come yet]	--
*ali**amka*** she woke up,]	*a**ka**la* [consecutive: she ate]
*wana**kuja*** [they are coming]	*wa**ki**kimbia* [continuous: running]

Verb	2nd Verb [type]
a*la* [he eats]	*na ku*nywa [concurrent: and drinks]
ali*kuja* [she came]	*ku*tukaribisha [intention: to welcome us]

Practice:

Fill in the conjugated form of *wa*, be, in the verb column below. An **example** is provided for the first entry.

[The correct answers are given at the beginning of the next Practice section.]

Noun	Verb	Adjective or noun
bamia	*ni* [timeless]	*mboga*, vegetable
bamia	_____ [negative timeless]	*nyekundu*, red
chumba	_____ [present]	*tayari*, ready
vyumba	_____ [negative present]	*tayari*, ready
chungwa	_____ [past]	*mbichi*, unripe
machungwa	_____ [negative past]	*tamu*, sweet
kuimba	_____ [future]	*kuzuri*, nice

Noun	Verb	Adjective or noun
mahali	_____ [negative future]	mbali, far
mbamia	_____ [present]	mwema, good
mibamia	_____ [negative present perfect]	myema, good
mdudu	_____ [present]	mkubwa, big
wadudu	_____ [past]	wafu, lifeless
ufunguo	_____ [future]	mzuri, nice
funguo	_____ [present perfect]	mbaya, bad

10.7.5 Wa na, have

In Swahili the verb "have" is an extension of the verb wa, be, by the addition of the conjunction word **na**, and/with, giving us wa **na**, be with, which really means, have. Its tenses are thus formed by conjugating the verb wa, be, followed by the word **na**, with, EXCEPT for the present and the timeless tenses where the verb (wa) is NOT USED and the pronoun prefix is simply attached to the above **na** (see * in the examples below). For example:

PEOPLE [Pp]: Mtu-Watu, person(s)

[*ana njaa, she / he is hungry] Present, Timeless

[alikuwa **na** njaa, she / he was hungry] Past

[*atakuwa **na** njaa*, she / he will be hungry] Future

[*amekuwa **na** njaa*, she / he has become hungry] Present Perfect

[**wana** njaa*, they are hungry] Present, Timeless

[*walikuwa **na** njaa*, they were hungry] Past

[*watakuwa **na** njaa*, they will be hungry] Future

[*wamekuwa **na** njaa*, they have become hungry] Present Perfect

VEGETATION [V]: *Mti-Miti*, tree(s)

[**una** matunda*, it has fruits] Present, Timeless

[*ulikuwa **na** matunda*, it had fruits] Past

[*utakuwa **na** matunda*, it will have fruits] Future

[*umekuwa **na** matunda*, it has borne fruits] Present Perfect

[**ina** matunda*, they have fruits] Present, Timeless

[*ilikuwa **na** matunda*, they had fruits] Past

[*itakuwa **na** matunda*, they will have fruits] Future

[*imekuwa **na** matunda*, they have borne fruits] Present Perfect

MIX+FLOWERS, FRUITS [xFF]: Tunda-Matunda, fruit(s)

[**lina** rangi*, it has colour(s)] Present, Timeless

[*lilikuwa **na** rangi*, it had colour(s)] Past

[*litakuwa **na** rangi*, it will have colour(s)] Future

[*limekuwa **na** rangi*, it has borne colour(s)] Present Perfect

[**yana** rangi*, they have colour(s)] Present, Timeless

[*yalikuwa **na** rangi*, they had colour(s)] Past

[*yatakuwa **na** rangi*, they will have colour(s)] Future

[*yamekuwa **na** rangi*, they have borne colour(s)] Present Perfect

THINGS [T]: Kitu-Vitu, things(s)

    [*_kina milango_, it has doors] Present, Timeless

    [_kilikuwa_ **_na_** _milango_, it had doors] Past

    [_kitakuwa_ **_na_** _milango_, it will have doors] Future

    [_kimekuwa_ **_na_** _milango_, it now has doors] Present Perfect

    [*_vina milango_, they have doors] Present, Timeless

    [_vilikuwa_ **_na_** _milango_, they had doors] Past

    [_vitakuwa_ **_na_** _milango_, they will have doors] Future

    [_vimekuwa_ **_na_** _milango_, they now have doors] Present Perfect

MIX+FAUNA, VEGGIES [xFV]: Nyanya-Nyanya, tomato(es)

    [*_ina miiba_, it has thorns] Present, Timeless

    [_ilikuwa_ **_na_** _miiba_, it had thorns] Past

    [_itakuwa_ **_na_** _miiba_, it will have thorns] Future

    [_imekuwa_ **_na_** _miiba_, it has borne thorns] Present Perfect

    [*_zina miiba_, they have thorns] Present, Timeless

    [_zilikuwa_ **_na_** _miiba_, they had thorns] Past

    [_zitakuwa_ **_na_** _miiba_, they will have thorns] Future

    [_zimekuwa_ **_na_** _miiba_, they have borne thorns] Present Perfect

U-WORDS [U]: Utenzi-Tenzi, poem(s)

    [*_una maneno_, it has words] Present, Timeless

    [_ulikuwa_ **_na_** _maneno_, it had words] Past

    [_utakuwa_ **_na_** _maneno_, it will have words] Future

    [_umekuwa_ **_na_** _maneno_, it now has words] Present Perfect

    [*_zina maneno_, they have words] Present, Timeless

*[zilikuwa **na** maneno, they had words]* Past

*[zitakuwa **na** maneno, they will have words]* Future

*[zimekuwa **na** maneno, they now have words]* Present Perfect

PLACE-ADVERBS [Pl]: *Mahali- Mahali*, place(s)

[**pana** *madirisha*, it/they has/have windows] Present, Timeless

[*palikuwa **na** madirisha*, it/they had windows] Past

> Note: Quite often a story begins: *Hapo zamani <u>palikuwa na mtu</u>,* here long ago <u>there was (literally, was with) a man</u>.

[*patakuwa **na** madirisha*, it/they will have windows] Future

[*pamekuwa **na** madirisha*, it/they now has/have windows] Present Perfect

pa- refers to a definite place. The PLACE-ADVERBS [Pl] group has two other pronouns: **ku**- referring to an unspecified place, and **m**- referring to the interior of a place e.g. *kuna mvua*, it (e.g. the tropics) has rain, *mna maji*, it (e.g. a tank) has water.

GERUNDS [G]: Kusoma- Kusoma, reading(s)

[*kuna faida*, it/they has/have benefits] Present, Timeless

[*kulikuwa **na** faida*, it/they had benefits] Past

[*kutakuwa **na** faida*, it/they will have benefits] Future

[*kumekuwa **na** faida*, it/they has/have borne benefits] Present Perfect

Negatives

The negatives are formed in the usual way by attaching the **ha**- prefix, for example:

PEOPLE [Pp]: *Mtu-Watu*, person(s)

> [**ha**na njaa, she / he is not hungry] Present, Timeless

> [**ha**kuwa na njaa, she / he was not hungry] Past

> [**ha**takuwa na njaa, she / he will not be hungry] Future

> [**ha**jawa na njaa, she / he has not yet become hungry] Present Perfect

> [**ha**wana njaa, they are not hungry] Present, Timeless

> [**ha**wakuwa na njaa, they were not hungry] Past

> [**ha**watakuwa na njaa, they will not be hungry] Future

> [**ha**wajawa na njaa, they have not yet become hungry] Present Perfect

Note: As shown before, 1st and 2nd person singulars have negative prefixes which are different from the above *ha*- prefixes. They are **si**- and **hu**-, respectively, as follows:

> [**si**na njaa, I am not hungry] Present, Timeless

> [**hu**na njaa, you are not hungry] Present, Timeless

The 1st and 2nd person plurals use the normal **ha**- suffix.

VEGETATION [V]: Mti-Miti, tree(s)

> [**ha**una matunda, it has no fruits] Present, Timeless

> [**ha**ukuwa na matunda, it did not have fruits] Past

> [**ha**utakuwa na matunda, it will not have fruits] Future

> [**ha**ujawa na matunda, it has not yet borne fruits] Present Perfect

[*haina matunda*, they have no fruits] Present, Timeless

[*haikuwa na matunda*, they did not have fruits] Past

[*haitakuwa na matunda*, they will not have fruits] Future

[*haijawa na matunda*, they have not yet borne fruits] Present Perfect

MIX+FLOWERS, FRUITS [xFF]: Tunda-Matunda, fruit(s)

[*halina rangi*, it has no colour(s)] Present, Timeless

[*halikuwa na rangi*, it had no colour(s)] Past

[*halitakuwa na rangi*, it will not have colour(s)] Future

[*halijawa na rangi*, it has not yet borne colour(s)] Present Perfect

[*hayana rangi*, they have no colour(s)] Present, Timeless

[*hayakuwa na rangi*, they had no colour(s)] Past

[*hayatakuwa na rangi*, they will not have colour(s)] Future

[*hayajawa na rangi*, they have not yet borne colour(s)] Present Perfect

THINGS [T]: Kitu-Vitu, things(s)

[*hakina miguu*, it has no legs] Present, Timeless

[*hakikuwa na miguu*, it had no legs] Past

[*hakitakuwa na miguu*, it will not have legs] Future

[*hakijawa na miguu*, it does not yet have legs] Present Perfect

[*havina miguu*, they have no legs] Present, Timeless

[*havikuwa na miguu*, they had no legs] Past

[*havitakuwa na miguu*, they will not have legs] Future

[*havijawa na miguu*, they do not yet have legs] Present Perfect

MIX+FAUNA, VEGGIES [xFV]: Nyanya-Nyanya, tomato(es)

>[*ha*ina mbegu, it has no seed(s)] Present, Timeless

>[*ha*ikuwa na mbegu, it did not have (a) seed(s)] Past

>[*ha*itakuwa na mbegu, it will not have (a) seed(s)] Future

>[*ha*ijawa na mbegu, it has not yet borne (a) seed(s)] Present Perfect

>[*ha*zina mbegu, they have no seed(s)] Present, Timeless

>[*ha*zikuwa na mbegu, they did not have (a) seed(s)] Past

>[*ha*zitakuwa na mbegu, they will not have (a) seed(s)] Future

>[*ha*zijawa na mbegu, they have not yet borne (a) seed(s)] Present Perfect

U-WORDS [U]: Utenzi-Tenzi, poem(s)

>[*ha*una maana, it has no meaning] Present, Timeless

>[*ha*ukuwa na maana, it had no meaning] Past

>[*ha*utakuwa na maana, it will have no meaning] Future

>[*ha*ujawa na maana, it yet has no meaning] Present Perfect

>[*ha*zina maana, they have no meaning] Present, Timeless

>[*ha*zikuwa na maana, they had no meaning] Past

>[*ha*zitakuwa na maana, they will not have meaning] Future

>[*ha*zijawa na maana, they yet have no meaning] Present Perfect

PLACE-ADVERBS [Pl]: Mahali- Mahali, place(s)

>[*ha*pana kitu, it/they do/does not have anything] Present, Timeless

>[*ha*pakuwa na kitu, it did not have anything] Past

>[*ha*patakuwa na kitu, it will not have anything] Future

[*hapajawa na kitu*, it does not yet have anything] Present Perfect

pa- refers to a definite place. The PLACE-ADVERBS [Pl] group has two other pronouns: *ku*- referring to an unspecified place, and *m*- referring to the interior of a place e.g. *hakuna kitu*, it/they do/does not have anything, *hamna kitu*, it/they do/does not have anything.

GERUNDS [G]: Kusoma- Kusoma, reading(s)

[*hakuna furaha*, it has no joy] Present, Timeless

[*hakukuwa na furaha*, it had no joy] Past

[*hakutakuwa na furaha*, it will have no joy] Future

[*hakujawa na furaha*, it has yet no joy] Present Perfect

10.7.5.1 *Exception: embedded object SUFFIXED to na*

The embedded object goes at the end of the verb AND for which the relative pronoun (see above section 10.3 Relative Pronouns) is used. For example:

[Reminder: the verb <u>wa</u>, be, which is part of the verb *wa na*, have, is NOT used in the present tense (it is implied as is the tense as well), but it IS used in other tenses e.g. the first example below, in the past tense would be *niliku<u>wa</u> naye*, I had her / him]

All examples are in the present tense. Negatives are not given for all plural objects, the plural ones being prefixed the same as the singulars as seen in the first group:

PEOPLE [Pp]

[*ninaye*, I have her / him]
[*sinaye*, I don't have her / him]
[*anaye*, she / he has her / him]
[*hanaye*, she / he doesn't have her / him]

Plural objects are prefixed the same as above:
[*ninao*, I have them]
[*sinao*, I don't have them]
[*anao*, she / he has them]
[*hanao*, she / he doesn't have them]

VEGETATION [V]

[*ninao*, I have it]
[*sinao*, I don't have it]
[*anao*, she / he has it]
[*hanao*, she / he doesn't have it]

[*ninayo*, I have them]
[*anayo*, she / he has them]

MIX+FLOWERS, FRUITS [xFF]

[*ninalo*, I have it]
[*sinalo*, I don't have it]
[*analo*, she / he has it]
[*hanalo*, she / he doesn't have it]

[*ninayo*, I have them]
[*anayo*, she / he has them]

THINGS [T]

[*ninacho*, I have it]
[*sinacho*, I don't have it]
[*anacho*, she / he has it]
[*hanacho*, she / he doesn't have it]

[*ninavyo*, I have them]
[*anavyo*, she / he has them]

MIX+FAUNA, VEGGIES [xFV]

[*ninayo*, I have it]
[*sinayo*, I don't have it]
[*anayo*, she / he has it]
[*hanayo*, she / he doesn't have it]

[*ninazo*, I have them]
[*anazo*, she / he has them]

U-WORDS [U]

[*ninao*, I have it]
[*sinao*, I don't have it]
[*anao*, she / he has it]
[*hanao*, she / he doesn't have it]

[*ninazo*, I have them]
[*anazo*, she / he has them]

PLACE-ADVERBS [Pl]

[*ninapo*, I have it / them]
[*sinapo*, I don't have it / them]
[*anapo*, she / he has it / them]
[*hanapo*, she / he doesn't have it / them]

GERUNDS [G]

[*ninako*, I have it / them]
[*sinako*, I don't have it / them]
[*anako*, she / he has it / them]
[*hanako*, she / he doesn't have it / them]

10.7.6 Practice: Verb *wa na*, have"

Answers to the previous practice of section 10.7.4 Practice: Verb wa, be(come)":

Noun	Verb	Adjective or noun
bamia	**_ni_** [timeless]	*mboga*, vegetable
bamia	**_si_** [negative timeless]	*nyekundu*, red
chumba	**_kinakuwa_** or *kinawekwa*, is being set [present]	*tayari*, ready

Noun	Verb	Adjective or noun
	– more on *weka* and other wide-use verbs in Appendix C: Wide-use Verbs	
vyumba	**haviwi** [negative present]	*tayari*, ready
chungwa	**lilikuwa** [past]	*mbichi*, unripe
machungwa	**hayakuwa** [negative past]	*tamu*, sweet
kuimba	**kutakuwa** [future]	*kuzuri*, nice
mahali	**hapatakuwa** [negative future]	*mbali*, far
mbamia	**unakuwa** [present]	*mwema*, good
mibamia	**haijawa** [negative present perfect]	*myema*, good
mdudu	**anakuwa** [present]	*mkubwa*, big
wadudu	**walikuwa** [past]	*wafu*, lifeless
ufunguo	**utakuwa** [future]	*mzuri*, nice
funguo	**zimekuwa** [present perfect]	*mbaya*, bad

Practice:

Fill in the blank spaces the conjugated form of *wa na*, be with i.e. have, in the verb column below. An **example** is provided for the first entry.

[The correct answers are given at the beginning of the next Practice section.]

Noun	Verb	Adjective or noun
bamia	***ina*** [present / timeless]	rangi kijani, green
bamia [plural]	_____ [negative present / timeless]	makoko, nuts
chumba	_____ [present / timeless]	kitanda, bed
vyumba	_____ [negative present / timeless]	madirisha, windows
chungwa	_____ [past]	bei juu, expensive
machungwa	_____ [negative past]	mbegu, seed(s)
kuimba	_____ [future]	sauti nzuri, nice sound
mahali	_____ [negative future]	maji, water
mbamia	_____ [present / timeless]	bamia, okra
mibamia	_____ [present perfect]	bamia, okra
mdudu	_____ [present / timeless]	kitu kinywani, thing in the mouth

Noun	Verb	Adjective or noun
wadudu	_____ [past]	vitu vinywani, things in the mouths
mimi	_____ [present / timeless]	kitu, thing
ufunguo	_____ [future]	kufuli, padlock
funguo	_____ [present perfect]	makufuli, padlocks

10.8 –po/ko/mo, ...is/are...

The phrase "Someone (or something) is in (or at, on, of) some place",
e.g. people are at the door, is constructed in Swahili as follows:

*watu **wapo** mlangoni*

where **wapo** has the pronoun prefix of PEOPLE [Pp]: *Mtu-Watu*, person(s)
namely **wa**-, they, and a **–po** suffix which is a relative pronoun of PLACE-
ADVERBS [Pl]: Mahali- Mahali, place(s) [which is explained above in
section 10.3 Relative Pronouns]. *Mlango*, door, is suffixed with -ni, in / at,
to refer to the location, thus "at the door". Notice: there is no tense infix
nor even a verb base, the present or timeless tense and the verb *wa*, be,
are implicit. Let's do another similar example:

*Tanzania **ipo** Afrika ya Mashariki*, Tanzania is in East Africa

where **ipo** has a pronoun prefix of MIX+FAUNA, VEGGIES [xFV]: Nyanya-
Nyanya, tomato(es) namely **i**-, it, and a **–po** suffix as described above.
[Reminder: as explained in section 3.6 U-WORDS [U]: Utenzi-Tenzi,
poem(s) under <u>Countries</u>, although country names belong to the U group
they follow the rules of the xFV group which includes the word *nchi*,
country!]

PLACE-ADVERBS [Pl]: Mahali- Mahali, place(s) has two other relative pronouns namely -*ko*-, referring to a general place, and -*mo*-, referring to the interior of a place, which are also used in the above construction in place of -*po*. Examples:

*nyanya **iko** hapa*, the tomato is here [*hapa*, here, is dealt with above in section 7.1 Demonstrative Adjectives (closer)]

*matunda **yamo** kikapuni*, the fruits are in the basket

More examples: [The subject of this section, namely "is", "are", "am", is **bolded**.]

PEOPLE [Pp]: *Mtu-Watu*, person(s)

[*watu wako nje*, people are outside]

[*Upo wapi*? Where are you? *Nipo hapa*, I am here]

[*Umo ndani*? Are you in there?]

Note: 3rd person singular uses subject prefix *yu*- instead of the usual *a*- e.g.

[*Yuko wapi Ali*? Where is Ali? *Yumo jikoni*, he is in the kitchen]

MIX+FLOWERS, FRUITS [xFF]: *Tunda-Matunda, fruit(s)*

[*matunda yamo kikapuni*, the fruits are in the basket]

Note: instead of the suffix -*ni*, in / at / on, we can use preposition *kwenye*, in / at, as in *matunda yamo kwenye kikapu*. But note that you either write *kwenye*, in, or add the suffix –*ni* to *kikapu*.

THINGS [T]: *Kitu-Vitu*, things(s)

[*Kitu kipo mezani*? Is the thing on the table? *Kipo*, it is]

MIX+FAUNA, VEGGIES [xFV]: *Nyanya-Nyanya*, tomato(es)

[*Twiga wako namna mbili huku*, giraffes are of two kinds here]

[*Nyanya iko wapi*? Where is the tomato? *Iko hapa*, it is here]

[*Kuku wapo*, chicken are (here, in stock; these adverbs are implied).] This is the wording of signs often posted on yard doors in Tanzania where chicken, skinned or live, are sold! It is abbreviated i.e. without an ending such as *hapa*, here. Note that if the implication is that chicken are 'in stock' it still refers to a place - the yard - and hence the correct use of *wapo*, but Swahili usage does not keep to this rule hard and fast and uses it without a place (implied or not) e.g. using *tayari*, ready:

[*magari yapo tayari*, the cars are ready]

Quite often the order "noun pronoun-*po/ko/mo*" is reversed, with an implicit "there" e.g.

wako twiga wa namna mbili huko (or, *wako namna mbili za twiga huko*), there are two kinds of giraffes there

iko amani hapa, there is peace here

Other Tenses

These are constructed using the verb *wa*, be [section 10.7.2 Wa, be] as follows:

Pronoun-prefix + tense-infix + *kuwa* + a relative pronoun (-*po*, -*ko*, or -*mo*) of PLACE-ADVERBS [Pl]: Mahali- Mahali, place(s)

Example:

PEOPLE [Pp]: *Mtu-Watu*, person(s)

[*Sisi tulikuwapo nyumbani*, we were at home] Past tense
[*Sisi tutakakuwapo nyumbani*, we will be at home] Future; the ~~ka~~ is euphoniously dropped
[*Sisi tumekuwapo nyumbani*, we have been at home] Pr. Perf.
[*Wageni wamekuwapo tangu jana*, the guests have been here since yesterday] Pr. Perf.

Often, usage changes the above -*wapo* to -*wepo*!

<u>Negatives</u>

The negative is formed by appending the prefix **ha-** to the corresponding positive e.g. [Reminder: as explained above in section 5.4 Negatives, the past and present perfect tense infixes for negatives are respectively –<u>ku</u>- and -<u>ja</u>-]

> [**ha**yupo* nyumbani, he is not at home] Present

> [**ha**tu<u>ku</u>wapo* nyumbani, we were not at home] Past
> The -<u>ku</u>- is the past tense infix, not the infinitive prefix for wa, be

> [**ha**tutakuwapo* nyumbani, we will not be at home] Future
> The -ku- here IS the infinitive prefix for wa, be

> [**ha**tu<u>ja</u>wapo* nyumbani, we are not yet at home] Pr. Perf.

> *nyumbani can mean at home or in the house. For the former "at" -po is suffixed, for the latter "in" -mo is suffixed.

[More in Appendix G: -po- infix / suffix.]

10.9 Pana/Kuna/Mna, There is/are…

The phrase "There is/are someone/something at/in/on somewhere", e.g. there are people at the door, is constructed in Swahili as follows:

pana watu mlangoni OR mlangoni **pana** watu

where **pana** has the pronoun prefix of PLACE-ADVERBS [Pl]: Mahali-Mahali, place(s) namely **pa**-, it, and a suffix **–na**, with. Notice: There is no tense infix nor even a verb base, the present tense and the verb wa, be, are implicit and which, together with the –na-, give us wa na, have [section 10.7.5 Wa na, have]. This produces a literal translation of "the door has people". Another example:

pana mtu nje, there is a man outside [Literally, it – the outside – has a man]

PLACE-ADVERBS [Pl]: Mahali- Mahali, place(s) has two other pronouns namely **ku**- (referring to a general place) and **m**- (referring to the interior of a place) and these two are also used in the above construction in place of **pa**-. Examples:

kuna watu mjini, there are people in town
nyumbani **mna** watu, there are people in the house
mna sukari humu? is there sugar in it?
mna maji kisimani? is there water in the well?
mna samaki ziwani? are there fish in the lake?
mna watu sokoni? are there people in the market?

Other Tenses

For other tenses, the **tense** infix and the verb <u>**wa**</u>, be, which both were implicit in the above present tense, are inserted [section 10.7.2 Wa, be] e.g.

pa**li<u>kuwa</u>** na mtu mlangoni, there was a man at the door
m**li<u>kuwa</u>** na maji mtoni, there was water in the river
pa**ta<u>kuwa</u>** na mtu nje, there will be a man outside

Negatives

The negative is formed by appending the prefix **ha-** as explained in section 5.4 Negatives e.g.

katika mto huu **ha**mna maji, in this river there isn't water
katika mto huu **ha**mkuwa na maji, in this river there wasn't water
hamna watu sokoni? aren't there people in the market?

pana watu hapa? are there people here? **hapana***, there aren't
*By usage, *hapana* is also used in a stand-alone manner for a reply "no"
i.e. a negative response [see section 9 Interrogatives].

kuna maji njiani? is there water along the way? **hakuna**, there isn't

10.10 Compare Sections 10.8 and 10.9

There is close resemblance between the two expressions:

Section 10.8: watu **wapo** mlangoni, people are at the door
and:
Section 10.9: **pana** watu mlangoni, there are people at the door

The former is in the active sense whereas the latter uses a generic "there are…". They both mean the same, only the construction involving **wapo** and **pana** are different. In both there is an implicit wa, be, but the latter uses –**na**, with, which together with the implied wa gives us wa na, have (literally, be with). Accordingly, their other <u>tenses</u> are constructed in the same way as wa and wa na. For example:

watu wa**lik**u**wa**po mlangoni, people were at the door
pa**lik**uwa na watu mlangoni, there were people at the door

10.11 Ya-/i-, It is…

When not referring to a specific thing (such as *mtu*, person, or *maji*, water, etc) a generic 'it' is used which is a pronoun **ya-** or **i-** plus use of the timeless tense. **ya-** is the MIX+FLOWERS, FRUITS [xFF] plural pronoun which may implicitly be taken to refer to *maarifa*, knowledge, in general, which in turn can be interpreted as any generic information entity. **i-** is the MIX+FAUNA, VEGGIES [xFV] singular pronoun which may implicitly be taken to refer to *habari*, news, in general, which again can be interpreted as any generic information entity. For example:

yafaa tuende, it is befitting we go

imejuliwa nani aliiba fedha, it has become known who stole the money

Negatives follow the rules given above in section 5.4 Negatives. For example:

haifai kuchelewa, it is not proper to be late

haiwezekani, it is not doable

haidhuru, literally it means 'it does no harm', and is translated as 'it is okay'

haijulikani nani alipiga simu, it is not known who made the phone call

10.12 Practice: …is/There is…/It is…

Answers to the previous practice of section 10.7.6 Practice: Verb wa na, have":

Noun	Verb	Adjective or noun
bamia	**ina** [present / timeless]	rangi kijani, green
bamia	**hazina** [negative present / timeless]	makoko, nuts
chumba	**kina** [present / timeless]	kitanda, bed
vyumba	**havina** [negative present / timeless]	madirisha, windows
chungwa	**lilikuwa na** [past]	bei juu, expensive
machungwa	**hayakuwa na** [negative past]	mbegu, seed(s)
kuimba	**kutakuwa na** [future]	sauti nzuri, nice sound
mahali	**hapatakuwa na** [negative future]	maji, water
mbamia	**una** [present / timeless]	bamia, okra
mibamia	**imekuwa na** [present perfect]	bamia, okra
mdudu	**ana** [present / timeless]	kitu kinywani, thing in the mouth

Noun	Verb	Adjective or noun
wadudu	***walikuwa na*** [past]	*vitu vinywani*, things in the mouths
mimi	***nina*** [present / timeless]	*kitu*, thing
ufunguo	***utakuwa na*** [future]	*kufuli*, padlock
funguo	***zimekuwa na*** [present perfect]	*makufuli*, padlocks

Practice:

Fill in the blank spaces one of the expressions indicated in square brackets (which were explained in sections 10.8 –po/ko/mo, …is/are, 10.9 Pana/Kuna/Mna, There is/are and 10.11 Ya-/i-, It is…] in the expression column below. An **example** is provided for the first entry.

[The correct answers are given at the beginning of the next Practice section.]

Noun or Pronoun	Expression	Noun or Verb	Adverb
John	*yumo* ["is"]	--	*dukani*, in the shop
--	_____ ["There were"]	*wageni*, guests	*hapa*, here
--	_____ ["It is"]	*-hitaji*, necessary	*tupumzike*, that we rest

Noun or Pronoun	Expression	Noun or Verb	Adverb
Bwana, the boss	_____ ["was not"]	--	**nyumbani**, at home
Yeye, she	_____ ["was"]	--	**kwenye mkutano**, in the meeting
--	_____ ["There are"]	**michicha**, spinach plants	**shambani**, in the farming plot
--	_____ ["There are no"]	**mimea**, plants	**shambani**, in the farming plot
--	_____ ["There were"]	**michicha**, spinach plants	**shambani**, in the farming plot
--	_____ ["There will not be"]	**michicha**, spinach plants	**shambani**, in the farming plot

11 ANATOMY OF VERBS

Maarifa ni mali,

Knowledge is wealth
[Knowledge is power]

This chapter is a review of the components of constructed verbs.

The verb attachments below are numbered in order of insertion left-to-right, that is, prefixes, then infixes, then suffixes:

1. **H**- Negative/Routine Prefix
2. **P**ronoun Prefix
3. **T**ense Infix
4. **R**elative Infix
5. **O**bject Infix
6. **C**onditional Infix

[verb base here]

7. **P**reposition Infix
8. **T**ransformation Infix
9. *Kuwa* na* Object Suffix, and *-po/ko/mo* Suffix
10. **T**imeless Relative Suffix
11. **S**ubjunctive-Imperative Suffix

A mnemonic for remembering the above is: [the infinitive form **kuwa*, to be, is used here (instead of *wa*, be, as found in the Dictionary in Volumes 2 and 3) to facilitate our mnemonic!]

AH[1]a! P[2]lease T[3]urn oveR[4] fO[5]r C[6]heaP[7] T[8]icK[9]eT[10]S[11]. [Think of a checkout receipt that has an offer for you on its reverse side!] Keep in mind that

NOT ALL OF THE ABOVE are present in every verb construction. It is essential to memorize this verb mnemonic!

The above numbers also match the sub-sections of section 22.2 Index tables: Verb e.g. "5. Object Infix" above matches sub-section 22.3.3 Index table: 5. Verb Object. These numbers make it easy below to refer to the corresponding index. If however you are up to speed on all the attachments of verb construction and just need a way to do a quick look-up, here below is a convenient table where all verb attachments are given under each part of the above mnemonic. It is a highly condensed table as compared to index tables of section 22 which have more detail including links back to the original text in the relevant chapters as well as examples for each attachment.

11.1 Quick Look-up Table of Verb Attachments

AH^{1}a! (negation, routine)							
ha/hu (negation)				*hu* (routine)			
P^{2}lease (**Pronoun**, by noun group)							
ni/u/a/tu/mn/wa (Pp) *si*,1st pers. sing. -ve	*u/i* (V)	*li/ya* (xFF)	*ki/vi* (T)	*i/zi* (xFV)	*u/zi* (U)	*pa/ku/m* (PI)	*ku* (G)
T^{3}urn (**Tense**)							
a/na/li/ta/me; -/-/ku/ta/me (negation); *ka/ki/ku* (immediate 2nd verb); *taka/si* (relative future/negation							
oveR^4 (**Relative**, by noun group)							
ye/o (Pp)	*o/yo* (V)	*lo/yo* (xFF)	*cho/vyo* (T)	*yo/zo* (xFV)	*o/zo* (U)	*po/ko/mo* (PI)	*ko* (G)
fO^{5}r (**Object**)							
ni/ku/m/tu/wa/wa (Pp)	*u/i* (V)	*li/ya* (xFF)	*ki/vi* (T)	*i/zi* (xFV)	*u/zi* (U)	*pa/ku/mu* (PI)	*ku* (G)
C^{6}heaP^7 (**Conditional**, **Preposition**)							
C^6: *ki/po/nge/ngali; si/sipo* (negation) P^7: *e/i*							
T^{8}icK^{9}etT^{10}S^{11} (**Transformation**, Kuwa na object & *po/ko/mo*, **Timeless** relative, **Subjunctive**)							
T^8: *je/ji/k(an)/man/na/pi/sh/u/w/z* K^9 object: same as R^4 above K^9: *po/ko/mo* T^{10}: see R^4 above S^{11}: *e/eni*							

11.2 Anatomy of Constructed Verbs

[verb bases used: *leta*, bring; *ja*, come]

Ha[1]leti, she does not bring: **H-** is 1. Negative Prefix. [Section 5.4 Negatives]

Hu[1]leta, she [always] brings: **Hu-** is 1. Routine Prefix. There is no tense infix, it is ANY tense. [Section 5.6 *Hu-* Routine Conjugation]

A[2]leta, she brings: **A-** is 2. Pronoun Prefix. [*A-* is either a tense prefix, or it is the timeless tense infix, because one of the two *a*'s in *a-a-leta* is euphoniously dropped.] [Section 5.1.1 Pronoun Prefixes]

Ana[3]kuja, she is coming: **-na-** is 3. Tense Infix, present tense in this case. [Section 5.1 Tenses] *Aki[3]leta*, bringing: **-ki-** is 3. Tense Infix, a continuous (in progress) action in this case. [Section 10.6 Immediate 2nd Verbs]

Kitu anacho[4]leta, the thing which she is bringing: **-cho-** is 4. Relative Infix. [Section 10.3 Relative Pronouns]

Kitu anachoki[5]leta, the thing which she is bringing (it): **-ki-** is 5. Object Infix. [Section 10.1 Embedded Object References]

Aki[6]leta, if she brings: **-ki-** is 6. Conditional Infix. [Section 10.4 Conditionals]

Akinilete[7]a, if she brings for me: **-e-** is 7. Preposition Infix. [Section 10.2 Prepositions]; *-ni-* is an object infix, similar to 5 above

Kitu kinacholetw[8]a, the thing which is being brought, or
Kitu kinaletw[8]a, the thing is being brought: **-w-** is 8. Transformation Infix. [Section 5.8 Verb Transformations]

Kitu ninacho[9], the thing which I have: **-cho-** is 9. *Kuwa na* Object Infix. [Section 10.1 Embedded Object References]

Kitu kiletwacho[10], the thing being brought: **-cho-** is 10. Timeless Relative Suffix. [Section 10.3 Relative Pronouns]

Alete[11], that she may bring: **-e-** is 11. Subjunctive-Imperative Suffix. [Section 10.5 Subjunctives]

11.3 Practice: Anatomy of Verbs

Answers to the previous practice of section 10.12 Practice: ...is/There is.../It is...:

Noun or Pronoun	Expression	Noun or Verb	Adverb
John	yumo ["is"]	--	dukani, in the shop
--	Kulikuwa na ["There were"]	wageni, guests	hapa, here
--	Ya ["It is"]	-hitaji, necessary	tupumzike, that we rest
Bwana, the boss	hakuwapo ["was not"]	--	nyumbani, at home
Yeye, she	alikuwamo ["was"]	--	kwenye mkutano, in the meeting
--	Mna ["There are"]	michicha, spinach plants	shambani, in the farming plot
--	Hamna ["There are no"]	mimea, plants	shambani, in the farming plot
--	Mlikuwa na ["There were"]	michicha, spinach plants	shambani, in the farming plot
--	Hamtakuwa na ["There will not be"]	michicha, spinach plants	shambani, in the farming plot

Practice:

For each of the verbs in **bold** which have been parsed into their components by hyphens write to the right of each parsed component its mnemonic letter and the corresponding number e.g. if the component is a tense infix write 3.**T**. The verb base is given in square brackets. The underlined wording in the English translation corresponds to the bold. An **example** is provided for the first entry.

[The correct answers are given at the beginning of the next Practice section.]

Mpishi **a**$^{2.P}$-**na**$^{3.T}$-**ye**$^{4.R}$-**tu**$^{5.O}$-pik$^{verb\ base}$-**i**$^{7.P}$-a ni Paulo, the cook <u>who is cooking for us</u> is Paul. [verb pika, cook]

Nyanya **a**___-**na**___-**zo**___-**zi**___-ona$^{verb\ base}$, tomatoes <u>which he is seeing them</u>. [verb ona, see]

A___-**na**___-**tu**___-let$^{verb\ base}$-**e**___-a, he is <u>bringing to us</u>. [verb leta, bring]

Ha___-**wa**___-**ja**___-ja$^{verb\ base}$, they <u>have not yet come</u>. [verb ja, come]

11.4 Verb Tense Deviation Summary

The two corelated tables below, "1: Tables of Rules" and "2: Table of Examples", highlight deviations from standard / normal tense rules. The purpose here is to show in one place deviations for a review by comparison, helping in their memorization.

Examples in the "2: Table of Examples" are ARBITRARILY based on the "THINGS [T]: Kitu-Vitu, things(s)" group e.g. the use of the ki- singular pronoun and the corresponding relative -cho- and object -ki-. This group stands in as a GENERIC group e.g. the example 1 (a) in the "Table of Examples": kinatosha, it suffices, is referring to a generic kitu, thing.

How to read the "1: Table of Rules"

Abbreviations: **Std?** = Standard? **Retd?** = Retained? **exc.** = exception; +ve = positive; -ve = negative; Tless = timeless; Rout. = routine; pron. = pronoun; vb = verb; Fut. = future

Negative in grey.

Column (a) is the 'benchmark' column, while columns (b), (c) and (d) override (a) as indicated in this table.

Under Tenses, the **+ve** row has the following:

(a) **Regular Verbs.** "**Std?** = Yes" e.g. in table 2, the present tense example 1 (a) *kinatosha*, it suffices, follows the standard rules of verb construction. "**exc.** = blank" means there are no exceptions for all the tenses.

(b) **Single Syllable Verbs.** *Ku* of the infinitive retained? "**Retd?** = Yes". Example 1 (b) *kinakula*, it is eating, retains the infinitive *ku*, as do all other tenses with the exceptions of the timeless and routine tenses ("**exc.** = Tless, Rout.") where it is NOT retained: Example 9 (b) *kila*, it eats, and example 11 (b) *hula*, it (always) eats.

(c) **Special Case of Single Syllable Verbs *wa*, be.** "Tless *ni*". The timeless tense (example 9 (c)) is conjugated as *ni*, is, there being no pronoun nor verb ("no pron./vb"). Other tenses follow the rules in (a) and (b) above e.g. present tense example 1 (c) *kinakuwa*, it is being.

(d) **Special Case of Single Syllable Verbs *wa na*, have.** "Pres., Tless, -*na*". The present and timeless tenses are conjugated with suffix -*na*, is, attached to a pronoun, there being no verb ("w.pron., no vb"): examples 1 (d) and 9 (d) *kina*, it has. Other tenses follow the rules in (a) and (b) above: past tense example 3 (d): *kilikuwa na*, it had (was with) it.

Under Tenses, the **-ve** row has the following:

(a) **Regular Verbs.** "**Std?** = No". Present tense example 2 (a) *hakitoshi*, it is insufficient, does NOT follow the standard rule of just prefixing a *ha-* to the +ve verb construction (which would have yielded *hakinatosha*), all of the other tenses also not abiding by the standard rule (either by changing the ending to -*i* as in the above example, or by using -***ku***- instead of -***li***- for the past tense and -***ja***- for -***me***- for the present perfect) with the exception of the future tense ("**exc.** = Fut.") which DOES follow the standard rule: future example 6 (a) *hakitatosha*, it will not suffice.

(b) **Single Syllable Verbs**. *Ku* of the infinitive retained? "**Retd?** = No". Present tense example 2 (b) *hakili*, it is not eating, does NOT retain the infinitive *ku*, as don't the other tenses with the exception of the future tense ("**exc.** = Fut.") which DOES retain it: future tense example 6 (b) *hakitakula*, it will not eat.

(c) **Special Case of Single Syllable Verbs *wa*, be**. "ditto *si*". The timeless tense, example 10 (c), is conjugated as *si*, is not, there being no pronoun nor verb ("ditto"). Other tenses follow the rules in (a) and (b) above e.g. present tense: example 2 (c) *hakiwi*, it is not being; future tense example 6 (c) *hakitakuwa*, it will not be.

(d) **Special Case of Single Syllable Verbs *wa na*, have**. "*ha*- ditto". The present and timeless tense are conjugated with the standard negative prefix *ha*- and a suffix -*na*, is, along with a pronoun, there being no verb ("ditto"): examples 2 (d) and 10 (d) *hakina*, it does not have. Other tenses follow the rules in (a) and (b) above: past tense example 4 (d) *haki**ku**wa na*, it did not have (was not with) it, where the *ku* is NOT retained, the *ku* being the past tense; future tense example 6 (d) *hakitakuwa na*, it will not have, where *ku* is retained.

Under with a Relative, the **+ve** row has the following:

(a) **Regular Verbs**. "**Std?** = Yes". Present tense example 13 (a) *kinachotosha*, it which is sufficient, follows the standard rules of verb construction, as do all other tenses with the exceptions of: future tense where -***taka***- is used ("**exc.** = Fut. -***taka***-"), instead of the standard -*ta*-, example 17 (a) *ki**taka**chotosha*, it which will suffice; and the timeless tense where the relative -*o* is suffixed ("**exc.** = Tless -*o*"), instead of being infixed, example 21 (a) *kitosha**cho***, it which suffices.

(b) **Single Syllable Verbs**. *Ku* of the infinitive retained? "**Retd?** = Yes". Present tense example 13 (b) *kinacho**ku**la*, it which is eating, retains the infinitive *ku*, as do all other tenses with the exception of the timeless tense ("**exc.** = Tless") where it is NOT retained: Example 21 (b) *kilacho*, it which eats.

(c) **Special Case of Single Syllable Verbs *wa*, be.** "Pres., Tless *-li-*". The present and timeless tenses are conjugated using the old *-li-* present tense of *wa*, there being no verb ("no verb"), PLUS ("+") the relative *-o* is suffixed, instead of being infixed: examples 13 (c) and 21 (c) *kilicho*, it which is. Other tenses follow the rules in (a) and (b) above e.g. past tense example 15 (c) *kilichok̲uwa*, it which was.

(d) **NO Special Case of Single Syllable Verbs *wa na*, have,** the rules of (c) above being used: the present and timeless tense examples 13 (d) and 21 (d) *kilicho na*, it which has; and other tenses e.g. past tense example 15 (d) *kilichok̲uwa na*, it which had.

Under **with a Relative**, the **-ve** row has the following:

(a) **Regular Verbs.** "**Std?** = No". Present tense example 14 (a) *kisichotosha*, it which is not sufficient, does not follow the standard rules of verb construction, using instead a *-si-*, as do all other tenses; and, in the timeless tense, in addition to the *-si-*, the relative *-o* is suffixed, instead of being infixed, example 22 (a) *kisitoshacho*, it which suffices.

(b) **Single Syllable Verbs.** *K̲u* of the infinitive retained? "**Retd?** = Yes". Present tense example 14 (b) *kisichok̲ula*, it which is not eating, retains the infinitive *k̲u*, as do all other tenses with the exception of the timeless tense ("**exc.** = Tless") where it is NOT retained: Example 22 (b) *kisilacho*, it which eats.

(c) **Special Case of Single Syllable Verbs *wa*, be.** "ditto *si*". The present and timeless tenses are conjugated using the *-si-*, there being no verb and the relative *-o* being suffixed, instead of being infixed ("ditto"): examples 14 (c) and 22 (c) *kisicho*, it which is not. Other tenses follow the rules in (a) and (b) above e.g. past tense example 16 (c) *kisichok̲uwa*, it which was not.

(d) **NO Special Case of Single Syllable Verbs *wa na*, have,** the rules of (c) above being used: examples 14 (d) and 22 (d) *kisicho na*, it which hasn't; and other tenses e.g. past tense example 16 (d) *kisichok̲uwa na*, it which hadn't.

The **with an Object** section is easy to follow, for BOTH **+ve** and **-ve** rows:

(a) **Regular Verbs**. Same rules as the **Tenses** section ("same as top").

(b) **Single Syllable Verbs**. _Ku_ of the infinitive retained? **"Retd?** = No / No"**, no exceptions.

(c) **NO Special Case of Single Syllable Verbs _wa_, be,** the rules of (a) and (b) above are used.

(d) **Special Case of Single Syllable Verbs _wa na_, have**. Same rules as in its corresponding **Tenses** section ("same as top"), PLUS ("+") the object reference uses a RELATIVE -_o_ which is suffixed e.g. present tense example 23 (d) _kinacho_, it has it; past tense -ve example 26 (d) _hakikuwa nacho_, it did not have it.

The other sections viz. **Conditional**, **Subjunctive** and **Immediate 2nd** are even easier to follow. Their construction is quite standard, using the attachments shown in the table, and there are NO Special Cases except under **Conditional** where the infinitive _ku_- IS retained for -ve e.g. example 34 (b) _kisipokula_, if it does not eat, otherwise the _ku_- is NOT retained e.g. example 33 (b) _kikila_, if it eats [note, this example is identical to 31 (b), as are 33 (c) and 31 (c), that is these are homonyms!]

The examples given above are a selective sub-set of the full set of examples in "2: Table of Examples" and which are numbered as referenced in the title **Tenses**: examples 1-12 of table 1. Also, the rules given in the "1: Table of Rules" below, which have been explained above, are again – fully! - explained by rows and columns after the "2: Table of Examples" under the heading "Explanation of Rules in the 2: Table of Examples", along with references to their covering sections!

1: Table of Rules

	(a) Regular Verbs *tosha*, suffice		Single Syllable Verb Deviations from Regular Verbs			
			(b) *la*, eat (*ku* retained?)		Special Cases	
	Std?	exc.	Retd?	exc.	(c) *wa*, be	(d) *wa na*, have
Tenses: examples 1-12						
+ve	Yes	-	Yes	Tless Rout.	Tless *ni* (no pron./vb)	Pres., Tless **-na** (w.pron., no vb)
-ve	No	Fut.	No	Fut.	ditto *si*	*ha-* ditto
with a Relative: examples 13-22						
+ve	Yes	Fut. *-taka-* Tless *-o*	Yes	Tless	Pres., Tless **-li-** (no verb) + *-o*	-
-ve	No *-si-*	Tless *-o*	Yes	Tless	ditto *-si-*	
with an Object: examples 23-32						
+ve	same as top		No	-	-	same as top +
-ve			No			*-o*
Conditional: examples 33, 34						
+ve	*-ki-*	-	No			-
-ve	*sipo-*		Yes			
Subjunctive: examples 35, 36						
+ve	*-e*	-	No	-	-	-
-ve	*-si-* +*-e*		No			
Immediate 2nd: examples 37, 38						
+ve	*-ka-*	-	No	-	-	-
-ve	*-si-* +*-e*		No			

A blank cell (showing a hyphen "-") in the table above propogates the rules to its left e.g. the +ve / -ve **Conditional** cell under (c) uses the rules to its left i.e. for the +ve we have in table 2, cell 33 (a), *kikitosha*, if it suffices, in 33 (b) *kikila*, if it eats (the inifinitve *ku* is not retained), and thus cell 33 (c) is *kikiwa*, if it is, and cell (d) is *kikiwa na*, if it has. Similarly, for the -ve, cell 34 (a) has *kisipotosha*, if it does not suffice, cell (b) has *kisipokula*, if it does not eat (but the infinitive *ku* here IS retained, as per the rule "Yes"), thus cell 34 is (c) *kisipokuwa*, if it is not, cell 34 (d) is *kisipokuwa na*, it does not have.

2: Table of Examples

All examples in the table below are for 3rd person singular, plurals being readily made by changing *ki* to *vi*, *cho* to *vyo*. The PEOPLE [Pp]: *Mtu-Watu*, person(s) group has three persons: 1st, 2nd and 3rd person singular and plural. These too are readily made by changing *ki* to one of *ni*, *I*, *u*, you (singular), *a*, she / he, *tu*, we, *m*, you (plural), *wa*, they. Note: for negation, the 1st and 2nd person singulars are exceptions: *si*, negation of *ni*, *hu*, negation of *u*, which is covered in section 5.4 Negatives.

Abbreviations: Pr: present; Fut = future; Pf = perfect; Tless = timeless; Rtne = routine; Cond = conditional; Subj = subjunctive; 2nd V = 2nd verb; +ve = positive; -ve = negative

Deviations **bolded**		(a) *tosha*, suffice	(b) *la*, eat (*ku-* retained, except*)	(c) *wa*, be (*ku-* retained, except*)	(d) *wa na*, have (*ku-* retained, **except***)
Tenses					
1	Pr. +ve	kinatosha	kinakula	kinakuwa	*kina
2	-ve	hakitosh**i**	*hakil**i**	*hakiw**i**	*hakina
3	Past +ve	kilitosha	kilikula	kilikuwa	kilikuwa na
4	-ve	hakikutosha	*hakikula	*hakikuwa	*hakikuwa na
5	Fut. +ve	kitatosha	kitakula	kitakuwa	kitakuwa na
6	-ve	hakitatosha	hakitakula	hakitakuwa	hakitakuwa na
7	Pr. Pf. +ve	kimetosha	kimekula	kimekuwa	kimekuwa na
8	-ve	hakijatosha	*hakijala	*hakijawa	*hakijawa na
9	Tless +ve	kitosha	*kila	ni	see Present
10	-ve	see Present	see Present	si	see Present
11	Rtne +ve	hutosha	*hula	*huwa	*huwa na
12	-ve	see Present	see Present	see Present	see Present
with Relative					
13	Pr. +ve-	kinachotosha	kinachokula	*kilicho	*kilicho na
14	-ve	kisichotosha	kisichokula	*kisicho	*kisicho na
15	Past +ve	kilichotosha	kilichokula	kilichokuwa	kilichokuwa na
16	-ve	see Present	see Present	kisichokuwa	kisichokuwa na
17	Fut. +ve	kitakachotosha	kitakachokula	kitakachokuwa	kitakachokuwa na
18	-ve	see Present	see Present	see Past	see Past
19	Pr. Pf. +ve	kimechotosha	kimechokula	kimechokuwa	kimechokuwa na

Deviations **bolded**		(a) *tosha*, suffice	(b) *la*, eat (*ku*- retained, **except***)	(c) *wa*, be (*ku*- retained, **except***)	(d) *wa na*, have (*ku*- retained, **except***)
20	-ve	see Present	see Present	see Past	see Past
21	Tless +ve	*kitoshacho*	**kilacho*	see Present	see Present
22	-ve	*ki**si**toshа**cho***	**ki**si**lacho***	see Present	see Present
	with Object				
23	Pr. +ve	*kinakitosha*	**kinakila*	**kinakiwa*	**kinacho*
24	-ve	*hakikitosh**i***	**hakikil**i***	**hakikiw**i***	**hakinа**cho***
25	Past +ve	*kilikitosha*	**kilikila*	**kilikiwa*	**kili**ku**wa* na**cho**
26	-ve	*haki**ku**kitosha*	**haki**ku**kila*	**haki**ku**kiwa*	**haki**ku**wa nаcho*
27	Fut. +ve	*kitakitosha*	**kitakila*	**kitakiwa*	**kita**ku**wa nacho*
28	-ve	*hakitakitosha*	**hakitakila*	**hakitakiwa*	**hakitа**ku**wa nаcho*
29	Pr. Pf. +ve	*kimekitosha*	**kimekila*	**kimekiwa*	**kime**ku**wa nacho*
30	-ve	*haki**ja**kitosha*	**haki**ja**kila*	**haki**ja**kiwa*	**haki**ja**wa nаcho*
31	Tless +ve	*kikitosha*	**kikila*	**kikiwa*	see Present
32	-ve	see Present	see Present	see Present	see Present
	Other				
33	Cond. +ve	*kikitosha*	**kikila*	**kikiwa*	**kikiwa na*
34	-ve	*ki**sipo**tosha*	*ki**sipo**kula*	*ki**sipo**kuwa*	*ki**sipo**kuwa na*
35	Subj. +ve	*kitoshe*	**kile*	**kiwe*	**kiwe na*
36	-ve	*ki**si**toshe*	**ki**si**le*	**ki**si**we*	**ki**si**we na*
37	2nd V. +ve	*kikatosha*	**kikala*	**kikawa*	**kikawa na*
38	-ve	see Subj.	see Subj.	see Subj.	see Subj.

Scan the body of the above table section-by-section (Tenses section first, then Relative, Object and Other sections), within each section scanning row-by-row each column and again column-by-column each row for the whole table, noting normal usage (unbolded) and deviations (**bolded**), including seeing patterns of deviation. Normal usage and deviations are summarized below, along with references to their covering sections in square brackets.

Explanation of Rules in 2: Table of Examples

"N" = normal, "D" = **deviation**: listed by row number first, then further below by column letters (lower case). Negative in grey. [Note that for negation, the normal rule is the use of a *ha*- prefix.]

1. N: uses -*na*- [5.1]; note the -*na*, with, in d1 is not the present tense
2. **D:** drops the -*na*- and changes the ending -*a* to -*i* [5.4]
3. N: uses -*li*- [5.1]
4. **D:** changes the -*li*- to -**ku**- [5.4]
5, 6. N: use -*ta*- [5.1, 5.4]

7. N: uses -me- [5.1]

8. D: changes the -me- to -ja- [5.4]

9, 21, 31. D: keeps the -i- of pronoun ki- instead the -a- of the tense e.g. kiatosha] [5.1]

10. D: same as 2 above [5.4]

11. N: uses hu- [5.6]

12. N: same as 2 above [5.4,5.6]

13, 15, 17, 19, 21. N: same as 1, 3, 5, 7, 9 plus -cho- infix (suffix in 21) [10.3]

17. D: changes the -ta- to -taka- [10.3]

14, 16, 18, 20, 22. D: uses -si- plus -cho- infix (suffix in 22) [10.3]

23-32. N: same as 1-10 plus an embedded object -ki- [10.1] and the infinitive ku- is NOT retained in columns c and d

33: N: uses -ki- [10.4, only -ki- examples shown here and not ikiwa, -po-, etc]

34: D: uses -sipo- [10.4]

35. N: doesn't use a tense but changes the ending -a to -e [10.5]

36: D: uses -si- [10.5]

37: N: uses -ka- [10.6, only -ka- examples shown here and not -ki- nor -ku-]

38. N: same as 36 above [10.6]

c9. D: uses ni [10.7.2]

c10. D: uses si [10.7.2]

c13. D: uses -li- [10.7.3]

d: all the -na are conjugations of kuwa na, have, and not the present tense

b, c, d. D: ku- retained (underlined) or not (flagged with *) [10.7]

d1, d2, d13, d14, d23, d24. D: do not use the wa portion of wa na, have, but simply attach its na portion to the pronoun [10.7.5]

d23-d32: D: relative -cho is suffixed instead of being embedded [10.7.5.1]

12 SENTENCE CONSTRUCTION ILLUSTRATION

Elimu ni bahari kubwa,

Education is a big ocean

By this point in the text, sentence construction has been dealt with in all its parts. Here we will use a couple of examples to illustrate the most common parts of it:

(1) "The animal which I saw there at Ngorongoro* was a rhino; I hear that only a few remain." [*Tanzania's world famous game park]

9: *Kifaru*, rhino. Ngorongoro Crater, Tanzania. A UNESCO World Heritage Site (crater wall in the distance).

Only a few dozen rhinos remain, having been dwindled by illegal poaching for their horns :-(

From the English-Swahili Dictionary (in Volume 3)we obtain the following words (type of word is flagged in brackets):

animal: *mnyama* (noun, Pp group)
see: *ona* (verb)
there: *kule* (demonstrative)
be: *wa* (verb)
rhino: *kifaru* (noun, T group)
hear: *sikia* (verb)
that: *kwamba* (conjunction)
only: *tu* (adverb)
few: *chache* (adjective)
remain: *baki* (verb)

From what we have learnt in the book we get the following (section references in brackets):

ni-, I [5.1.1 Pronoun Prefixes]
*a-, it [5.1.1 Pronoun Prefixes]
*wa-, they [5.1.1 Pronoun Prefixes]
-li-, past tense [5.1 Tenses]
-na-, present tense [5.1 Tenses]
*-ye-, whom/which [10.3 Relative Pronouns]
*-mw-, him/it [10.1.1 Object References for PEOPLES: Mtu-Watu, person(s)]
*wa-, plural [4 Adjectives]
*reminder: all animates follow PEOPLE [Pp] rules [3.9 Animates outside of PEOPLE [Pp]]

Note: except for the tenses, which are independent of noun groups, all of the above could also have been obtained from chapter 23 Index table of Noun Groups, all in one place (but only after you become familiar with how it is organized). Similarly, tenses could have been obtained from section 22.3.1 Index table: 3. Verb Tense Infix.

Sentence construction

Now we can use the above to string together the following:

Mnyama [1]ni+li+ye+mw+ona kule Ngorongoro [2]a+li+kuwa kifaru; ni+na+sikia kwamba wa+na+baki wa+chache tu.

[1]"he / she whom I saw" This is the most complicated construction here. You can review it under <u>As Object</u> in section 10.3 Relative Pronouns. [2]"he was" The infinitive *ku-* of the verb is retained. See section 10.7 Exceptions: Single Syllable Verbs.

Another example:

    (2) "Next week I will try to climb Kilimanjaro the tallest* mountain in the world." [*i.e. free-standing]

10: **Kilimanjaro**, western face. Tanzania. A UNESCO World Heritage Site.

It is the tallest free-standing mountain in the world and yet a lot of people of average fitness or better have climbed it.

juma, week (noun, xFF group)
ja, come (verb)
jaribu, try (verb)
panda, climb (verb)
refu, tall (adjective)
mlima, mountain (noun, V group)
katika, in (preposition)
dunia, world (noun, xFV group)

-*ta*-, future tense [5.1 Tenses]
-*yo*, which [10.3 Relative Pronouns]
li-, it [5.1.1 Pronoun Prefixes]
u-, it [5.1.1 Pronoun Prefixes]
-*li*-, old present tense for *wa* (10.7.3 Old -li- Present Tense of *wa*, be, with Relatives)
m-, singular [4 Adjectives]

Sentence construction

Now we can use the above to string together the following:

Juma ¹li+ja+yo ni+ta+jaribu ²kupanda Kilimanjaro ³ulio mlima m+refu ⁴<u>kuliko yote</u> katika dunia.

¹"it which comes i.e. next" See section 10.3 Relative Pronouns.
²"to climb" See section 10.6 Immediate 2nd Verbs.
³"it which is" See section 10.7.3 Old -li- Present Tense of *wa*, be, with Relatives.
⁴"<u>than all</u>" Superlatives are made up thus. See section 4.3 Making Up Adjectives.

Tip: Plural prefix *ma*- can be used to construct the equivalent of the English ~s e.g. the English 'hundreds' has its equivalent: *mamia,* as in *mamia walijeruhiwa katika ajali,* hundreds were injured in the accident. See the *ma*-/~s entry in the dictionary volumes.

13 Numbers

Cardinal adjectives from 1 to 11 are:

1 –moja [mtu mmoja, one person; ndizi moja, one banana]
2 –wili [miti miwili, two trees; ndizi mbili, two bananas]
3 –tatu [matunda matatu, three fruits; ndizi tatu, three bananas]
4 –nne [vitu vinne, four things; nyanya nne, four tomatoes]
5 –tano [ndovu watano, five elephants; nyanya tano, five tomatoes]
6 **sita** [watu sita, six persons]
7 **saba** [miti saba, seven trees]
8 –nane [matunda manane, eight fruits; nyanya nane, eight tomatoes]
9 **tisa** [mahali tisa, nine places]
10 kumi [watu kumi, ten persons]
Note: Only the single digit numbers (except for the three foreign ones which are shown in bold) take on adjectival prefixes as seen in the examples above.
Multiple digit numbers can optionally take on adjectival prefixes in the <u>single digit</u> portion:
15 kumi na –moja [miti kumi na <u>mi</u>tano, 15 trees]
Two-digit numbers are of the form base-and-number e.g. 11 is kumi na –moja, ten and one. The bases up to one million are:
20 ishirini
30 thelathini
40 arobaini
50 hamsini
60 sitini
70 sabini
80 themanini
90 tisini
100 mia
1,000 elfu
100,000 laki
1,000,000 milioni

<u>Ordinal numbers:</u>
These are constructed in Swahili using the possessive connector –**a**, of, together with a cardinal number. For example:
-**a** tano, fifth [kitabu cha tano, fifth book]
But "first" and "second" are exceptions:
-a **kwanza** (not moja) [kitabu cha **kwanza***, first book]
-a **pili** (not wili) [kitabu cha **pili**, second book]

[*A week-long African-American festival is called **Kwanzaa**, an additional **a** tacked on to the end of *kwanza* in order to have seven letters symbolizing the seven day festival.]

Fractions:
nusu, a half
theluthi or *thuluthi*, a third
robo, a quarter
thumni, an eighth

Decimals:
nukta, decimal point [*mbili nukta nne tano*, 2.45]

Percent:
kwa mia, out of 100 [*saba nukta tano kwa mia*, 7.5%]
OR:
asilimia, per cent [*asilimia saba nukta tano*, 7.5%]

Summary:

	Counting	Adjectives	Ordinals
1	*moja*, one	−*moja*	−*a kwanza*
2	*mbili*, two	-*wili*	-*a pili*, second
3	*tatu*, three	-*tatu*	-*a tatu*, third
4	Here onwards it's the same word for counting, adjectives and ordinals: e.g. *nne*, four/fourth		

For example:
1: as noun, for counting: *moja*, one; as adjective: *kitu kimoja**, one thing; as ordinal adjective: *kitu cha kwanza*, first thing [*this adjective has a foreign equivalent *mosi* e.g. *Jumamosi*, Saturday – literally, week one, meaning first day of the week, *Ijumaa*, Friday, being the culmination of a week.]
2: as noun, for counting: *mbili*, two; as adjective: *vitu viwili*, two things; as ordinal adjective: *kitu cha pili*, second thing

3: as noun, for counting: *tatu*, three; as adjective: *vitu vitatu*, three things; as ordinal adjective: *kitu cha tatu*, third thing

4: as noun, for counting: *nne*, four; as adjective: *vitu vinne*, four things; as ordinal adjective: *kitu cha nne*, fourth thing

14 Calendar, Seasons

Swahili calendar is as follows:

Weekdays
Ijumaa, Friday, a holiday in the Muslim world
Jumamosi, Saturday, a half-day workday in East Africa. [*mosi*, 1*]
Jumapili, Sunday, a holiday in East Africa. [*pili*, 2nd*]
Jumatatu, Monday. [*tatu*, 3*]
Jumanne, Tuesday. [*nne*, 4*]
Jumatano, Wednesday. [*tano*, 5*]
Alhamisi, Thursday.

[*There are two ways to interpret these numbers: (a) using *juma*, week e.g. *juma-mosi*, day 1 of the (Swahili) week, or (b) using *Ijumaa*, Friday e.g. Friday+1.]

Months
Januari, Februari, Machi, Aprili, Mei, Juni, Julai, Agosti, Septemba, Oktoba, Novemba, Desemba

Date
The numeric form DD-<u>MM</u>-YYYY is used preceded by the word *tarehe*, date. For example,

Tarehe kumi na saba <u>mwezi wa tano</u> mwaka wa elfu mbili kumi na tano*, Date 17 <u>fifth month</u>* year 2015 [that is 17-<u>5</u>-2015]. *or, <u>Mei</u>, May.

Seasons [*majira / msimu*, season]
December-February: **kaskazi**, monsoon (northerly) / **kiangazi**, hot & dry
March-May: **masika**, long rains
June-August: **kipupwe**, cool / **kusi**, monsoon (southerly)
September-October: **demani**, warm / **kusi**, monsoon (southerly)
November-December: **vuli**, short rains

[<u>The Serengeti Migration</u>: The above semi-annual rains – that is, when they don't fail – are what drives the famous, ageless, wildebeest-zebra-antelope migration. It takes place over the Serengeti National Park in north-western Tanzania and, across the international border with Kenya, the much smaller Maasai Mara National Reserve. These two parks are contiguous. The migration is an annual, cyclical trek, clockwise along a wriggly loop, roughly parallel with the limits of the two parks, the animals rarely straying out to the surrounding human habitation. Its pattern is basically one of pursuing the next greener pasture, after having grazed the previous to the ground, and in pursuit of drinking water. During the *masika*, long rains, the horde is generally south of the east-west Grumeti River in the western portion of Serengeti. Towards the end of the year, they are found grazing at the top of the trek, straddling the international border. Following the *vuli*, short rains, they slowly move down the eastern portion of the loop, all the way to the bottom of the trek, early in the New Year, completing the migration loop. But what thrills tourists the most is the crossing of the east-west Grumeti River, in a northerly direction, in approximately June-July. The over-two-million-strong migrating horde is preys-galore for the basking crocodiles and the salivating lions.]

15 Time

Swahili day ends at sunset which hovers around 6 pm (give or take an hour) due to being on or close to the Equator. When the day ends and a new one commences, so does the clock start ticking anew. Thus, one hour after sunset (which is nominally at 6 pm) the time is *saa moja jioni*, literally hour **one** in the evening, which according to the usual (international) reckoning is **7** pm, a difference of six hours. Thus, to convert international time to Swahili time you <u>shift</u> it by six hours. [Don't be surprised to occasionally see someone in East Africa wearing their wrist watches upside down so they can read the hour (the shorter) hand in Swahili time! But it is tricky as the minute (longer) hand must still be read in the usual way. That was partly tongue in cheek, but presumably the wearer wants to flip wearing it

Saa tisa na nusu, 3:30

without having to change the time every time he wants to switch between Swahili and international time. In the best-of-both-worlds category, it is better to relabel the numerals to reflect Swahili time – easy to do with a wall clock whose cover opens, see image alongside here. This way you can read BOTH Swahili and international times, the former by reading the relabelled numerals, the latter visually by looking at the positions of the time hands!] The typical practice is that when speaking Swahili you use Swahili time, and when speaking other languages you use international time.

To indicate PM or AM you have to state the time period of the day which is divided into the following periods:

Time Periods:

Name	From	To	
jioni	6 pm	8 pm	evening
usiku*	8 pm	4 am	night
usiku wa manane	12 midnight, or dead of the night		literally, night of the eights, eight in Swahili time i.e. 2 am
alfajiri	4 am	6 am	pre-dawn = *asubuhi sana*, very (early) morning
macheo	6 am		= *kucha*, sunrise = *mapambazuko*, dawn
asubuhi*	6 am	12 noon	morning
adhuhuri	12 noon		literally, midway
mchana*	12 pm	3:30 pm	early afternoon
alasiri	3:30 pm	6 pm	late afternoon
machweo	6 pm		= *kuchwa*, sunset = *magharibi*, dusk

*These three are the **key time periods** which can be broadened out to cover all 24 hours:

asubuhi, morning
mchana, afternoon [*mchana* is also the term for day e.g. *mchana na usiku*, day and night]
usiku, night time

Examples:

saa moja (1) *jioni*, or **usiku** = 7 pm
saa mbili (2) **usiku** = 8 pm
saa kumi (10) *alfajiri* or **usiku** = 4 am
saa moja (1) **asubuhi** = 7 am
saa sita (6) *adhuhuri* or **mchana** = 12 noon
saa kumi (10) *alasiri* or **mchana** = 4 pm

Off-the-hour time:

nukta, second(s)
dakika, minute(s)

Examples:

[time periods not shown; note the six hour difference between **Swahili** time and **international*** time]
barabara, sharp (literally, exactly)
kamili, on-the-dot (literally, complete, as in 'the hour complete')
saa tano na nusu, literally hour **5** and a half = **11:30***
saa tano kasoro dakika kumi barabara, literally hour **5** less 10 minutes exactly = 10 to **11*** sharp
saa tano kasarobo, literally hour **5** less a quarter = quarter to **11***
saa nne kamili, literally hour **4** complete = **10*** on-the-dot

Relative Time:

sasa, now
halafu, later
leo, today
kesho, tomorrow
kesho kutwa, day after tomorrow
jana, yesterday
juzi, day before yesterday
usiku wa kuamkia, eve [literally, night of awakening]
wiki or *juma, week*
mwezi, month
mwaka, year
karne, century
iliyopita / hii / ijayo, last / this / next *e.g. wiki iliyopita*, last week

16 Greeting

In East Africa, as in many parts of the world, the custom is to have an opening exchange of greetings before going on to the subject of the conversation even if it is simply asking the price or for directions :-)

The opening greeting is:

To an individual of your age or lower:

hujambo? * Everything's okay?
*strictly speaking it would be *huna jambo?* you do not have a problem?

To a group of your age or lower: *hamjambo?* meaning same as above

The individual's reply is:

sijambo, no problem, the group's is:

hatujambo, no problem

If the other party is your junior, their response will be a return greeting:

shikamuu – see next below

To a senior person:

shikamuu, a shortened form of *nashika miguu yako*, I grip your feet, to which the reply is:

marahaba, it is welcomed, I am pleased

In places of greater Arabic influence such as Zanzibar and the Kenyan coast:

salaam alekum / salaamu, peace be with you
reply: *alekum issalaam*, and with you peace

sabalkheri, good morning

Close friends may use a shortened greeting: *vipi?* how? Or: *mambo?* problems? Reply: *sawa*, okay Or: *zuri*, fine Or: *poa*, cool

Next:

habari za asubuhi / mchana / leo? News of the morning / afternoon / day? [Or simply, *habari gani?* what news?]

The responses are varied e.g.

kama kawaida or *kama kila siku*, the usual

Next:

hali yako njema? your condition (state) is good?

Or:

hali gani? how are you? [Literally, what is the state?]

The responses again are varied e.g.

[*na*] *shukuru* [*mungu*], [I] am thankful [of god]

Next: [optional, for close acquaintances]

bibi, watoto wote wako salama? Wife, children all okay (literally, safe)?

A short response is:

wako, they are

If you are offered anything e.g.

keti, invited to have a seat, or

onja, asked to taste a sample, etc, you say:

asante, thank you, to which the reply will be:

karibu, you're welcome

The ending greeting is:

kwa heri, goodbye

Or:
usiku mwema, good night

Finishing off the above is:

ya kuonana tena, of seeing each other again

17 Simple Swahili for Beginners

Simple Swahili is a rough-n-ready approach which does not use all its rules yet is easily understood. Here are tips on using Simple Swahili.

Skeletal form: Use only the **bases** of nouns and adjectives straight off the dictionary, that is without attaching prefixes e.g.

chungwa tatu, three orange [correct form: *machungwa matatu*), three oranges]

Same for verbs: Use verb **bases** without any prefixes / infixes / suffixes e.g.

taka chungwa tatu, want three orange [correct form: *ninataka machungwa matatu*), I want three oranges]

For other tenses use a relative time indicator (see chapter 15 Time) e.g. use *jana* (yesterday) to indicate past tense:

jana taka chungwa tatu, yesterday want three orange [correct form: *jana nilitaka machungwa matatu*), yesterday I wanted three oranges]

Swahili verb construction takes time to understand and master, so allow yourself the requisite time to achieve it.

Use *ya-* for all **possessives** e.g.

kitu yangu [correct form: *kitu changu*], my thing
kitu ya mwalimu [correct form: *kitu cha mwalimu*], teacher's thing

Use *hii-* for all 'this' / 'these' **demonstratives** e.g.

kitu hii [correct form: *kitu hiki*], this thing
vitu hii [correct form: *vitu hivi*], these things

Use *ile-* for all 'that' / 'those' **demonstratives** e.g.

kitu ile [correct form: *kitu kile*], that thing
vitu ile [correct form: *vitu vile*], those things

Negative **hapana** can be used for just about all negative constructs e.g.

hapana taka [correct form: *sitaki, hataki,* etc], I / she / etc do(es) not want

Use the possessor adjectives of section 8.2 Possessor Adjective –ake, her, his, its and section 8.3 "1st / 2nd / 3rd Possessor Adjectives" as-is, that is without attaching any prefixes e.g.

taka zigo angu, want my luggage [correct form: *ninataka mzigo* (plural: *mizigo*) *wangu* (plural: *yangu*), I want my luggage(s)]

You WILL be understood because bases will be recognized (as long as you clearly pronounce them as per chapter 19 Pronunciation). The only ambiguity is whether you meant one piece of luggage or many pieces but other than that "want my luggage" is understood.

In general, say only the key words of your thoughts e.g. you are thinking "Where is the station?" but you say only "*Stesheni*?" station? or "*Kituo?*" bus stop? and perhaps hand-signing a "Where?" by shaking a flat, palm opened upwards, or if you remember it say the word for it "*Stesheni wapi*?" station where? [Correct form: *Stesheni iko wapi?* Where is the station?]

Carry a printed / written list of Swahili words for very common English words, including at least the numbers (section 13 Numbers) and the interrogative adjectives (section 9 Interrogatives).

When a word eludes you try using the English word you have in mind. There is a chance it will be understood especially in urban areas. For example, "bus" in Swahili is *basi* and so if you said bus there is a chance it will be understood. [Actually, *basi,* bus, is a good example of converting a foreign word, bus, into its Swahili equivalent, *basi.* This was tackled in 3.11 Making Up Nouns under "Borrowed foreign words" e.g. if you were looking for the word for 'ticket', you would just attach an 'i' at end (which in Swahili results in 'tiketi', but in oral usage its exact spelling does not matter).]

Ask people to speak at slow speed:

sema polepole, speak slowly

or if you want to be very clear about this:

tafadhali sema polepole na mimi, kwa sababu ni bado mwanafunzi, please speak slowly with me, because I am still a student

And you too want to speak slowly so as not to pressure yourself trying to speak rapidly. And, slow speed signals to the listener that you are a learner, thus preparing her for an appropriate conversation speed!

What you will get out of all this initial simple approach is mastery of the base words of Swahili which are the essential foundation blocks on which grammatical Swahili can be constructed.

On the other hand, if you do want to make use of Good Swahili right from the start:

Penye nia, pana njia,

Where there is a will, there is a way!

18 Good Swahili

Jembe halimtupi mkulima,

A hoe does not let a farmer down
[Your resources are your allies]

As you get the hang of Simple Swahili as explained above, you will be building a 'critical mass' of the language base whereby the right words (albeit only in root form) are quickly recalled whenever needed. As soon as you feel this confidence, start fleshing out this base by filling in the correct grammar (in the form of prefixes, etc) and you are on your way to Good Swahili :-)

Why is good Swahili ultimately essential? Because good grammar is necessary for clarity and meaning, and additionally, in the case of Swahili, for its euphony!

Immersion: reading (aloud) as much as you can (even repeats) is a sure way to immerse yourself into a Swahili milieu. Of course the ultimate way of immersion is to go to East Africa and converse only in Swahili which, if nothing else, will let you, later on, cherish your Swahili memories.

BUT, be prepared to occasionally encounter bad grammar, even from locals, just like you encounter in English-speaking countries. And there always is conflation e.g. *rafiki*, friend, belongs to **MIX+FAUNA, VEGGIES [xFV]** whereas *rafiki*, ally, belongs to **MIX+FLOWERS, FRUITS [xFF]**, same singular spelling but different plurals: *rafiki* and *marafiki* respectively, the former being human(s), the latter figurative(s). [Note: The xFF group is sometimes assigned to nouns which in the Dictionary (Volumes 2 and 3) are assigned to the xFV group e.g. *johari*, jewel, is assigned therein to xFV but is also seen assigned in usage to the xFF group, thus the plural under xFV would be *johari* and under xFF *majohari!* Richard F. Burton commented on Swahili inconsistencies in his "Zanzibar: City, Island and Coast", 1872, but also refers to the "...anomalous orthography and cacography of our English". The moral of the story: no language is perfectly consistent!]

And there are spelling variations especially the use of _mu_ instead of **mw**, or _mi_ instead of **my** e.g.

nili_mu_uliza, nili**mw**uliza, I asked her

milia m_i_eupe na m_i_eusi, milia m**y**eupe na m**y**eusi, black and white stripes

And the swapping of _l_ and **r**, and of _f_ and **v** e.g.

te_l_emka, te**r**emka, come down
mpumba_f_u, mpumba**v**u, fool

And the dropping of **y** e.g.

onesha, on**y**esha, point out

Using _a_ in place of **e** or **i** typically with foreign words e.g.

sam_a_h_a_ni, sam**e**h**e**ni, I beg your pardon
fik_a_ra, fik**i**ra, thought

There is also a patois, similar to the English-Jamaican one, called _Sheng_ which is quite hard to understand, like the Jamaican variety which no English-speaking foreigner can understand ;-) _Sheng_, originating in Nairobi, Kenya, is only spoken between young acquaintances who choose to do so but not with other people especially foreigners such as tourists, expatriates, volunteers, etc.

19 Pronunciation

Swahili is pronounced **syllable-by-syllable** as spelt AND there are no un-emphasized neutral vowels e.g. *kijiji*, village, is pronounced ki-ji-ji [as in **Ki**pling **Ji**m **Ji**m, syllable by syllable, with equal emphasis], and NOT as is popularly pronounced: k-jiji as in kijiji.com.

The first order of business: what is a syllable in Swahili? Much like in English, it is a consonant followed by a vowel as in the solfege syllables Do, Re, Mi, Fa, So, La, Ti which are pronounced exactly the same in Swahili. [I would change the So to Su thereby making it a complete set of Swahili vowels: a, e, i, o, u.] Having said that, exceptions immediately arise:

1. **Repeated** vowels [see summary table below for how vowels are pronounced]: e.g. *saa*, clock, *mzee*, elder or old person, *tii*, obedient, *jogoo*, rooster, *kuu*, great, where the repeated vowels *a*, *e*, etc are part* of the syllable formed with the preceding consonant and that such syllables are to be pronounced as if there were only ONE* vowel but spoken ever so slightly LONGER than for single such vowels (cf. beach and bitch, where the former has a longer vowel sound). For example, *saa* is pronounced as the sa- in salmon with the *a* being a slightly stretched out sound. [*Repeated vowels are not always single vowel sounds as in the examples above but often are two or more separate vowels e.g. *sikuuuza*, I did not sell it, where the first -*u*- is part of the negative past tense -*ku*-, the second -*u*- is an object reference (for say *mchoro*, drawing) and the third -*u*- is the beginning of the verb base -*uza*, sell, are **three separate vowels** and are pronounced accordingly: *siku-u-uza!*]
2. Consecutive **different** vowels: e.g. *heroe*, flamingo, *toboa*, bore a hole, *amua*, decide. In each of these cases, the consecutive vowels belong to SEPARATE syllables e.g. the *oe* vowels of *heroe* each belong to separate syllables: *ro* and a standalone *e*. If you take the English word heroin and split it into two parts hero-in, then substitute the "in" with the quintessential Canadianese "eh" but without its questioning tone, you get hero-eh and that's

how it is pronounced in Swahili. Similarly, with *to-bo-a*, the *bo-a* is pronounced as in boa constrictor. The *mu-a* in *a-mu-a* is pronounced as in the cow "moo" sound plus a satisfaction "ah" sound but not prolonged, fore nor aft: ah-moo-ah.

3. **M**- or **n**- followed by a consonant act as separate nasal consonants. Think of the word teamster: the -m- is a separate nasal consonant preceding the consonant -st-. In the same way, *mzee*, old man, consists of two syllables *m-ze*, the nasal *m-* (think of 'mmm' when one ponders or finds something delicious) and -*ze* (as in zephyr but with a slightly prolonged *e*). Other examples: *m**guu***, leg = mmm-gu (as in good, with its slightly prolonged *u*) *n**dugu***, brother, = nnn-dugu (think of do Gulag; it is not pronounced 'an dugu' the way Jack Nicholson addresses his foster child in Tanzania in the movie "About Schmidt"; presumably his character is pronouncing it as any foreigner would, not being accustomed to it). An interesting extension of this is, for example, *mtu **m**moja*, one person, where the nasal *m-* is followed by a syllable beginning with *m-!* Try pronouncing it.

4. The Roman alphabet was deemed to be better suited in representing Swahili sounds than Arabic (which is how it used to be written in). But better suited does not mean perfect, resulting in the use of two or three consonants plus a vowel to represent one sound, such as the bolded consecutive consonants plus vowel in the following examples: *ny**oka*** (think Ferri**gno** **ca**rtoon), snake, *kw**eli*** (think **qua**ck **li**ttle), true. But there are some tough ones too: *ng'**ombe*** (think si**ng** oh cl**imb eh**), *m**bwa*** (think **mmm-bois** where **bois** is French for wood), *g**hafula*** (think Af**gha**nistan **full a**rmy), suddenly, *d**hani*** (think **the** Ali **Ni**nja, **A**li as in Muhammad **A**li), think. [*ng'ombe* is to be compared with *ndugu* given above, the distinction being made with the use of an apostrophe in the former.]

5. Again, suitability not being perfection, there are a number of letters which have **two different sounds** for the **same letter**! e.g. *changu*, my/mine, where the *ch* is pronounced similar to 'change' but *changu*, snapper fish, is pronounced with the forceful *ch* of Aachoo!; *kanga*, guinea-fowl, where the *k* is pronounced similar to Jakarta but *kanga*, printed shawl, is

pronounced as **kha** as in **Kh**an. Although you can't tell which sound to make for a **ch** or a **k** the good news is that besides these two cases above, there is only a couple more to my knowledge: *chini*, down / low, where the **ch** is pronounced forcefully as explained above, and *mbaya/mbali* given in the table below. [Sometimes, infrequently, you will find *kanga*, printed shawl, spelled *khanga* to indicate the emphatic *k*.]

6.   -*j*- is a softer version of the English one, not at the back of the oral cavity but in front and closer to the English -ch-.

7.   -*gi*- is not the -*j*- of English but as in "**gi**ddy up". [John Wayne in "Hatari" pronounces it perfectly in *tingisha chupa*, shake the bottles, but then butchers it in *wacha mama – akili mingi*, let madam alone – too clever! where he pronounces the -*gi* as -*ji*; but also to be noted is that, *mingi* should be *nyingi*, *akili* being a member of the xFV noun group – refer to 4.1 Summary of Vowel-adjectives. This latter likely was a script error, perhaps a deliberate one as *mingi* is easier on a foreign tongue and yet would be easily understood.] A good example (but initially tricky) to practise and memorize is **Ubelgiji**, Belgium, where again the "**gi**" is pronounced as in "**gi**ddy up" while the "*ji*" as in English but with a softer "j" as explained in the point above.

Summary:

*First pronounce the whole English word(s), then just what is **bolded**

Category	E.g.	*Pronounced
Repeated vowels	*tii*, obedient	**tea**ch
Two different consecutive vowels	*heroe*, flamingo	**hero**in **e**h
Leading nasal *m-*, *n-*	*mzee*, old person	**mmm**-**ze**ppelin, the 'e' in -ze is a long one
	ndugu, brother	**nnn**-**do Gu**lag
Multi-consonant single sound	*kweli*, true	**qua**ck little
	twiga, giraffe Similarly, *bwana*, *gwaride*, *pwani*, *swala*	**twig** arch

Category	E.g.	*Pronounced
	mbwa, dog	**mmm-bois*** *French for wood
	mnyama, animal	**mmm**-Ta**nya ma**
	ng'ombe, cow	si**ng** oh cli**mb** eh the 'g' is almost silent
	nyoka, snake	Ferri**gno car**toon
	nywa, drink	Ta**nya Waal*** *river in Holland
	nywele, hair	Ta**nya well** eh
Consonant+*h*-	*chai*, chai	same word in English
	dhani, think	**Th**e Ali* Ninja *as in Muhammad Ali, not ~~Ally McBeal~~
	ghafula, suddenly	Af**gha**nistan **full** army
	shamba, farming plot	**sha**man **Barb**
	thelathini, thirty	**the**ft larceny **thi**ef **ni**x
Two-sound consonants	*changu*, 1. mine, 2. Snapper fish	1. **cha**i and **Gu**lag 2. Aa**ch**oo **Assam** and **Gu**lag
	kanga, 1. guinea-fowl, 2. shawl & sarong (named so, as the original prints resembled the spotted pattern of a guinea-fowl)	1. **Kant** tango army 2. **Kha**n tango army
	tunda mbaya, bad fruit	**mmm-bark Ya**!
	mahali mbali, far place	**mmm-Bh**utan army list
gi-	*giza*, darkness	**Giza** (pyramids of)
j-	*juu*, up	**Ju**jistu, the 'u' is a long one; this is a tough one: the 'j' is in

Category	E.g.	*Pronounced
		between the English 'ch' and 'j'
Vowel sounds	_afya_, health	**Af**rica **Ya**maha
	elfu, thousand	**Elf U**ber
	iba, steal	**Iba**dan (Nigeria)
	oga, bathe	**Oga**den (Ethiopia)
	_ua_, flower	**oo**h **aah**, **oo** and **aa** are not prolonged
Neutral, unemphasized vowel [the schwa, ə]	There is NO NEUTRAL VOWEL in Swahili thus _kijiji_, village is pronounced:	**Ki**pling **Jim Jim**, the 'i' pronunciation is identical in all three syllables [again, 'j' is softer than in English]
	and not as is popularly pronounced in kijiji.com:	~~Katrina Jim Jim~~
All other consonants		Same or close to as in English
The **Internet** is a very good complement to the above guide. See Chapter 20 Internet Resources.		

All Swahili words end in a vowel (for euphony) and all syllables must be pronounced with equal emphasis with, usually, an extra emphasis on the **penultimate** syllable e.g. sa-**FA**-ri, journey. There is an odd exception to note: _barabara_, which has two meanings: road (noun) or properly / exactly (adverb). The 'road' version is pronounced as usual: ba-ra-**BA**-ra BUT the 'properly' version is pronounced as two words ba-**RA** ba-**RA** in quick succession, taking the cue from its foreign origin (Arabic)!

Like with all languages, foreigners speak with an accent. However, accent is not as important as clarity where the key thing is whether a syllable is recognized or not. For example, if you pronounce safari as you would in English, where the first 'a' is a neutral schwa ə, it will not be as a local would pronounce it but it will be understood.

Beyond that, if you do want to try to speak like a local it would have to be through the process of listen-n-repeat. [The Internet, including YouTube, has a plethora of Swahili pronunciation help, which is most useful for listen-n-repeat exercises.] One of the things to listen to is Swahili words that begin with a nasal consonant *m-* or *n-* e.g. *mzee*, elder, or *ndugu*, brother (see these consonants in the table above for how they are pronounced). [A little more challenging is when the nasal consonant is followed by an *m-* or *n-* syllable e.g. *mmoja*, one, an adjective used for the singulars of the PEOPLE [Pp] or VEGETATION [V] groups. Give it a try.] And when these are followed by a multi-consonant syllable having a *-y-* in it, it is a little harder but it is a precious sound in Swahili. For example, *mnyama*, animal (see it in the above table). And if the second syllable is a multi-consonant one the sound is even more endearing. For example, *Mnyamwezi*, a member of the huge *Wanyamwezi* tribe of western Tanzania. And when you are able to pronounce *ng'ombe*, cattle, you will have 'arrived' :-) Interestingly, the *ng'o* in *ng'ombe* is onomatopoeic, being the 'moo' of a cow!

20 Internet Resources

For recent and latest material on Swahili, including new words, the Internet is an invaluable resource, keeping in mind though that Swahili not being one of the widely-used global languages (such as English, French, Spanish) it accordingly does not have as many resources nor much competition nor profit which are necessary for producing works of very high quality such as the Merriam-Webster or Oxford English dictionaries.

For starters one can look up an Internet search engine with key words that begin with "Swahili..." e.g. "Swahili dictionary / stories / blogs / newspapers / wikipedia / etc". And, the Internet being audio-visual, it is a very good resource for Swahili sounds especially vowel and syllable pronunciation e.g. You Tube, BBC Swahili, VOA Swahili (Sauti ya Amerika), etc. Transcribing a few sentences from such resources is an excellent way to being able to hear and process Swahili. For example VOA *Alfajiri*, dawn or pre-dawn, service begins:

Kucha Afrika, Sunrise Africa!

Hii ni idhaa ya Kiswahili Sauti ya Amerika VOA ikitangaza kutoka hapa mjini Washington DC, This is the Swahili radio broadcast of Voice of America VOA being broadcast from here downtown Washington DC!

Ni saa kumi na moja alfajiri kwa Saa za Afrika ya Kati na saa kumi na mbili asubuhi kwa Saa za Afrika Mashariki, It is 11* o'clock Central African Time and 12* o'clock East African Time in the morning! [*These are Swahili times which in international reckoning are 5 o'clock and 6 o'clock, respectively, in the morning. See Chapter 15 Time.]

Nakukaribisha msikilizaji katika matangazo kumekucha Afrika kutoka hapa VOA Swahili, I welcome you listener [in]to announcements already arisen / arising [in] Africa from here VOA Swahili!

Admittedly, this is not easy to do the first time, but with experience it becomes relatively easier, paying off big dividends in becoming good in oral Swahili :-) And, as always, read the Swahili out aloud, which is another solid way to getting a good grip on oral Swahili.

Videos on You Tube: You Tube presents much material in Swahili, supplementing the material in these volumes, some examples being, from basic to advanced:

- alphabet, numbers and syllables
- word groups e.g. shapes
- lessons
- children's stories
- documentaries
- short films
- feature films

The first three bullets are easy to use and understand. It's the remaining which can be difficult, in the early going, as they often have modulated / animated speeches to suit the context, as well as rapid speech that native speakers use, requiring much rewinding and repeating to catch the words.

As an example of animated / modulated / rapid speech, below is a children's story on You Tube for which I have provided its Swahili text. [The video on You Tube has captions, but in English. It does have an auto-translate into Swahili but I couldn't get it to work and / or it was garbled or had unrelated text :-( ] All words in this story are found in the dictionary (Volume 2 of the three volume set), nouns in singular form, verbs in root form.

Story Title: **"Simba na Panya"** ["Lion and Mouse"]

Elapsed Time m:ss	Narration and Dialogue [the latter in double-quotes] Dialogues are prefixed *S:* or *P:* standing for *Simba* or *Panya*. Entries in square brackets show a variation in pronunciation by the narrator e.g. *Siku [sku]* in which the 'i' is dropped.
0:00	*Hapo zamani za kale, kwenye msitu palishi simba aliyeongoza msitu. Siku [sku] moja baada ya chakula chake, simba alilala chini ya mti kupumzika. Panya mdogo akaja. Akaona itakuwa wema kucheza juu ya simba.*
0:30	*Akaanza kukimbia juu chini kwenye mwili wa yule simba. Alikimbia huku akitembea juu hadi chini kwa mkia wa simba. Simba aliamka kwa hasira huku akinguruma kwa ngumu. Alimbana yule panya kwa mkono wake. Panya alijaribu*

Elapsed Time m:ss	Narration and Dialogue [the latter in double-quotes] Dialogues are prefixed *S:* or *P:* standing for *Simba* or *Panya*. Entries in square brackets show a variation in pronunciation by the narrator e.g. *Siku [sku]* in which the 'i' is dropped.
	kujinasua lakini wapi. Simba alifungua mdomo wake, tayari kumla.
1:00	*Panya aliogopa sana.* *P: "Ai, mfalme wangu tafadhali usimile. Tafadhali nisamehe kwa leo. Niachilie. Na kwa hivi sitawahi kusahau. Labda siku [sku] moja nitakusaidia [nitaksadia]."* *Simba alisajabishwa na wazo la panya kuweza kumsaidia. Kisha, kafungua* (sic) *mdomo wake na kumachilia.* *P: "Ahsante, mfalme wangu. Sitawahi kusahau ukarimu wako."* *S: "Unabahati sana rafiki kwani tayari nimeshiba. [continues]*
1:30	*Nenda zako sasa. Lakini wacha nikuambie usiwahi nichezea."* *Siku chache baadaye, simba alikuwa anatembea [natembea] kwenye msitu. Wawindaji wakaweka mtego kumshika yule simba. Wawindaji hao walijificha nyuma ya mti kumsubiri simba akaribie kwenye mtego. Alipokaribia wawindaji walivuta kamba na kumkamata yule simba ndani ya wavu.*
2:00	*Simba alianza kunguruma kwa nguvu na kujaribu kujiokoa. Lakini wawindaji walizidi kukaza wavu. Wawindaji walirudi kijijini kuchukua mkokoteni watakaotumia kumsafirisha simba.* *Simba bado alikuwa ananguruma [nanguruma] kwa nguvu. Kwenye mawote walimsikia, na pia yule panya alimsikia.* *P: "Mfalme yuko kwenye matatizo. Lazima nirudishe fadhila."*
2:30	*Muda si mrefu panya alimfikia simba.* *P: "Mfalme wangu usijali mimi nitakusaidia uwe huru."* *Panya alipanda juu ya ule mtego. Akatumia meno yake kali kuzitafuna zile kamba. Mwishowe alimnasua yule simba*

Elapsed Time m:ss	Narration and Dialogue [the latter in double-quotes] Dialogues are prefixed *S:* or *P:* standing for *Simba* or *Panya*. Entries in square brackets show a variation in pronunciation by the narrator e.g. *Siku [sku]* in which the 'i' is dropped.
	kutoka kwa ule mtego akawa huru. Simba aligundua kwamba hata panya mdogo anaweza kuwa msaada mkubwa.
3:00	*S: "Ahsante panya. Sitawahi kukusumbua wewe tena. Ishi kwa furaha kwenye msitu wangu. Umeokoa maisha ya mfalme. Na sasa wewe mwanamfalme wa msitu huu."* *P: "Ahsante mfalme. Kwaheri. Tuonane karibuni."* *S: "Aah, kwenda wapi? Ungependa kucheza juu ya mgongo wangu na kutembea hadi kwenye mkia wangu."*
3:30	*Panya alipanda kwenye mgongo wa simba na kubembea hadi kwenye mkia. Baada ya muda [mda], wawindaji walirudi na mkokoteni mkubwa ili wambebe simba. Simba na panya waliwaona na wakaanza kuwakimbilia. Simba alitoa ngurumo kubwa na wale wawindaji waliogopa na wakakimbia kurudi kijijini.*
4:00	*Simba na panya wakawa marafiki milele.*

TIP: In You Tube settings is an option called "Playback speed": try lowering the speed to 0.75 or 0.5, which is still understandable but lets you focus word-by-word.

Aside from illustrating modulated / animated / rapid speech, the above can be used as an exercise to start bringing yourself up to speed in spoken Swahili!

Note: Yale University's Kamusi Project (*kamusi*, dictionary) was a very good resource but unfortunately it has not been functioning for many years now.

21 Dictionary

Kuuliza si ujinga,

Asking is not stupidity

How were the words in the Dictionary (Volumes 2 and 3) selected? A rule of thumb says only a fraction of all existing words are in practical, daily use, so for starters I used a list of 100 most common English nouns, 100 adjectives, 100 verbs, etc. Next I used words from categories such as professions (teacher, farmer, etc), family (father, mother, etc), fauna (i.e. animal kingdom names), flora (plant kingdom names), household items, school items, office items, health items, etc – which represented a starting milieu. I went through scenarios for more words: one day in my life, in an artisan's life, in the kitchen, etc. All along the way as other words popped up in my head (especially while coming up with the numerous examples and practice text for this book, or I came across words in what I happened to be reading) they got added to the dictionary. This then is the 'practical' aspect of this dictionary.

Interestingly, only just over 200 of the words herein were not to be found in Madan's classic dictionary*, most likely as his was an early attempt – albeit a tremendous one, I will be quick to add – and so some words were bound to have slipped through the cracks, some of the common ones being: *duma*, cheetah, *janja*, cunning, *jinga*, stupid, *kanyaga*, step on, *kaptura*, shorts, *karanga*, peanuts, *kasuku*, parrot, *kutoka*, from (although *toka*, from, was found), *muhimu*, important, *swala*, gazelle, *tania*, tease, *toka*, come out / from. But it is to be noted that *asumini*, jasmine, was found as *yasmini*, *forodha*, customs, as *forotha*, *hadhari*, caution, as *hathari*, *hewa*, air, as *hawa*, *msichana*, girl, as *msijana*, etc. Also, *fyata*, slingshot, could be derived from *fyatua*, fire a gun; *eleza*, explain, was found as the causative form under *elea*, be lucid, and not as a separate entry as is common now, *nyesha*, rain, as a causative under *nya*, excrete, and not as a regular action verb. Having said all that, this textbook is dedicated to Madan (and Steere and Krapf) in recognition of pioneering efforts in the Swahili language – and to that giant of our language, Shaaban Robert.

[*A. C. Madan's 450 page "Swahili-English dictionary" 1903 is more than a dictionary. It has embedded in it Swahili grammar. For example, among the entries for letter "K" is found this grammatical note: "**Ka**, *1*. Is a verbal connective prefix, except in the cases noted below. In general, it connects two or more verbs together in such a way as either (*a*) to carry on the construction (mood and tense) of the first verb to those following with *ka-*, or (*b*) to supply in those verbs the construction appropriate to the context. But most commonly it is used (*1*) to connect a verb in the Past (Narrative) Tense Indicative with others following, or else (*2*) to connect a verb in the Imperative Mood with another in the Subjunctive, or Imperative. Thus...", a full page of notes on just this one item! A classic work in the fullest sense!]

My objective was to come up with a good set of common words whose knowledge would arm the student with a solid, practical, daily-use dictionary. Given these few thousand words you are ready to take off! I am confident that these represent at least 95% of the most common words in daily use.

The next step was to test this dictionary against something. I settled on testing it against short stories as that would be appropriate for a student readership (whereas formal reports, academic papers, etc come later for the student and which would be termed as the advanced/literary level). [Additional words, as encountered by the student in daily usage and their meanings determined, would augment this foundational dictionary. This augmentation, as with all languages, is a lifetime process and not a once-and-for-all.]

Test results:

(1) Story length: 330 words. Only one word was not in this dictionary (a hit rate of 99.7%) but even there it was obvious what the writer was intending: *kambia* a word made up from the word *kamba*,

rope, by inserting a preposition *-i-* giving the meaning "to tie up with rope". This is covered in section 10.2 Prepositions.

(2) Story length: 367 words. Seven words were not in this dictionary, which is a hit rate of 98%.

(3) Story length: 404 words. Only one word was not in this dictionary, a hit rate of 99.75%.

Derived words: Like in English, Swahili has many derived words e.g. from *jamaa*, society, we get *ujamaa*, socialism. These are 'made up' words as seen in sections 3.11 Making Up Nouns, 4.3 Making Up Adjectives, 5.12 Making Up Verbs, 6.1 Making Up Adverbs and Appendix B: Nouns/Verbs Made Up From Each Other. Other derivations are from transforming active verbs into passive, etc e.g. from *shinda*, win, we get *shindwa*, fail (literally, be won over) as seen in section 5.8 Verb Transformations. Only a selected representation of such derived words is included in the dictionary, as most derivatives are recognizable e.g. *pumu*, lung, and its related words *pumua*, breathe, *pumzi*, breath, and even *pumzika*, rest, which for illustrative purpose are all included in the dictionary. [A corollary of this is that the dictionary is actually much longer if all derived words were added!] Caution: what is recognizable is not always as straight-forward e.g. *ongoza*, lead, *kiongozi*, leader, *mwongozo*, direction, etc where the derived words are modified fore-n-aft! BUT, after encountering a few of these you will get to be on the lookout for different patterns of similarity of related words. [Note: keep in mind that just because there is a similarity it may only be superficial e.g. *pamba*, decorate, and *pambana*, encounter!] The moral of the story is: if a word is not found in the dictionary herein, try to make up another word or to transform it (as per sections listed at the beginning of "Derived words:" above) e.g. *utengano* is not listed in the dictionary. Reversing the 'making up' or transformation process, we get (after becoming good* at doing this!) *tenga*, set apart, and thus the made-up noun *utengano*, separation. Appendix B: Nouns/Verbs Made Up From Each Other and Appendix F: Widely-used *Ki-* Prefix present patterns which can be studied for becoming good at this. [*This skill is valuable in becoming good in Swahili!]

Gerunds are NOT listed in the dictionary as they are readily derived from their verb bases which ARE listed e.g. verb base *soma*, read, is listed from which the gerund *kusoma*, reading, is derived, always by prefixing the base with *ku-*. Note that *kusoma* is both the infinitive, to read, and the gerund, reading.

Built-in mini-thesaurus: a sort of built-in mini-thesaurus is embedded in the Dictionary in Volumes 2 and 3. This is of two forms: (1) **Related Words**, including antonyms. (2) **Categories** which are as follows: **body, building structure, fauna, food, number, person, produce, terrain, tool, utensil, vegetation** (including flowers) and for adjectives, **colours** e.g. you can look up the Swahili word for say teacher or if you want to know the Swahili words for similar professions you look up the **person:** entries. There are over 600 words in these categories. This mini-thesaurus should help the beginner find common related words by browsing them in these lists. To further facilitate such find-by-browsing, words other than nouns and verbs are also presented in a separate, shorter table in the Adjectives, Adverbs section of the English-Swahili Dictionary (in Volume 3). Take a moment now to familiarize yourself with these features.

TIP: Swahili has several wide-use verbs which are used with other words to make up new verbs. Refer to Appendix C: Wide-use Verbs.

Examples: All entries in the dictionary, except for nouns, have examples (commencing with "e.g."); in fact, many of the nouns have examples too.

21.1 Using The Dictionary

Prefixes, infixes, suffixes (attachments) that modify Swahili words must be stripped off before looking them up here, except for nouns which are listed with singular prefixes*. This stripping/de-construction process is thoroughly explained in section 22.1 How to Use the Index Tables which must be learnt in order to be able to look up constructed words in the dictionary (or for that matter, any Swahili dictionary).

[*Exceptions are nouns with a plural connotation e.g. *maji*, water, which belongs to the MIX+FLOWERS, FRUITS [xFF] group, is always plural. There is no singular for it. It is thus listed as *maji* along with a label "(plu)" next to it indicating the plural connotation.]

The dictionary is presented in the following parts:

(1) Swahili-English order (Volume 2) with the Swahili entries bolded;
(2) English-Swahili order with the English entries bolded (Volume 3);
(3) Words other than nouns & verbs, in English-Swahili order (in the Adjectives, Adverbs section of Volume 3). The purpose of this is to have a short list of adjectives, etc to facilitate browsing to find an adjective, etc of which you have only a vague idea but when it catches your eye while scanning this short list you would know it.

In all of the above parts the column order from left to right remains the same:

Columns:
Swahili [- **SORTED**[1]]: Swahili words[4]
F(oreign): Foreign-origin words are flagged "F" in this column
Type (of Word): The table below lists all the different types of words[5]
English [- **SORTED**[1]]: English words[2]
(Noun) **G**(rou)**p**: The group that a noun entry belongs to[3]

[1]When either of these column is labelled "- **SORTED**" the table is sorted by the column's entries AND its column entries are ALL **bolded**.

[2]over 600 entries are ALSO listed under the following categories **body, building structure, fauna, food, person, produce, terrain, tool, utensil, vegetation** (including flowers) and for adjectives, **colours**.

[3]In addition to the eight noun groups [described in chapter 3 Nouns], there is the special case of counting numbers *moja* or *mosi*, one, and *mbili*, two, which are NOUNS and are flagged as (**#**). [These two are to be compared with their corresponding ADJECTIVES *moja* and *wili*. From *tatu*, three, onwards the noun and adjective forms are identical and only the adjective forms are listed herein. This is covered in chapter 13 Numbers.]

[4]right after a Swahili noun its singular and plural prefixes are shown in brackets e.g.

mti(m,mi) where *m* indicates the singular prefix found in the entry, and *mi* indicates the plural prefix that replaces that singular prefix, that is the singular *mti* becomes the plural *miti*

nyanya(-) indicates this noun does NOT have a singular nor a plural prefix, *nyanya* being singular or plural

tunda(-,ma) indicates there is NO singular prefix and the plural is formed by simply prefixing *ma* to the word, that is the singular *tunda* becomes the plural *matunda*

utenzi(u,-) indicates there is NO plural prefix and the plural is formed by just removing the singular prefix, that is the singular *utenzi* becomes the plural *tenzi*

Where applicable a Swahili word has one of the following entries right after it:
(aug) meaning augmentative (i.e. bigger); belongs to xFF group
(dim) meaning diminutive (i.e. smaller); belongs to T group
(dis) meaning disability; belongs to T group
(plu) meaning noun is always plural in usage

[5]Word Type	Denotes
adj	adjective
adv	adverb
cond	conditional
conj	conjunction
dem	demonstrative adjective
iadj	interrogative adjective
ij	interjection

[5]Word Type	Denotes
n	noun
ppro	personal pronoun
prep	preposition
resp	response word
rpro	relative pronoun

v[.**vt**]	verb
	
	v(erb)**t**(ype):
	    blank=active & can take a direct object
	    v(erb).**c**(au)**s**(ative) i.e. to cause to ~
	    v(erb.)**i**(n)**t**(ransitive) i.e. can not have a direct object
	    v(erb).**p**(a)**s**(sive) i.e. "to be ~(ed)"
	    v(erb).**r**(e)**fl**(exive) i.e. ~self
	    v(erb).**r**(e)**c**(i)**p**(rocal) i.e. each other
	    v(erb).**st**(ative) i.e. "to be ~(ed)"
	where ~ represents the verb entry
	This is covered in section 5.8 Verb Transformations.

21.2 Swahili-English Dictionary

Please refer to Volume 2.

21.3 English-Swahili Dictionary

Please refer to Volume 3.

21.4 English-Swahili Adjectives, Adverbs, etc

Please refer to Volume 3.

22 Index of Attachments (alphabetical)

Mvumilivu hula mbivu,

A patient person eats ripe
[Patience is rewarded]

This index is designed keeping in mind that the reader is a student of the Swahili language which has the key peculiarity of extensive use of attachments (prefixes, infixes and suffixes) in the construction of words especially of verbs. The student will have seen this throughout the textbook and will no doubt have felt the constant need to know and sort them out in the head. This index then is precisely for facilitating that need.

This index is a set of tables of prefixes, infixes and suffixes, grouped by grammar components to which they belong: nouns, adjectives, verbs, etc. This brings all the attachments here in one place, alphabetically, for efficient referencing and, in turn, for referring back to the source chapters using the references given in the table entries (but only if the examples given in these tables are insufficient illustrations).

The index is also very handy for revision study.

22.1 How to Use the Index Tables

First of all, the importance of the study of attachments can not be over-emphasized because Swahili grammar is all about them, ALL of which – including, very importantly, homonyms – are presented here for matching against a word being analyzed as well as for scanning and selecting when constructing a word.

We will use an example to illustrate how to use these tables: [The goal in this example is to parse (de-construct) the constructed verb so that its meaning can be accurately analyzed]

nyanya anazoziona ni kubwa sana

Before we can proceed, the sentence has to be broken down into its components:

nyanya, tomato(es) = object [not subject because it would have required pronoun prefix *i-* instead of the *a-* used in the verb that follows]
anazoziona = some verb in a constructed form
ni, is = verb
kubwa, big = adjective
sana, very = adverb

This first breakdown was achieved by looking up the individual words in the Swahili-English Dictionary (in Volume 2), all of which were found except *anazoziona* which we assume is a constructed verb since the dictionary (like any other dictionary) lists only verb bases. [By the way, had it been found it would have had to be the imperative form of the verb! See section 5.10 Imperatives.]

Next, we parse this constructed verb so as to understand what it means and to extract from it the verb base for looking it up in the dictionary.

Recall the mnemonic in chapter 11 ANATOMY OF VERBS:

AH[1]a! P[2]lease T[3]urn oveR[4] fO[5]r C[6]heaP[7] T[8]icK[9]etT[10]S[11],

where the bold letters are indicative of all the different verb attachments in the order of insertion left-to-right (that is, prefixes, then infixes, then suffixes), which is also the order in which the tables below are presented in the sections that follow. Note: not all of these prefixes, etc are present in every verb construction.

The index tables are numbered in the same order as the above mnemonic's bold letters e.g. the <u>third</u> bold letter in the mnemonic is **T[3]** (= Tense) whose corresponding index is Index table: 3. Verb Tense Infix (section 22.3.1). Let's start parsing the constructed verb: [If however, you are up to speed on all the attachments of verb construction, you may want to use section 11.1 Quick Look-up Table of Verb Attachments, instead of the detailed tables of this chapter.]

anazoziona

(a) The first thing to parse is usually the easiest*: it is the leading prefix which is to be found either in section 22.2.1 Index table: 1. H- Negative, Routine Prefix or in section 22.2.2 Index table: 2. Verb Pronoun Prefix. [*unless it happens to be a second concurrent or intended verb following a first verb in which case the second verb has no pronoun at the front and always begins with *ku-*. This was covered above in section 10.6 Immediate 2nd Verbs e.g. concurrent 2nd action: *alisoma na kuandika*, he read **and** wrote; intended 2nd action *alikuja kupumzika*, he came **to** rest.] Since the above example does not begin with an *h-* nor even a *k-*, we proceed to look up its leading letter(s) in the pronoun index table 2 and find that there is only one entry that begins with *a-* namely:

(b) *a-nazoziona*, where *a-* according to index 2 is a 3rd person pronoun which in the example given therein is "she / he". Thus, we get:

(c) *a-nazoziona*, **she/he** ...

(d) Now we enter the realm of infixes which besides being presented type by type in index tables 3 through 7 are also presented in one combined MASTER table in section 22.3 Master Infix table for a more efficient identification of the infixes in a constructed verb. Thus, we look up our next letter *-n-* in the master table. We find a number of *-n-* entries in it but none as a single letter AND the only two-letter infix that matches is *-na-* which in the table is indicated as the present tense. Thus, we now have:

(e) *a-na-zoziona*, she/he [**present tense**] ... [we park the tense info in square brackets for now, until we come to the verb base when we can translate it as such]

(f) Carrying right along, we look up our next letter *-z-* and again there are a few entries beginning with that letter of which two match our case, namely *-zo-* which according to the master table are relative pronouns (both labelled with superscripts [4.R] denoting table **4. Relative**), respectively belonging to two noun groups, xFV and U, which in this case doesn't matter as they both mean the same thing: who(m)/which. Thus, we have:

(g) *a-na-zo-ziona*, **who(m)/which** she/he [present tense] … Out of curiosity, which of the two noun groups does -**zo**- refer to? The answer lies in the dictionary look up for *nyanya*, tomato: xFV. Next we again consult the master table for our next letter, again a -**z**- and again it shows a number of entries with that letter and again two of which match our case, namely -**zi**- which according to the master table are object references (both labelled with superscripts [5.O] denoting table **5. O**bject) belonging respectively to the same two noun groups as previous, xFV and U, meaning 'them'. Thus we have:

(h) *a-na-zo-zi-ona*, who(m)/which she/he [present tense] **them** … Next we again consult the master table for our next letter, an -**o**- and find a number of entries all of which are flagged [4.R] meaning they are relative pronouns of which we already have one above, so it can't be a relative pronoun, meaning there are no more matches and that we have hit the beginning of the verb base. Looking it up in the Swahili-English Dictionary (Volume 2) we find a perfect match for it, namely *ona*, see, giving us:

(i) *a-na-zo-zi-**ona***, who(m)/which she/he **sees** them… [the present tense is now applied to the verb: **sees**]

Putting all the words together we get:

nyanya, tomatoes = object
anazoziona, who(m)/which she/he sees them = constructed verb
ni, is = verb
kubwa, big = adjective
sana, very = adverb

nyanya anazoziona ni kubwa sana, the tomatoes which he/she sees them are very big

Phew! That's it! But keep in mind that such tedious processes are only for revision of what has been previously learnt in this book and that in due time you will get the hang of it and it WILL become second nature and you WILL be on your way to becoming very good at it. The moral of the story: this short-term pain is for a long term gain AND there are no short cuts to it, gotta pay your dues ;-) Besides, you HAVE TO strip off the prefixes, etc from a word, especially verbs, in order to be able to look it up in any Swahili dictionary! Without doing that the dictionary (or any other Swahili dictionary) is useless. So, keep in mind that the price you pay for diligently learning and mastering prefixes, etc WILL pay off handsomely down the road :-) [Even after you only occasionally use these index tables, the **mnemonic** we have been using continues to be very useful for parsing in the head.]

The above constructed verb example did not have any suffix modifications, it ended in the verb base *ona*. Let's tackle an example in which it does not:

mwite atupikie chakula

Looking up the dictionary, only one of the above three words is found: the noun *chakula*, food. The first two words we assume are constructed verbs. Using the technique described above we can parse them as far as possible resulting in:

mw-ite a-tu-pikie, where the initial parsing tells us:

mw-, you (plural) [this is a false hit! see **TIP** below]
a-, he/she = pronoun
-tu-, us = object

But when we look up the remaining words, - *ite* and - *pikie*, the dictionary does NOT have any exact matches. The closest matches are *ita*, call, and *pika*, cook. Seeing that only the ending vowel *-a* is different from the *-e* and *-ie-* in our two words, *ita* and *pika* are the only possible candidates for the verbs we are seeking.

TIP: Verbs that end in *-e* (but also see * below for those ending in *-ye* or -*je*) indicate that they are either **subjunctive** verbs, or they are **imperatives** which use subjunctive forms. If it is a subjunctive and it has an attached prefix, that prefix is a pronoun, found in table 2 and explained in section 10.5 Subjunctives. Or if it is an imperative and it has an attached prefix, that prefix is an object reference found in table 5 and explained in section

5.10 Imperatives. [There is also a very slight possibility of the verbs being one of a very few foreign-origin verbs that end in -e e.g. *samehe*, forgive, *starehe*, be comfortable, but which in our example they obviously are not.] To convert the subjunctive or object+imperative form back to its verb base, we simply change the -e back to -**a** reversing the process explained in section 10.5 Subjunctives or in section 5.10 Imperatives. [*If a verb ends in -**ye** a possibility is that it is the 3rd person singular relative pronoun used at the end of a verb for the timeless tense e.g. *atoshaye*, she/he who suffices; see section 10.3 Relative Pronouns. Or, if a verb ends in -**je** a possibility is that it is a verb transformed into a question e.g. *fungaje*, shuts how? See section 5.8 Verb Transformations. Again, neither of these possibilities, -ye or -je, is true of our case.] By the way, all of the above -e endings are found in section 22.4 Master Suffix table of indexes 9 to 11.

As to whether the first of our two constructed verbs has either a pronoun or an object prefixed to the front (the second word has already been parsed into a pronoun prefix and an object infix), we try for a match in the pronoun table 2 and the object table 5 and find matches in both for the *mw-* in *mwite*. The plot thickens! The pronoun table 2 tells us that the *mw-* is a 2nd person plural pronoun while the object table 5 tells us that it is a 3rd person singular object reference. As to which it is, section 10.5 Subjunctives under Explicit Imperatives states a 2nd person plural command does NOT use a prefix but a suffix -ni. Thus, our *mw-* is a 3rd person singular object reference!

Reversing the -e endings of our two constructed verbs to -a, and detaching the *mw-* prefix we get:

Ita and *pikia*, of which *ita* matches one of our two candidate verbs, but not *pikia*. One down, one to go!

TIP: If the vowel preceding the ending vowel of a verb is -e- or -i-, it is quite possible that these are **prepositional** inserts as given below in section 22.3.5 Index table: 7. Verb Preposition Infix. To convert the prepositional form back to its verb base, we simply remove the -e- or -i- reversing the process explained in section 10.2 Prepositions.

Thus, *pikia* becomes *pika* which IS found in the dictionary.

Putting our findings together:

mwite, call him/her
atupikie, that he/she cook for us = constructed verb [preposition -*i*- = for]
chakula, food

TIP: Most of the **foreign-origin** verbs do not end in –*a* but during insertion of a preposition the ending gets changed to –*a* or –*e* e.g. *jibu*, reply, changes to *jibia*, reply **to**. Thus, when the constructed form *jibia* is encountered the changed ending vowel must be factored in when looking it up in the dictionary. The simplest way to do this is to ignore the last vowel, and the inserted preposition, and look up just *jib*: there is only one verb in the dictionary whose first three letters match: *jibu* which when you insert a preposition into, gives you *jibia*.

TIP: Watch out for a few of the prefixes, etc which are **homonyms** and thus can initially be very confusing. The most confusing of the homonyms is the *ku*- prefix or infix which can be ANY one of the following:

- Negative past tense e.g. *hakupenda*, he **did not** like
- 2nd person singular object e.g. *hakukupenda*, he did not like **you**
- PLACE-ADVERBS [Pl] pronoun e.g. *kunatosha*, **it** (some place in general) suffices
- PLACE-ADVERBS [Pl] object e.g. *hakukupenda*, he did not like **it** (some place in general)
- GERUNDS [G] object e.g. *hakukupenda*, he did not like **it** (e.g. singing)
- Infinitive form of single syllable verbs e.g. *alikula*, he ate. But note that it disappears in the negative form: *hakula*, he did not eat, where the -*ku*- here is the negative past tense. But then it IS present in the negative future tense: *hatakula*, he will not eat!
- Second verb denoting a concurrent action e.g. *alikuja na* **ku***kaa*, he came and he sat
- Second verb denoting an intended action e.g. *alikuja* **ku***pumziga*, he came to rest

Add to that, there are a few verb bases that begin with *ku*- e.g. *kuta*, meet (whose infinitive form is *kukuta*). Thus, we can have *uli*****kuta***, you met, where -*ku*- is part of the verb base! [Another type of confusion is with the verbs *pa*, give, and *tupa*, throw e.g. *alitupa* where -*tu*- can be the object "us" attached to the verb *pa*, he/she gave us, OR -*tu*- is simply part of the verb *tupa*, he/she threw!]

TIP: Also to watch out for, especially in literary writing, are truncations. See 'truncation' under 'tip' in the Index at the end.

TIP: If in a constructed verb you see any consonant(s) *b* through *g* inclusive (except *ch*) it/they are part of the verb base! Thus, you don't have to try and identify it/they as potential attachments.

Nouns: The nouns used in the above examples were deliberately chosen to be easy to handle: they were either singular (*chakula*) or had the same singular / plural forms (*nyanya*), which meant they could be looked up as-is in the dictionary. But nouns of course will also be encountered in plural forms which may be different from their singular. If you are not sure whether they are singular or plural, try looking them up as-is and if that fails, matching their prefixes with the noun index table below in section 22.5 Index table: Noun Prefix e.g. *matunda* will not be found in the dictionary but the noun index table has two *ma*- entries, one for the xFF group, the other U group. We strip off *ma*- from *matunda* and look up *tunda* and we get a hit: fruit, and that it belongs to the xFF group!

Adjectives: The scenario above with nouns is also the case with adjectives except the adjective index table is used, in section 22.6 Index table: Adjective Prefix e.g. *nzuri* will not be found in the dictionary but the adjective index table has several entries beginning with *n*, two of which match our case, one for the xFV group, the other U group. We strip off *n*- from *nzuri* and look up *zuri* in the dictionary and we get a hit for it, meaning nice. As to which **group rules** it has to abide by, we would need to know what noun it describes and the group the noun belongs to e.g. xFV group: *nyanya nzuri*, nice tomato(es); xFF group: *matunda **mazuri***, nice fruits; U group: *utenzi **mzuri***, nice poem.

Adverbs: There is nothing to this! It is used as found in the dictionary e.g. *sana*, very, in our first example above.

Demonstratives: These are easy to recognize: 'this' or 'these' begin with *h*- followed by two or three letters and 'that' or 'those' end with -*le* preceded by one or two letter e.g. *huu*, this, or *hii*, these, or *ule*, that, or *ile*, those, referring in all cases to say a tree(s). To confirm that a word you are dealing with is a demonstrative, strip off the *h-* prefix or *-le* suffix and match the remainder with an entry in section 22.7 Index table: Demonstrative Adjective.

Possessives: Possessives end with *-a*, of, or *-ake*, her / his / its, or *-ao*, their, and additionally for persons *-angu*, my, *-ako*, your (singular), *-etu*, our, *-enu*, your (plural). These suffixes are preceded by one or two letters e.g. *kitu changu*, my thing. Again, same as with the Demonstratives above, to confirm you do have a possessive you strip off the suffix and match the remainder with an entry in section 22.8 Index table: Possessives.

Special case of adjective (-o) -ote: Adjectives *-ote*, all / whole, and *-o -ote*, any, do NOT follow the rules given above under Adjectives (which conform to the singular / plural rules of the noun they are describing). Instead, they follow the rules given above under Possessives e.g. *vitu vyote*, all things (and not *vitu viote* if it had followed the normal adjectival rules), or *kitu cho chote*, any thing (and not *kitu kio kiote*). The *-o* and *-ote* are very easy to recognize when encountered but to confirm their identification you just strip them off and match the remainder with an entry in section 22.9 Index table: Adjective (–o) -ote, (any) all / whole.

Thought process: The de-construction examples presented above are not exhaustive but are very useful illustrations of what to do when tackling a constructed word. They are good models of the **thought process** necessary to analyzing and understanding constructed Swahili words, especially verbs.

Abbreviated column headings of the index tables:

p(a)g(e)

T = T(ense)

SP = S(ingular), P(lural)

Gp = Noun G(rou)p

The sort order (identified in the column headings by superscripts) of these tables is: [1]Prefix (the first column), [2]SP, [3]pg

Neg(ative): shown in grey below, is formed with a leading prefix: *h(a)-* [except for the subjunctive, where a *–si–* is inserted after the pronoun prefix] and in the present tense the tense infix is DROPPED and the last vowel is changed to "*i*", which was covered in section 5.4 Negatives].

22.2 Index tables: Verb

22.2.1 Index table: 1. H- Negative, Routine Prefix

¹Verb H- Prefix	³pg	T	²S P	Gp	[Comment] Eg
ha-	80				Neg. Eg *hautoshi*, it does not suffice p82
hu-	88				Routine Eg *hupita kila siku*, I / we / it / they / etc [will] [have] pass[ed] by everyday p88
hu-	81		S	Pp	Neg. 2nd Person Eg *hutoshi*, you don't suffice p81

22.2.2 Index table: 2. Verb Pronoun Prefix

¹Verb Pronoun Prefix	³pg	T	²S P	Gp	[Comment] Eg
a-ᵖʳᵒⁿ	65		S	Pp	3rd Person Eg *anatosha*, she / he suffices p65
ch-ᵖʳᵒⁿ	70		S	T	Timeless tense Eg *kisu **chakata***, the knife cuts p70
i-ᵖʳᵒⁿ	66		P	V	Eg *inatosha*, they suffice p66
i-ᵖʳᵒⁿ	66		S	xFV	Eg *inatosha*, it suffices p66
ki-ᵖʳᵒⁿ	66		S	T	Eg *kinatosha*, it suffices p66
ku-ᵖʳᵒⁿ	67			G	Eg *kunatosha*, it suffices p67

¹Verb Pronoun Prefix	³pg	T	²SP	Gp	[Comment] Eg
ku-*pron*	67			Pl	Eg *kunatosha*, it (e.g. some place) suffices p67
Kuna-*pron*	191				Eg *kuna watu mjini*, there are people in town p192
li-*pron*	66		S	xFF	Eg *linatosha*, it suffices p66
m-*pron*	66		P	Pp	2nd Person Eg *mnatosha,* you suffice p66
Mna,	191			Pl	Eg *nyumbani mna watu*, there are people in the house ***mna** sukari humu*? is there sugar in it? ***mna** maji kisimani*? is there water in the well? ***mna** samaki ziwani*? are there fish in the lake? ***mna** watu sokoni*? are there people in the market? P192
m-*pron*	67			Pl	Eg [mnatosha, it (e.g. interior space) suffices p67
m-*pron*	69	Tl	P	Pp	2nd Person Eg *mw*<u>atosha</u>,* you suffice *The -w- is euphoniously added p69
n-*pron*	68	Tl	S	Pp	1st Person Eg *n*atosha*, I suffice 68
ni-*pron*	172	Tl			*wa*, be, Eg *mpishi ni muhimu hotelini*, a cook is important in a hotel p172

[1]Verb Pronoun Prefix	[3]pg	T	[2]SP	Gp	[Comment] Eg
ni-*pron*	65		S	Pp	1st Person Eg *ninatosha*, I suffice p65
pa-*pron*	67			Pl	Eg *panatosha*, it suffices p67
si-*pron*	172	Tl			Neg. *wa*, be, Eg *mpishi si muhimu dukani*, a cook is not important in a shop p172
si-*pron*	81	Pr Tl	S	Pp	1st Person Eg *sitoshi*, I don't suffice p81
tu-*pron*	65		P	Pp	1st Person Eg *tunatosha,* we suffice p65
tw-*pron*	68	Tl	P	Pp	1st Person Eg *tw*<u>atosha</u>,* we suffice 68
u-*pron*	67		S	U	Eg *unatosha*, it suffices p67
u-*pron*	66		S	V	Eg *unatosha*, it suffices p66
u-*pron*	65		S	Pp	2nd Person Eg *unatosha,* you suffice p65
vi-*pron*	66		P	T	Eg *vinatosha*, they suffice p66
ch-*pron*	71		P	T	Timeless tense Eg *visu **vy**akata*, the knives cut p71
w-*pron*	69	Tl	S	Pp	2nd Person Eg *w*<u>atosha</u>*, you suffice 69
wa-*pron*	65		P	Pp	3rd Person Eg *wanatosha*, they suffice p65
ya-*pron*	66		P	xFF	Eg *yanatosha*, they suffice p66

¹Verb Pronoun Prefix	³pg	T	²SP	Gp	[Comment] Eg
ya-	193				Eg *yafaa tuende*, it is befitting we go *haifai kuchelewa*, it is not proper to be late haiwezekani, it is not doable *haidhuru*, literally it means 'it does no harm', and is translated as 'it is okay' P193
zi-ᵖʳᵒⁿ	67		P	U	Eg *zinatosha*, they suffice p67
zi-ᵖʳᵒⁿ	66		P	xFV	Eg *zinatosha*, they suffice p66

22.3 Master Infix table of indexes 3 to 8

¹Verb All Infixes	³pg	T	²S P	Gp	[Comment] Eg
--³.T	172	TI			wa, be, just ni, no verb base nor prefixes Eg mpishi ni muhimu hotelini, a cook is important in a hotel p172
--³.T	172	TI			Neg. wa, be, just si, no verb base nor prefixes Eg mpishi si muhimu dukani, a cook is not important in a shop p172
--³.T	176	Pr			wa na, have, see suffix –na below Eg ana njaa, she / he is hungry p176
-a-³.T	65	TI			Eg a*tosha, he / she
-cho-⁴.R	142		S	T	Eg Kitu kinachotosha, thing which suffices p142
-e/i-⁷.P	136				Eg Pata, get, becomes patia, get for p136
-i-⁵.O	125		S	xFV	Eg ninaiona, I see it p133
-i-⁵.O	132		P	V	Eg ninaiona, I see them p132
-ja-³.T	80	PP			Neg. Eg hajatosha*, she / he has not yet suffice p81
-ji-⁸.T	93				Reflexive Eg Mwanamke anajipenda, the woman likes herself p93 Mlango inajifunga, the door shuts by itself p93
-k-⁸.T	92				Stative Eg pendeka, be likable. Mwanamke anapendeka, the

¹Verb All Infixes	³pg	T	²SP	Gp	[Comment] Eg
					woman is likable p92 *Mlango unafungika*, the door is closable p92 **Mlango* umefungika, the door has become closed p92
-ka-³·ᵀ	164				for 2ⁿᵈ serial action verb Eg *alifika akapumzika*, he arrived then/and he rested p164
-ka-³·ᵀ	164	Pa			in narration Eg *akaondoka*, she left 164
-kan-⁸·ᵀ	92				Stative Eg *Kurudi kesho kunawezekana?* To return tomorrow is doable/possible? p92
-ki-³·ᵀ	164				for 2ⁿᵈ continuous action verb Eg *alikuja akikimbia*, he came running p164
-ki-³·ᵀ	165				continuous action verb Eg *jozi ni vitu viwili vikiwa pamoja*, a pair is two things being together p165
-ki-⁵·ᴼ	132		S	T	Eg *ninakiona*, I see it p132
-ki-⁶·ᶜ	153				Eg *nikitaka nitakuambia*, if I want I will tell you p153 *akiwa nyumbani nitamwona*, if she is at home I will see her p153
-ko-⁴·ᴿ	139			Pl	Eg *Mahali kunakotosha*, place(s) which suffice(s) p144
-ko-⁴·ᴿ	144			G	Eg *Kusoma kunakotosha*, reading(s) which suffice(s) p144

¹Verb **All** Infixes	³pg	T	²S P	Gp	[Comment] Eg
-kuku- 3.T	164				for 2nd intended action verb Eg *alikuja kupumzika*, he came to rest p164
-ku-3.T	164				for 2nd same-time action verb Eg *alisoma na kuandika*, he read and wrote p164
-ku-3.T	80	Pa			Neg. Eg *haukutosha*, it did not suffice p82
-ku-5.O	133			G	Eg *ninakuona*, I see it p133
-ku-5.O	133			Pl	Eg *ninakuona*, I see it p133
-ku-5.O	134		S	Pp	2nd Person Eg *ninakupenda*, I love you (singular) p134
-l-7.P	137				Euphonious* filler for preposition Eg *tia*, put: tilia, put into p137 *tembea*, walk: *tembelea,* walk to (i.e. to visit) p137 *nunua*, buy: nunulia, buy for p137 Foreign vowel not ending in –a Eg *jibu*, reply: jibia, reply to p137
-li-3.T	57	Pr			Rare relative present tense of *wa*, be Eg *maneno yaliyo kweli*, words which are true i.e. true words p57
-li-3.T	65	Pa			Eg *kiatu kilichakaa*, a shoe wore out p70
-li-5.O	132		S	xFF	Eg *ninaliona*, I see it p132

¹Verb All Infixes	³pg	T	²SP	Gp	[Comment] Eg
-lo-⁴·ᴿ	141		S	xFF	Eg *Tunda linalotosha*, fruit which suffices p141
-m(w)-⁵·ᴼ	134		S	Pp	3ʳᵈ Person Eg *ninampenda*, I love her / him p134
-man-⁸·ᵀ	92				Passive Eg *Mfupa uliovunjika umeungamana*, the broken bone has set p92
-me-³·ᵀ	65	PP			Eg *kiatu* kimechakaa, a shoe has p70
-mo-⁴·ᴿ	139			PI	Eg *Nyumbani mnamotosha*, house interior(s) which suffice(s) p144
-mu-⁵·ᴼ	133			PI	Eg *ninamuona*, I see them p133
-na-³·ᵀ	65	Pr			Eg *anatosha*, she / he suffices p65
-ngali-⁶·ᶜ	154	P			Eg *ningalijua unakuja ningalipika chakula*, if I had known you were coming I would have cooked food p155
-nge-⁶·ᶜ	154				Eg *ningejua unakuja ningepika chakula*, if I knew you were coming I would have cooked food p154
-ni-⁵·ᴼ	134		S	Pp	1ˢᵗ Person Eg *ninanipenda*, I love myself p134
-o-⁴·ᴿ	140		P	Pp	All Persons Eg *Watu wanaotosha*, persons who suffice p140

¹Verb All Infixes	³pg	T	²S P	Gp	[Comment] Eg
*-o-*⁴·ᴿ	141		S	V	Eg *Mti unaotosha*, tree which suffices p141
*-o-*⁴·ᴿ	143		S	U	Eg *Utenzi unaotosha*, poem which suffices p143
*-pa-*⁵·ᴼ	133			Pl	Eg *ninapaona*, I see it p133
-po- ⁶·ᶜ	155				Eg *nitakapofika nitakupiga simu*, when I arrive I will phone you p155
*-po-*⁴·ᴿ	143			Pl	Eg *Mahali panapotosha*, place(s) which suffice(s) p143
*-sh-*⁸·ᵀ	92				Causative Eg *angusha*, fell. Mlimaji *aliangusha miti*, the farmer felled the trees p93
*-si-*³·ᵀ	148				Relative neg. Eg *miti isiyotosha*, trees which are not, or will not be, or have not been, or were not sufficient! P148
si⁻⁶·ᶜ	155				Neg. Eg *nisingejua unakuja nisingeweza kupika chakula*, if I did not know you were coming I would not have been able to cook food p155 *nisingalikuwa mgonjwa ningalikuja nawe*, if I had not been sick I would have come with you p155
sipo⁻⁶·ᶜ	154				Neg. Eg *negative: asipokuwa nyumbani nitamngojea*, if she is

¹Verb **All** Infixes	³pg	T	²SP	Gp	[Comment] Eg
					not at home I will wait **for her** p169
-ta-^{3.T}	65	Fu			Eg *kiatu* kitachakaa, a shoe will p70
-taka-^{3.T}	140	Fu			Relative construction future tense Eg *atakayetosha*, person who will suffice p140
-tu-^{5.O}	134		P	Pp	1st Person Eg *ninatupenda*, I love us p134
-u-^{5.O}	132		S	V	Eg *ninauona*, I see it p132
-u-^{5.O}	133		S	U	Eg *ninauona*, I see it p133
-u-^{8.T}	93				Antonym Eg *Mlinzi alifungua mlango*, the watchman opened the door p93
-u-^{8.T}	93				Synonym Eg *Msichana anakam(u)a ng'ombe*, the girl is milking the cow p94
-vi-^{5.O}	132		P	T	Eg *ninaviona*, I see them p132
-vyo-^{4.R}	142		P	T	Eg *Vitu vinavyotosha*, things which suffice p142
-w-^{8.T}	91				Passive Eg *pendwa, be liked. Mwanamke anapendwa na wote*, the woman is liked by all p91 . *fungwa*, be closed. Mlango *unafungwa na mlinzi*, the door is being closed by the watchman. Mlango *imefungwa na mlinzi*, the door has been closed by the watchman p91

[1]Verb All Infixes	[3]pg	T	[2]S P	Gp	[Comment] Eg
-wa-[5.O]	134		P	Pp	2nd Person Eg *ninawapenda*, I love you (plural) p134
-wa-[5.O]	134		P	Pp	3rd Person Eg *ninawapenda*, I love them p134
-ya-[5.O]	132		P	xFF	Eg *ninayaona*, I see them p132
-ye-[4.R]	140		S	Pp	All Persons Eg *Mtu anayetosha*, person who suffices p140
-yo-[4.R]	141		P	V	Eg *Miti inayotosha*, trees which suffice p141
-yo-[4.R]	141		P	xFF	Eg *Matunda yanayotosha*, fruits which suffice p141
-yo-[4.R]	142		S	xFV	Eg *Nyanya inayotosha*, tomato which suffices p142
-z-[8.T]	92				Causative Eg *pendeza*, make likable. *Nguo zinampendeza mwanamke*, clothes make the woman attractive p93
-zi-[5.O]	133		P	U	Eg *ninaziona*, I see them p133
-zi-[5.O]	133		P	xFV	Eg *ninaziona*, I see them p133
-zo-[4.R]	143		P	U	Eg *Tenzi zinazotosha*, poems which suffice p143
-zo-[4.R]	143		P	xFV	Eg *Nyanya zinazotosha*, tomatoes which suffice p143

22.3.1 Index table: 3. Verb Tense Infix

Tenses:

T(ime)l(ess), Pr(esent), Pa(st), P(resent)P(erfect), Fu(ture)

¹Verb Tense Infixes	³pg	T	²SP	Gp	[Comment] Eg
_-³·ᵀ	172	Tl			*wa*, be, just *ni*, no verb base nor prefixes Eg *mpishi ni muhimu hotelini*, a cook is important in a hotel p172
_-³·ᵀ	172	Tl			Neg. *wa*, be, just *si*, no verb base nor prefixes Eg *mpishi si muhimu dukani*, a cook is not important in a shop p172
_-³·ᵀ	176	Pr			*wa na*, have, see suffix *–na* below Eg *ana njaa*, she / he is hungry p176
-a-³·ᵀ	65	Tl			Eg *a*tosha*, he / she
-ja-³·ᵀ	80	PP			Neg. Eg *hajatosha**, she / he has not yet suffice p81
-ka-³·ᵀ	164				for 2ⁿᵈ serial action verb Eg *alifika akapumzika*, he arrived then/and he rested p164
-ka-³·ᵀ	164	Pa			in narration Eg *akaondoka*, she left 164
-ki-³·ᵀ	164				for 2ⁿᵈ continuous action verb Eg *alikuja akikimbia*, he came running p164
-ki-³·ᵀ	165				continuous action verb Eg *jozi ni vitu viwili vikiwa pamoja*, a pair

[1]Verb Tense Infixes	[3]pg	T	[2]SP	Gp	[Comment] Eg
					is two things being together p165
-kuku- 3.T	164				for 2nd intended action verb Eg *alikuja kupumzika*, he came to rest p164
-ku-3.T	164				for 2nd same-time action verb Eg *alisoma na kuandika*, he read and wrote p164
-ku-3.T	80	Pa			Neg. Eg *haukutosha*, it did not suffice p82
-li-3.T	65	Pa			Eg *kiatu kilichakaa*, a shoe wore out p70
-li-3.T	57	Pr			Rare relative present tense of *wa*, be Eg *maneno yaliyo kweli*, words which are true i.e. true words p57
-me-3.T	65	PP			Eg *kiatu* kimechakaa, a shoe has p70
-na-3.T	65	Pr			Eg *anatosha*, she / he suffices p65
-si-3.T	148				Relative neg. Eg *miti isiyotosha*, trees which are not, or will not be, or have not been, or were not sufficient! P148
-ta-3.T	65	Fu			Eg *kiatu* kitachakaa, a shoe will p70

¹Verb Tense Infixes	³pg	T	²SP	Gp	[Comment] Eg
-taka- 3.T	140	Fu			Relative construction future tense Eg *atakayetosha*, person who will suffice p140

22.3.2 Index table: 4. Verb Relative Infix

¹Verb Relative Infixes	³pg	T	²SP	Gp	[Comment] Eg
-cho-⁴·ᴿ	142		S	T	Eg *Kitu kinachotosha*, thing which suffices p142
-ko-⁴·ᴿ	139			Pl	Eg *Mahali kunakotosha*, place(s) which suffice(s) p144
-ko-⁴·ᴿ	144			G	Eg *Kusoma kunakotosha*, reading(s) which suffice(s) p144
-lo-⁴·ᴿ	141		S	xFF	Eg *Tunda linalotosha*, fruit which suffices p141
-mo-⁴·ᴿ	139			Pl	Eg *Nyumbani mnamotosha*, house interior(s) which suffice(s) p144 *Nyumbani mnamotosha*, house interior(s) which suffice(s) p144
-o-⁴·ᴿ	140		P	Pp	All Persons Eg *Watu wanaotosha*, persons who suffice p140
-o-⁴·ᴿ	141		S	V	Eg *Mti unaotosha*, tree which suffices p141

¹Verb Relative Infixes	³pg	T	²SP	Gp	[Comment] Eg
-o-⁴·ᴿ	143		S	U	Eg *Utenzi unaotosha*, poem which suffices p143
-po-⁴·ᴿ	143			Pl	Eg *Mahali panapotosha*, place(s) which suffice(s) p143
-vyo-⁴·ᴿ	142		P	T	Eg *Vitu vinavyotosha*, things which suffice p142
-ye-⁴·ᴿ	140		S	Pp	All Persons Eg *Mtu anayetosha*, person who suffices p140
-yo-⁴·ᴿ	141		P	V	Eg *Miti inayotosha*, trees which suffice p141
-yo-⁴·ᴿ	141		P	xFF	Eg *Matunda yanayotosha*, fruits which suffice p141
-yo-⁴·ᴿ	142		S	xFV	Eg *Nyanya inayotosha*, tomato which suffices p142
-zo-⁴·ᴿ	143		P	U	Eg *Tenzi zinazotosha*, poems which suffice p143
-zo-⁴·ᴿ	143		P	xFV	Eg *Nyanya zinazotosha*, tomatoes which suffice p143

22.3.3 Index table: 5. Verb Object Infix

¹Verb Object Infixes*	³pg	T	²SP	Gp	[Comment] Eg
-i-⁵·ᴼ	132		P	V	Eg *ninaiona*, I see them p132
-i-⁵·ᴼ	125		S	xFV	Eg *ninaiona*, I see it p133

[1]Verb Object Infixes*	[3]pg	T	[2]SP	Gp	[Comment] Eg
-ki-[5.O]	132		S	T	Eg *ninakiona*, I see it p132
-ku-[5.O]	133			G	Eg *ninakuona*, I see it p133
-ku-[5.O]	133			Pl	Eg *ninakuona*, I see it p133
-ku-[5.O]	134		S	Pp	2nd Person Eg *ninakupenda*, I love you (singular) p134
-li-[5.O]	132		S	xFF	Eg *ninaliona*, I see it p132
-m(w)-[5.O]	134		S	Pp	3rd Person Eg *ninampenda*, I love her / him p134
-mu-[5.O]	133			Pl	Eg *ninamuona*, I see them p133
-ni-[5.O]	134		S	Pp	1st Person Eg *ninanipenda*, I love myself p134
-pa-[5.O]	133			Pl	Eg *ninapaona*, I see it p133
-tu-[5.O]	134		P	Pp	1st Person Eg *ninatupenda*, I love us p134
-u-[5.O]	132		S	V	Eg *ninauona*, I see it p132
-u-[5.O]	133		S	U	Eg *ninauona*, I see it p133
-vi-[5.O]	132		P	T	Eg *ninaviona*, I see them p132
-wa-[5.O]	134		P	Pp	2nd Person Eg *ninawapenda*, I love you (plural) p134
-wa-[5.O]	134		P	Pp	3rd Person Eg *ninawapenda*, I love them p134
-ya-[5.O]	132		P	xFF	Eg *ninayaona*, I see them p132
-zi-[5.O]	133		P	U	Eg *ninaziona*, I see them p133

¹Verb Object Infixes*	³pg	T	²S P	Gp	[Comment] Eg
-zi-⁵·ᴼ	133		P	xFV	Eg *ninaziona*, I see them p133

*Object references for *wa na*, have, are SUFFIXED. See below in section 22.4.2 "Index table: 10. Verb Timeless Relative".

.

22.3.4 Index table: 6. Verb Conditional Infix

¹Verb Cond. Infixes	³pg	T	²S P	Gp	[Comment] Eg
-ki-⁶·ᶜ	153				Eg *nikitaka nitakuambia*, if I want I will tell you p153 *akiwa nyumbani nitamwona*, if she is at home I will see her p153
-ngali-⁶·ᶜ	154	P			Eg *ningalijua unakuja ningalipika chakula*, if I had known you were coming I would have cooked food p155
-nge-⁶·ᶜ	154				Eg *ningejua unakuja ningepika chakula*, if I knew you were coming I would have cooked food p154
-po-⁶·ᶜ	155				Eg *nitakapofika nitakupiga simu*, when I arrive I will phone you p155
si-⁶·ᶜ	155				Neg. Eg *nisingejua unakuja nisingeweza kupika chakula*, if I did not know you were coming I would not have been able to cook food p155 *nisingalikuwa mgonjwa ningalikuja*

¹Verb Cond. Infixes	³pg	T	²S P	Gp	[Comment] Eg
					nawe, if I had not been sick I would have come with you p155
sipo- 6.C	154				Neg. Eg *negative: asipokuwa nyumbani nitamngojea*, if she is not at home I will wait **for her** p169

22.3.5 Index table: 7. Verb Preposition Infix

¹Verb Prep. Infixes	³pg	T	²S P	Gp	[Comment] Eg
-e/i-[7.P]	136				Eg *Pata*, get, becomes patia, get for p136
-l-[7.P]	137				Euphonious filler for preposition Eg *tia*, put: tilia, put into p137 *tembea*, walk: *tembelea,* walk to (i.e. to visit) p137 *nunua*, buy: nunulia, buy for p137 Foreign vowel not ending in *–a* Eg *jibu*, reply: jibia, reply to p137

22.3.6 Index table: 8. Verb Transformation Infix

These are infixes which are included in the master infix table, except for two suffixes, *-je* and *-pi*, which of course are shown in the master <u>suffix</u> table.

¹Verb Transf. Infixes	³pg	T	²S P	Gp	[Comment] Eg
-je[8.T]	94				How, what Eg *pendaje?*, like how? *Anapendaje?* How does she like (it)? p94 *fungaje?*, shut how? *Alifungaje?* How did he shut (it)? p94
-ji-[8.T]	93				Reflexive Eg *Mwanamke anajipenda*, the woman likes herself p93 *Mlango inajifunga*, the door shuts by itself p93
-k-[8.T]	92				Stative Eg *pendeka*, be likable. Mwanamke *anapendeka,* the woman is likable p92 *Mlango unafungika*, the door is closable p92 *Mlango* umefungika, the door has become closed p92
-kan- 8.T	92				Stative Eg *Kurudi kesho kunawezekana?* To return tomorrow is doable/possible? p92
-man- 8.T	92				Passive Eg *Mfupa uliovunjika umeungamana*, the broken bone has set p92
-na[8.T]	93				Reciprocal Eg *Mwanamke na mwanamume wanapendana,* the woman and the man like each other p93
-pi[8.T]	94				How, what Eg *wezapi?*, be able to how? *Atawezapi?* How will he be able to? p94

[1]Verb Transf. Infixes	[3]pg	T	[2]SP	Gp	[Comment] Eg
-sh-[8.T]	92				Causative Eg *angusha*, fell. Mlimaji *aliangusha miti*, the farmer felled the trees p93
-u-[8.T]	93				Antonym Eg *Mlinzi alifungua mlango*, the watchman opened the door p93
-u-[8.T]	93				Synonym Eg *Msichana anakam(u)a ng'ombe*, the girl is milking the cow p94
-w-[8.T]	91				Passive Eg *pendwa, be liked. Mwanamke anapendwa na wote, the woman is liked by all* p91 . *fungwa, be closed.* Mlango *unafungwa na mlinzi,* the door is being closed by the watchman. *Mlango imefungwa na mlinzi,* the door has been closed by the watchman p91
-z-[8.T]	92				Causative Eg *pendeza*, make likable. *Nguo zinampendeza mwanamke*, clothes make the woman attractive p93

22.4 Master Suffix table of indexes 9 to 11

[1]Verb All Suffixes	[3]pg	T	[2]S P	Gp	[Comment] Eg
-cho[10.T]	142	Pr TI	S	T	Relative construction for: (a) timeless tense Eg *Kitu kitoshacho*, thing which suffices p142. (b) *wa* present tense which uses the *-li-* tense infix q.v. in Master Infix table.
-cho[9.K]	184		S	T	Embedded object for *wa na*, have, using relative pronoun. Eg *ninacho*, I have it p184
-e[11.S]	157	S			Subjunctive last vowel change Eg *afanye kazi*, [I suggest] that he work p157
-e[11.S]	157	S			Neg. subjunctive last vowel change Eg *asifanye kazi*, [I suggest] that he not work p157
-e[12.I]	97	Pr			Object+imperative last vowel change Eg *kichukue kisu*, carry it the knife p97
-e[12.I]	157	Pr			Neg. imperative last vowel change Eg *usinunue mboga*, [I wish] that you not buy vegetables p157
-eni[12.I]	97	Pr	P		*chukueni*, carry p97

¹Verb All Suffixes	³pg	T	²SP	Gp	[Comment] Eg
-je⁸·ᵀ	94				How, what Eg *pendaje?*, like how? *Anapendaje?* How does she like (it)? p94 *fungaje?*, shut how? *Alifungaje?* How did he shut (it)? p94
--ko¹⁰·ᵀ	144	Pr Tl		Pl	Relative construction for: (a) timeless tense Eg *Mahali kutoshako*, place(s) which suffice(s) p144. (b) *wa* present tense which uses the -*li*- tense infix q.v. in Master Infix table.
-ko¹⁰·ᵀ	144	Pr Tl		G	Relative construction for: (a) timeless tense Eg *Kusoma kutoshako*, reading(s) which suffice(s) p144. (b) *wa* present tense which uses the -*li*- tense infix q.v. in Master Infix table.
-ko⁹·ᴷ	188				"...is" + Preposition Eg *nyanya iko hapa*, the tomato is here 189
-ko⁹·ᴷ	185			G	Embedded object for *wa na*, have, using relative pronoun. Eg *ninako*, I have it / them p185
-ko⁹·ᴷ	185			G	Embedded object for *wa na*, have, using relative pronoun. Eg *ninako*, I have it / them p185

[1]Verb All Suffixes	[3]pg	T	[2]S P	Gp	[Comment] Eg
-lo[10.T]	141	Pr TI	S	xFF	Relative construction for: (a) timeless tense Eg *Tunda litoshalo*, fruit which suffices p141. (b) *wa* present tense which uses the *-li-* tense infix q.v. in Master Infix table.
-lo[9.K]	184		S	xFF	Embedded object for *wa na*, have, using relative pronoun. Eg *ninalo*, I have it p184
-mo [10.T]	144	Pr TI		Pl	Relative construction for: (a) timeless tense Eg *Nyumbani mnatoshamo*, house interior(s) which suffice(s) p144. (b) *wa* present tense which uses the *-li-* tense infix q.v. in Master Infix table.
-mo[9.K]	188				"...is" + Preposition Eg matunda yamo kikapuni, the fruits are <u>in</u> the basket P189
-na[8.T]	93				Reciprocal Eg *Mwanamke na mwanamume wanapendana,* the woman and the man like each other p93
-na[9.K]	176	Pr			*wa na*, have, no tense infix, just this suffix Eg *ana njaa*, she / he is hungry p176
-o[10.T]	141	Pr TI	P	Pp	Relative construction for: (a) timeless tense Eg *Watu watoshao*, persons who suffice p141. (b) *wa* present

¹Verb **All** Suffixes	³pg	T	²S P	Gp	[Comment] Eg
					tense which uses the -li- tense infix q.v. in Master Infix table.
$-o^{10.T}$	141	Pr Tl	S	V	Relative construction for: (a) timeless tense Eg *Mti utoshao*, tree which suffices p141. (b) *wa* present tense which uses the -li- tense infix q.v. in Master Infix table.
$-o^{10.T}$	143	Pr Tl	S	U	Relative construction for: (a) timeless tense Eg *Utenzi utoshao*, poem which suffices p143. (b) *wa* present tense which uses the -li- tense infix q.v. in Master Infix table.
$-o^{9.K}$	184		P	Pp	Embedded object for *wa na*, have, using relative pronoun. Eg *ninao*, I have them p184
$-o^{9.K}$	184		S	V	Embedded object for *wa na*, have, using relative pronoun. Eg *ninao*, I have it p184
$-o^{9.K}$	185		S	U	Embedded object for *wa na*, have, using relative pronoun. Eg *ninao*, I have it p185
$-pi^{8.T}$	94				How, what Eg *wezapi?*, be able to how? Atawezapi? How will he be able to? p94
$-po^{10.T}$	144	Pr Tl		Pl	Relative construction for: (a) timeless tense Eg *Mahali patoshapo*, place(s) which

¹Verb All Suffixes	³pg	T	²S P	Gp	[Comment] Eg
					suffice(s) p144. (b) *wa* present tense which uses the *-li-* tense infix q.v. in Master Infix table.
-po⁹·ᴷ	188				"...is" + Preposition Eg *Tanzania ipo Afrika ya Mashariki*, Tanzania is in East Africa p188
-po⁹·ᴷ	185			Pl	Embedded object for *wa na*, have, using relative pronoun. Eg *ninapo*, I have it / them p185
-vyo¹⁰·ᵀ	142	Pr Tl	P	T	Relative construction for: (a) timeless tense Eg *Vitu vitoshavyo*, things which suffice p142. (b) *wa* present tense which uses the *-li-* tense infix q.v. in Master Infix table.
-vyo⁹·ᴷ	184		P	T	Embedded object for *wa na*, have, using relative pronoun. Eg *ninavyo*, I have them p184
-ye¹⁰·ᵀ	140	Pr Tl	S	Pp	Relative construction for: (a) timeless tense Eg *Mtu atoshaye*, person who suffices p140. (b) *wa* present tense which uses the *-li-* tense infix q.v. in Master Infix table.

¹Verb All Suffixes	³pg	T	²SP	Gp	[Comment] Eg
-ye⁹·ᴷ	183		S	Pp	Embedded object for *wa na*, have, using relative pronoun. Eg *ninaye*, I have her / him 183
-yo¹⁰·ᵀ	141	Pr TI	P	V	Relative construction for: (a) timeless tense Eg *Miti itoshayo*, trees which suffice p141. (b) *wa* present tense which uses the *-li-* tense infix q.v. in Master Infix table.
-yo¹⁰·ᵀ	142	Pr TI	P	xFF	Relative construction for: (a) timeless tense Eg *Matunda yatoshayo*, fruits which suffice p142. (b) *wa* present tense which uses the *-li-* tense infix q.v. in Master Infix table.
-yo¹⁰·ᵀ	143	Pr TI	S	xFV	Relative construction for: (a) timeless tense Eg *Nyanya itoshayo*, tomato which suffices p143. (b) *wa* present tense which uses the *-li-* tense infix q.v. in Master Infix table.
-yo⁹·ᴷ	184		P	V	Embedded object for *wa na*, have, using relative pronoun. Eg *ninayo*, I have them p184
-yo⁹·ᴷ	184		P	xFF	Embedded object for *wa na*, have, using relative pronoun. Eg *ninayo*, I have them p184

¹Verb All Suffixes	³pg	T	²S P	Gp	[Comment] Eg
-yo⁹·ᴷ	184		S	xFV	Embedded object for *wa na*, have, using relative pronoun. Eg *ninayo*, I have it p184
-zo¹⁰·ᵀ	143	Pr TI	P	xFV	Relative construction for: (a) timeless tense Eg *Nyanya zitoshazo*, tomatoes which suffice p143. (b) *wa* present tense which uses the *-li-* tense infix q.v. in Master Infix table.
-zo¹⁰·ᵀ	143	Pr TI	P	U	Relative construction for: (a) timeless tense Eg *Tenzi zitoshazo*, poems which suffice p143. (b) *wa* present tense which uses the *-li-* tense infix q.v. in Master Infix table.
-zo⁹·ᴷ	185		P	xFV	Embedded object for *wa na*, have, using relative pronoun. Eg *ninazo*, I have them p185
-zo⁹·ᴷ	185		P	U	Embedded object for *wa na*, have, using relative pronoun. Eg *ninazo*, I have them p185

¹Verb Suffixes	³pg	T	²SP	Gp	[Comment] Eg
-cho⁹·ᴷ	184		S	T	Embedded object for *wa na*, have, using relative pronoun. Eg *ninacho*, I have it p184
-ko⁹·ᴷ	188				"...is" + Preposition Eg *nyanya iko hapa*, the tomato is here 189
-ko⁹·ᴷ	185			G	Embedded object for *wa na*, have, using relative pronoun. Eg *ninako*, I have it / them p185
-ko⁹·ᴷ	185			G	Embedded object for *wa na*, have, using relative pronoun. Eg *ninako*, I have it / them p185
-lo⁹·ᴷ	184		S	xFF	Embedded object for *wa na*, have, using relative pronoun. Eg *ninalo*, I have it p184
-mo⁹·ᴷ	188				"...is" + Preposition Eg *matunda yamo kikapuni*, the fruits are in the basket P189
-na⁹·ᴷ	176	Pr Tl			*wa na*, have, no tense infix, just this suffix Eg *ana njaa*, she / he is hungry p176.
-o⁹·ᴷ	184		P	Pp	Embedded object for *wa na*, have, using relative pronoun. Eg *ninao*, I have them p184
-o⁹·ᴷ	184		S	V	Embedded object for *wa na*, have, using relative pronoun. Eg *ninao*, I have it p184

¹Verb Suffixes	³pg	T	²S/P	Gp	[Comment] Eg
-o$^{9.K}$	185		S	U	Embedded object for *wa na*, have, using relative pronoun. Eg *ninao*, I have it p185
-po$^{9.K}$	188				"...is" + Preposition Eg Tanzania ipo Afrika ya Mashariki, Tanzania is in East Africa p188
-po$^{9.K}$	185			Pl	Embedded object for *wa na*, have, using relative pronoun. Eg *ninapo*, I have it / them p185
-vyo$^{9.K}$	184		P	T	Embedded object for *wa na*, have, using relative pronoun. Eg *ninavyo*, I have them p184
-ye$^{9.K}$	183		S	Pp	Embedded object for *wa na*, have, using relative pronoun. Eg *ninaye*, I have her / him 183
-yo$^{9.K}$	184		P	V	Embedded object for *wa na*, have, using relative pronoun. Eg *ninayo*, I have them p184
-yo$^{9.K}$	184		P	xFF	Embedded object for *wa na*, have, using relative pronoun. Eg *ninayo*, I have them p184
-yo$^{9.K}$	184		S	xFV	Embedded object for *wa na*, have, using relative pronoun. Eg *ninayo*, I have it p184
-zo$^{9.K}$	185		P	xFV	Embedded object for *wa na*, have, using relative pronoun. Eg *ninazo*, I have them p185

¹Verb Suffixes	³pg	T	²SP	Gp	[Comment] Eg
-zo⁹·ᴷ	185		P	U	Embedded object for *wa na*, have, using relative pronoun. Eg *ninazo*, I have them p185

22.4.2 Index table: 10. Verb Timeless Relative Suffix

¹Verb Suffixes	³pg	T	²SP	Gp	[Comment] Eg
-cho¹⁰·ᵀ	142	Pr TI	S	T	Relative construction for: (a) timeless tense Eg *Kitu kitoshacho*, thing which suffices p142. (b) *wa* present tense which uses the *-li-* tense infix q.v. in Master Infix table.
-ko¹⁰·ᵀ	144	Pr TI		Pl	Relative construction for: (a) timeless tense Eg *Mahali kutoshako*, place(s) which suffice(s) p144. (b) *wa* present tense which uses the *-li-* tense infix q.v. in Master Infix table.
-ko¹⁰·ᵀ	144	Pr TI		G	Relative construction for: (a) timeless tense Eg *Kusoma kutoshako*, reading(s) which suffice(s) p144. (b) *wa* present tense which uses the *-li-* tense infix q.v. in Master Infix table.
-lo¹⁰·ᵀ	141	Pr TI	S	xFF	Relative construction for: (a) timeless tense Eg *Tunda litoshalo*, fruit which suffices p141. (b) *wa* present tense

¹Verb Suffixes	³pg	T	²S P	Gp	[Comment] Eg
					which uses the -li- tense infix q.v. in Master Infix table.
-mo [10.T]	144	Pr Tl		Pl	Relative construction for: (a) timeless tense Eg *Nyumbani mnatoshamo*, house interior(s) which suffice(s) p144. (b) *wa* present tense which uses the -li- tense infix q.v. in Master Infix table.
-o[10.T]	141	Pr Tl	P	Pp	Relative construction for: (a) timeless tense Eg *Watu watoshao*, persons who suffice p141. (b) *wa* present tense which uses the -li- tense infix q.v. in Master Infix table.
-o[10.T]	141	Pr Tl	S	V	Relative construction for: (a) timeless tense Eg *Mti utoshao*, tree which suffices p141. (b) *wa* present tense which uses the -li- tense infix q.v. in Master Infix table.
-o[10.T]	143	Pr Tl	S	U	Relative construction for: (a) timeless tense Eg *Utenzi utoshao*, poem which suffices p143. (b) *wa* present tense which uses the -li- tense infix q.v. in Master Infix table.
-po[10.T]	144	Pr Tl		Pl	Relative construction for: (a) timeless tense Eg *Mahali patoshapo*, place(s) which

¹Verb Suffixes	³pg	T	²SP	Gp	[Comment] Eg
					suffice(s) p144. (b) *wa* present tense which uses the *-li-* tense infix q.v. in Master Infix table.
-vyo¹⁰·ᵀ	142	Pr Tl	P	T	Relative construction for: (a) timeless tense Eg *Vitu vitoshavyo*, things which suffice p142. (b) *wa* present tense which uses the *-li-* tense infix q.v. in Master Infix table.
-ye¹⁰·ᵀ	140	Pr Tl	S	Pp	Relative construction for: (a) timeless tense Eg *Mtu atoshaye*, person who suffices p140. (b) *wa* present tense which uses the *-li-* tense infix q.v. in Master Infix table.
-yo¹⁰·ᵀ	141	Pr Tl	P	V	Relative construction for: (a) timeless tense Eg *Miti itoshayo*, trees which suffice p141. (b) *wa* present tense which uses the *-li-* tense infix q.v. in Master Infix table.
-yo¹⁰·ᵀ	142	Pr Tl	P	xFF	Relative construction for: (a) timeless tense Eg *Matunda yatoshayo*, fruits which suffice p142. (b) *wa* present tense which uses the *-li-* tense infix q.v. in Master Infix table.
-yo¹⁰·ᵀ	143	Pr Tl	S	xFV	Relative construction for: (a) timeless tense Eg *Nyanya itoshayo*, tomato which suffices

¹Verb Suffixes	³pg	T	²SP	Gp	[Comment] Eg
					p143. (b) *wa* present tense which uses the *-li-* tense infix q.v. in Master Infix table.
-zo[10.T]	143	Pr Tl	P	xFV	Relative construction for: (a) timeless tense Eg *Nyanya zitoshazo*, tomatoes which suffice p143. (b) *wa* present tense which uses the *-li-* tense infix q.v. in Master Infix table.
-zo[10.T]	143	Pr Tl	P	U	Relative construction for: (a) timeless tense Eg *Tenzi zitoshazo*, poems which suffice p143. (b) *wa* present tense which uses the *-li-* tense infix q.v. in Master Infix table.

22.4.3 Index table 11: Verb Subjunctive-Imperative Suffix

¹Verb Suffixes	³pg	T	²SP	Gp	[Comment] Eg
_[12.I]	97	Pr	S		Eg infinitive *kuchukua*, to carry, becomes imperative: *chukua*, carry (addressed to a 2nd person singular) It is a homonym of the verb base, only the moods are different p97

¹Verb Suffixes	³pg	T	²S P	Gp	[Comment] Eg
-e¹¹·ˢ	157	S			Subjunctive last vowel change Eg *afanye kazi*, [I suggest] that he work p157
e¹¹·ˢ	157	S			Neg. subjunctive last vowel change Eg *asifanye kazi*, [I suggest] that he not work p157
-e¹²·ᴵ	97	Pr			Object+imperative last vowel change Eg *kichukue kisu*, carry it the knife p97
-e¹²·ᴵ	157	Pr			Neg. imperative last vowel change Eg *usinunue mboga*, [I wish] that you not buy vegetables p157
-eni¹²·ᴵ	97	Pr	P		*chukueni*, carry p97

22.5 Index table: Noun Prefix

¹NOUN Prefix	³pg	T	²SP	Gp	[Comment] Eg
_noun	32			xFV	Eg *nyanya*, tomato *nyanya*, tomatoes p32
_noun	36			PI	Eg *mahali*, place(s) p36
_noun	38			G	Eg *kusoma*, reading(s) p38
_noun	33		P	U	Eg *utenzi*, poem *tenzi*, poems p33
_noun	28		S	xFF	Eg *tunda*, fruit *matunda*, fruits p28
ch-*noun*	30		S	T	Eg *chumba*, room *vyumba*, rooms p30
ja-*noun*	28		S	xFF	Eg *jambo*, issue / problem / matter *mambo*, issues / problems / matters p28
ji-*noun*	28		S	xFF	Eg *jicho*, eye *macho*, eyes p28 *jina*, name *majina*, names p28 *jino*, tooth *meno*, teeth p28
ki-*noun*	30		S	T	Eg *kiti*, chair *viti*, chairs p30
ku-*noun*	37			G	Eg *kusema*, talking pg38, *kusamehe*, forgiving pg38
kuto-*noun*	38			G	Eg *kutosamehe*, unforgiving pg38

¹NOUN Prefix	³pg	T	²SP	Gp	[Comment] Eg
kutoku- noun	38			G	Eg *kutokusema*, silence pg38
*m-*noun	23		S	Pp	Eg *mtoto*, child *watoto*, children p23
*m-*noun	26		S	V	Eg *mmea*, plant *mimea*, plants p26
*ma-*noun	28		P	xFF	Eg *tunda*, fruit *matunda*, fruits p28
*ma-*noun	34		P	U	Eg *uvuno*, harvesting *mavuno*, harvest p34
*mb-*noun	34		P	U	Eg *The* uw- is dropped and a prefix *mb-* is attached: *uwinda*, hunting *mbinda*, huntings p34
*me-*noun	28		P	xFF	Eg *jino*, tooth *meno*, teeth p28
*mi-*noun	24		P	Pp	Eg *mtume*, prophet *mitume*, prophets p24
*mi-*noun	26		P	V	Eg *mmea*, plant *mimea*, plants p26
*mu-*noun	26		S	V	Eg *muhogo*, cassava plant *mihogo*, cassava plants p26
*mw-*noun	26		S	V	Eg *mwembe*, mango tree *miembe*, mango trees p26
mwa- noun	23		S	Pp	Eg *mwalimu*, teacher *walimu*, teachers p23

¹NOUN Prefix	³pg	T	²SP	Gp	[Comment] Eg
Mwi- _{noun}	24		S	Pp	Eg *Mwislamu*, Muslim *Waislamu*, Muslims p24
n-^{noun}	33		P	U	Eg *uyoga*, mushroom *nyoga*, mushrooms p33
nd-^{noun}	34		P	U	Eg *ulimi*, tongue *ndimi*, tongues p34
-ni^{noun}	36			Pl	Eg *kikapu*, basket, results in: *kikapuni*, in(side) basket pg36
ny-^{noun}	33		P	U	Eg *uwanda*, plateau, plain *nywanda*, plains [sometimes *nyanda*] p33 *ungu*, pot (native) *nyungu*, pots p33 *uso*, face *nyuso*, faces p33 *uma*, fork *nyuma*, forks p34
u-^{noun}	33		S	U	Eg *utenzi*, poem *tenzi*, poems p33
ul-^{noun}	34		S	U	Eg *ulimi*, tongue *ndimi*, tongues p34
uw-^{noun}	34		S	U	Eg *The* uw- is dropped and a prefix *mb-* is attached: *uwinda*, hunting *mbinda*, huntings p34
vi-^{noun}	30		P	T	Eg *kiti*, chair *viti*, chairs p30

¹NOUN Prefix	³pg	T	²SP	Gp	[Comment] Eg
vy-noun	30		P	T	Eg *chumba*, room *vyumba*, rooms p30
w-noun	34		S	U	Eg *wimbo*, song *nyimbo*, songs p34
wa-noun	23		P	Pp	Eg *mtoto*, child *watoto*, children p23
we-noun	24		P	Pp	Eg *mwizi* or *mwivi*, thief *wezi* or *wevi*, thieves p24

22.6 Index table: Adjective Prefix

¹ADJECT. Prefix	³pg	T	²SP	Gp	[Comment] Eg
_adj	55				Foreign-origin Eg *kitabu safi*, clean book [not *kisafi*] p55 *vitabu safi*, clean books [not *visafi*] p55
_adj	49		S	xFF	Eg *dafu zuri*, nice unripe coconut p49
_adj	52			xFV	Eg *ndizi kubwa*, big banana(s) p52
ch-adj	50		S	T	e-adjective Eg *kisu chema*, good knife p50
j-adj	49		S	xFF	Vowel-adjective Eg *debe jangavu*, shining can p49

¹ADJECT. Prefix	³pg	T	²SP	Gp	[Comment] Eg
ki-*adj*	50		S	T	Eg *kitabu kizuri*, nice book p50 vowel-adjective Eg *kisu ki*(i)*ngine*, other knife p50
ku-*adj*	53			G	Eg *kucheza kuzuri*, nice playing(s) p53
kw-*adj*	54			G	e&i-adjective Eg *kufanya kwema*, good doing(s) p54 *kufanya kwingine*, other doing(s) p54
m-*adj*	48		S	Pp	Eg *mke mzuri*, pretty wife p48
m-*adj*	52		S	U	Eg *ufagio mzuri*, nice broom p52
m-*adj*	49		S	V	Eg *mwitu mzuri*, beautiful forest p49
m-*adj*	52			xFV	Eg *mboga mbaya*, bad vegetable(s) 52
ma-*adj*	49		P	xFF	Eg *madafu mazuri*, nice unripe coconuts p49
me-*adj*	49		P	xFF	e&i-adjective Eg *maembe me(e)ma*, good mangoes (-e-dropped from the adjective) p50 *maembe me(i)ngine*, other mangoes (-i- dropped from the adjective) p50
mi-*adj*	49		P	V	Eg *miitu mizuri*, beautiful forests p49
mw-*adj*	48		S	Pp	Vowel-adjective Eg *mvulana mwangalifu*, careful boy p48

¹ADJECT. Prefix	³pg	T	²SP	Gp	[Comment] Eg
mw-*adj*	53		S	U	Vowel-adjective Eg *ufunguo mwingine*, other key p53 *ufunguo mweupe*, white key; *funguo nyeupe*, white keys] [*ufunguo* mwema, good key p53
mw-*adj*	49		S	V	Vowel-adjective Eg *mkuki mwangavu*, shining spear p49
my-*adj*	49		P	V	e-adjective Eg *mikuyu myema*, good sycamore / fig trees p49
n-*adj*	52		P	U	Eg *fagio nzuri*, nice brooms p52
n-*adj*	51			xFV	Eg *nyanya ndogo / ngumu / njazi / nzuri*, small / hard / plentiful / nice tomato(es) p51
nj-*adj*	53		P	U	e-adjective Eg *funguo njema*, good keys p53
nj-*adj*	52			xFV	e-adjective Eg *karafuu njema*, good clove(s) p52
ny-*adj*	53		P	U	Vowel-adjective Eg *funguo nyingine*, other keys p53
ny-*adj*	52			xFV	Vowel-adjective Eg *chupa nyangavu*, shining bottle(s) p52 *karafuu nyingine*, other clove(s) p52 *karafuu nyororo*, soft clove(s) p52
pa-*adj*	53			Pl	Eg *mahali pazuri*, nice plac(e)s p53
pe-*adj*	53			Pl	e&i-adjective Eg *mahali pe(e)ma*, good place(s) (-e-

¹ADJECT. Prefix	³pg	T	²SP	Gp	[Comment] Eg
					dropped from the adjective) p53 *mahali pe(i)ngine*, other place(s) (-i- dropped from the adjective) p53
vi-ᵃᵈʲ	50		P	T	Eg *vitabu vizuri*, nice books p50 vowel-adjective Eg *visu vi(i)ngine*, other knives p50
vy-ᵃᵈʲ	50		P	T	e-adjective Eg *visu vyema*, good knives p50
wa-ᵃᵈʲ	48		P	Pp	Eg *wake wazuri*, pretty wives p48
we-ᵃᵈʲ	48		P	Pp	e&i-adjective Eg *wavulana we(e)ma*, good boys (-e- dropped from the adjective) p48 *wavulana we(i)ngine*, other boys (-i- dropped from the adjective) p48

22.7 Index table: Demonstrative Adjective

Demonstrative adjectives: *h-*, this, these, *−le*, that, those

¹DEMO. Prefix	³pg	T	²SP	Gp	[Comment] Eg
-i, i-	106, 108		P	V	Eg *miti hii*, these trees p106 *miti ile*, those trees p108
-i, i-	107, 109		S	xFV	Eg *nyanya hii*, this tomato p107 *nyanya ile*, that tomato p109

¹DEMO. Prefix	³pg	T	²SP	Gp	[Comment] Eg
-ki, ki-	107, 108		S	T	Eg *kitu hiki*, this thing p107 *kitu kile*, that thing p108
-ku, ku-	107, 109			G	Eg *kusoma huku*, this/these reading(s) p107 *kusoma kule*, that/those reading(s) p109
-ku, ku-	107, 109			Pl	Eg *mahali huku*, this/these place(s) speaking generally p107 *mahali kule*, that/those place(s) speaking generally p109
-li, li-	106, 108		S	xFF	Eg *tunda hili*, this fruit p106 *tunda lile*, that fruit p108
-mu, m-	107, 109			Pl	Eg *mahali humu*, this/these place(s) inside p107 *mahali mle*, that/those place(s) inside p109
-o	109				Specific demonstrative Eg [mtu huyo; watu hao: this / these person(s) p110
-pa, pa-	107, 109			Pl	Eg *mahali hapa*, this/these place(s) p107 *mahali pale*, that/those place(s) p109
-u, u-	106, 108		S	V	Eg *mti huu*, this tree p106 *mti ule*, that tree p108
-u, u-	107, 109		S	U	Eg *utenzi huu*, this poem p107 *utenzi ule*, that poem p109

¹DEMO. Prefix	³pg	T	²SP	Gp	[Comment] Eg
-vi, vi-	107, 108		P	T	Eg *vitu hivi*, these things p107 *vitu vile*, those things p108
-wa, wa-	106, 108		P	Pp	Eg *watu hawa*, these persons p106 *watu wale*, those persons p108
-ya, ya-	108, 108		P	xFF	Eg *matunda haya*, these fruits p106 *matunda yale*, those fruits p108
-yu, yu-	106, 108		S	Pp	Eg *mtu huyu**, this person p106 *mtu yule**, that person p108
-zi, zi-	107, 109		P	U	Eg *tenzi hizi*, these poems p107 *tenzi zile*, those poems p109
-zi, zi-	107, 109		P	xFV	Eg *nyanya hizi*, these tomatoes p107 *nyanya zile*, those tomatoes p109

22.8 Index table: Possessives

Possessives: possessives –*a* and possessors –*ake*, etc

Animate exception Egs are commented "animate" below:

¹POSS. Prefix	³pg	T	²SP	Gp	[Comment] Eg
ch-	115		S	T	Possessive Eg *Kiti cha mwalimu*, teacher's chair p115

¹POSS. Prefix	³pg	T	²S P	Gp	[Comment] Eg
ch-	117		S	T	Possessor Eg *Kiti chake*, her/his/its chair p117
kw-	115			G	Possessive Eg *Kusoma kwa mwalimu*, teacher's reading(s) p115
kw-	115			Pl	Possessive Eg *mahali kwa wanyama* wa pori, wild animals' land (but not stated exactly where or which) p115
kw-	117			G	Possessor Eg *Kusoma kwake*, her/his reading(s) p117
Kw-*	118			Pl	Possessor Eg *tunda la kwangu*, fruit of mine *tunda la kwangu*, fruit of mine p118 *vitu vya kwangu*, things of mine p118
l-	115		S	xFF	Possessive Eg *Tunda la mwalimu*, teacher's fruit p115
l-	116		S	xFF	Possessor Eg *Tunda lake*, her/his/its fruit p116
mw-	115			Pl	Possessive Eg *ndani mwa nyumba*, inside of house p115

¹POSS. Prefix	³pg	T	²SP	Gp	[Comment] Eg
p-	115			Pl	Possessive Eg *Mahali *pa mwalimu*, teacher's place(s) p115
p-	117			Pl	Possessor Eg *Mahali *pake*, her/his/its place(s) p117
vy-	115		P	T	Possessive Eg *Viti vya mwalimu*, teacher's chairs p115
vy-	117		P	T	Possessor Eg *Viti vyake*, her/his/its chairs p117
w-	114		P	Pp	Possessive Eg *Mtoto wa mwalimu*, teacher's child p114
w-	116		P	Pp	Possessor Eg *Watoto wake*, her/his/its children p116
w-	114		S	Pp	Possessive Eg *Watoto wa mwalimu*, teacher's children p114
w-	114		S	V	Possessive Eg *Mti wa mwalimu*, teacher's tree p114
w-	115		S	U	Possessive Eg *Utenzi wa mwalimu*, teacher's poem p115

¹POSS. Prefix	³pg	T	²SP	Gp	[Comment] Eg
w-	116		S	Pp	Possessor Eg *Mtoto wake*, her/his/its child p116
w-	117		S	U	Possessor Eg *Utenzi wake*, her/his/its poem p117
w-	116		S	V	Possessor Eg *Mti wake*, her/his/its tree p116
w-	116			xFF	Possessor, animate Eg *kobe wake*, his tortoise p121
w-	121			xFF	Possessive, animate Eg *kobe wa mwalimu*, teacher's tortoise p121
y-	114		P	V	Possessive Eg *Miti ya mwalimu*, teacher's trees p114
y-	115		P	xFF	Possessive Eg *Matunda ya mwalimu*, teacher's fruits p115
y-	116		P	V	Possessor Eg *Miti yake*, her/his/its trees p116
y-	116		P	xFF	Possessor Eg *Matunda yake*, her/his/its fruits p116
y-	115		S	xFV	Possessive Eg *Nyanya ya mwalimu*, teacher's tomato p115

¹POSS. Prefix	³pg	T	²SP	Gp	[Comment] Eg
y-	117		S	xFV	Possessor Eg *Nyanya yake*, her/his/its tomato p117
y-	120		S	xFV	Possessive, animate Eg *rafiki ya mwalimu*, teacher's friend p120
y-	120		S	xFV	Possessor, animate Eg *rafiki yake*, his friend p120
z-	115		P	U	Possessive Eg *Tenzi za mwalimu*, teacher's poems p115
z-	115		P	xFV	Possessive Eg *Nyanya za mwalimu*, teacher's tomatoes p115
z-	117		P	U	Possessor Eg *Tenzi zake*, her/his/its poem p117
z-	117		P	xFV	Possessor Eg *Nyanya zake*, her/his/its tomatoes p117
z-	120		P	xFV	Possessive, animate Eg *rafiki za mwalimu*, teacher's friends p120
z-	120		P	xFV	Possessor, animate Eg *rafiki zake*, his friends p120

22.9 Index table: Adjective (–o) -ote, (any) all / whole

These use possessive prefixes instead of the usual adjectival prefixes!

[1]Any / All / Whole Prefix	[3]pg	T	[2]S P	Gp	[Comment] Eg
ch-	124		S	T	Eg *Kitu kizuri chote*, whole nice thing p124
ch-	124		S	T	Eg *Kitu kizuri cho chote*, any nice thing p124
kw-	126		P	G	Eg *Kusoma kuzuri kwo kwote*, any nice readings p126
kw-	126		P	G	Eg *Kusoma kuzuri kwote*, all nice readings p126
kw-	126		S	G	Eg *Kusoma kuzuri kwo kwote*, any nice reading p126
kw-	126		S	G	Eg *Kusoma kuzuri kwote*, whole nice reading p126
l-	122		S	xFF	Eg *tunda lote*, whole fruit p122
l-	122		S	xFF	Eg *tunda lo lote* p122
mw-	123		S	Pp	1st person Eg *mimi mwenyewe*, I myself p123
ny-	123		P	Pp	2nd person Eg *ninyi wote*, you all, but also *ninyi nyote* p123

[1]Any / All / Whole Prefix	[3]pg	T	[2]Sp	Gp	[Comment] Eg
p-	126		P	Pl	Eg *Mahali pazuri po pote*, any nice places p126
p-	126		P	Pl	Eg *Mahali pazuri pote*, all nice places p126
p-	125		S	Pl	Eg *Mahali pazuri po pote*, any nice place p125
p-	125		S	Pl	Eg *Mahali pazuri pote*, whole nice place p125
s-	123		P	Pp	3rd person Eg *sisi wote*, we all, but also *sisi sote* p123
vy-	124		P	T	Eg *Vitu vizuri vyo vyote*, any nice things p124
vy-	124		P	T	Eg *Kitu chenye thamani*, thing of value. *Vitu vizuri vyote*, all nice things p124
w-	124		P	Pp	1st person Eg *ninyi wote*, you all, but also *ninyi nyote* [2nd person plural] *ninyi wenye afya*, you of health, but also *ninyi nyenye afya* [2nd person plural]

¹Any / All / Whole Prefix	³pg	T	²S P	Gp	[Comment] Eg
					More examples: *sisi wo wote*, any of us p123
w-	124		P	Pp	3rd person Eg *watu wote*, all persons p124
w-	125		S	U	Eg *Utenzi mzuri wo wote*, any nice poem p125
w-	125		S	U	Eg *Utenzi mzuri wote*, whole nice poem p125
w-	124		S	V	Eg *Mti mzuri wo wote*, any nice tree p124
w-	124		S	V	Eg *Mti mzuri wote*, whole nice tree p124
y-	122		P	xFF	Eg *matunda yo yote*, any fruits p122
y-	122		P	xFF	Eg *matunda yote*, all fruits p122
y-	124		P	V	Eg *Miti mizuri yo yote*, any nice trees p124
y-	124		P	V	Eg *Miti mizuri yote*, all nice trees p124
y-	125		S	xFV	Eg *Nyanya nzuri yo yote*, any nice tomato p125
y-	125		S	xFV	Eg *Nyanya nzuri yote*, whole nice tomato 125

¹Any / All / Whole Prefix	³pg	T	²S P	Gp	[Comment] Eg
ye	123		S	Pp	3rd person Eg *mtu mwenye afya*, healthy person, but *also mtu yenye afya*, the ye- also being used in *mtu ye yote*, any person p123
z-	125		P	xFV	Eg *Nyanya nzuri zo zote*, any nice tomatoes p125
z-	125		P	xFV	Eg *Nyanya yenye mbegu*, tomato having seeds. *Nyanya nzuri zote*, all nice tomatoes p125
z-	125		P	U	Eg *Tenzi nzuri zo zote*, any nice poems p125
z-	125		P	U	Eg *Tenzi nzuri zote*, all nice poems p125

22.10 Practice: Parsing Words, Translations

Answers to the previous practice of section 11.3 Practice: Anatomy of Verbs:

Mpishi a²·ᴾ-na³·ᵀ-ye⁴·ᴿ-tu⁵·ᴼ-pik^{verb base}-i⁷·ᴾ-a ni Paulo, the cook <u>who is cooking for us</u> is Paul. [verb *pika*, cook]

Nyanya a²·ᴾ-na³·ᵀ-zo⁴·ᴿ-zi⁵·ᴼ-ona^{verb base}, tomatoes <u>which he is seeing them</u>. [verb *ona*, see]

A²·ᴾ-na³·ᵀ-tu⁵·ᴼ-let^{verb base}-e⁷·ᴾ-a, he is <u>bringing to us</u>. [verb *leta*, bring]

Ha¹·ᴴ-wa²·ᴾ-ja³·ᵀ-ja^{verb base}, they <u>have not yet come</u>. [verb *ja*, come]

Practice:

Translate the following sentences, using – as needed - the parsing method and tips given above in section 22 Index of Attachments (alphabetical). An **example** is provided for the first entry.

[The correct answers follow on the next page.]

Mtu aliyetupikia amerudi kwake, <u>the man who cooked for us has returned to his (place)</u>.

Tukinywa maji machafu tutaugua, _____.

Nitakapofika nyumbani nitakupiga simu,

_____.

Hatukumletea kitu, _____.

Huyu husoma wakati wote lakini wewe husomi tu, _____.

Shamba ni eneo linalolimwa,

_____.

Mtu aliyetusalimu mlangoni alikuwa rafiki yangu,

_____.

Answers to the above practice:

Mtu aliyetupikia amerudi kwake, <u>the man who cooked for us has returned to his (place)</u>.

Tukinywa maji machafu tutaugua, <u>if we drink dirty water we will become sick</u>.

Nitakapofika nyumbani nitakupiga simu, <u>when I reach home I will give you a call</u>.

Hatukumletea kitu, <u>we did not bring for him anything</u>.

Huyu husoma wakati wote lakini wewe husomi tu, <u>this (person) always reads but you never read</u>.

Shamba ni eneo linalolimwa, <u>a farming plot is a place that is being cultivated</u>.

Mtu aliyetusalimu mlangoni alikuwa rafiki yangu, <u>the person who greeted us at the door was my friend</u>.

<u>More Translation Practice:</u>

Translation of course is the ultimate test of accomplishment. You pass it and you can say you know Good Swahili.

Reminder: always read out aloud every Swahili phrase.

Translate the text below:

[The correct answers follow this text.]

Maembe!

Huyu ni mvulana. Jina lake ni Ali.
Huyu ni msichana. Jina lake ni Mariamu.

Hao ni kaka na dada, watoto wa Bwana Salehe. Wote wavili wana afya njema, tena ni wanafunzi wema. Wanasoma shule ya msingi inayoitwa Darajani *huko Tanga. Inaitwa* Darajani *kwa sababu ni karibu na daraja lililopo juu ya njia ya reli. Ali anasoma katika darasa la sita na dadaye la tatu.*

Joni ni jirani wa Ali, pia rafiki yake. Jamaa yake Joni imeishi hapa kwa miaka michache tu. Zamani walikuwa wakikaa ng'amboni mwa mto. Walihama hapo kwa kusudi la kuwa karibu kidogo na shule ya watoto. Lakini wakina Ali wamekuwa hapo hapa daima.

Kila asubuhi Mariamu huamsha kakaye: "Amka uoge na ule kifungua kinywa".

Leo juma pili hao watatu wanakwenda msituni karibu na mto Sigi kuangua maembe. Wanakwenda wakiendesha baisikeli. Ali na Joni ni hodari kwa kazi hii lakini Mariamu hajui kuyaangua maembe kwa kuwa bado mtoto mdogo. Basi hiyo ndiyo tabia yao, yaani kufanya vitu mbalimbali wote watatu kwa pamoja.

Kule ukingo na mto kuna mwembe mkubwa. Kabla ya kuangua maembe yanawapasa kuomba ruhusa na mwenyeji wa mti. Basi, wakaenda kwake Bwana Kasimu, wakabisha mlango. Punde mwanawe aliufungua.

"Hujambo?" wakamwamkia. "Babao yumo nyumbani?"

"Yumo uani" kijana kajibu.

Basi, wakazunguka nyumba, pia ukuta wa ua, wakapigia hodi mlango wa nyuma. Mzee akafungua mlango.

Wakamwamkia "Shikamuu, mzee".

Naye mzee akaitikia "Marahaba." Akaendelea "Nadhani mmekuja kuomba ruhusa kwa maembe", kwa kuwa siyo mara ya kwanza watoto wamekuja kwa ajili ya maembe. Akawaambia "Haya, kila mmoja ninyi mnaweza kuangua maembe matatu. Sawa?"

Wote watatu walitabasamu wakionyesha meno na kumjibu "Ndiyo, mzee!" Wakamshukuru mzee kwa kumwinamia. Kwa furaha mno wakaondoka wakielekea ule mwembe.

Answers to the above practice:

Mangoes!

This is a boy. His name is Ali.
This is a girl. Her name is Mariam.

They are elder brother and sister, children of Mr Salehe. Both are healthy, also good students. They study at a primary school called Darajani there in Tanga. It is called Darajani because it is near a bridge over a railroad. Ali studies in standard (or grade) six and his sister standard three.

John is Ali's neighbour, also his friend. His family has lived here for only a few years. Before, they were staying on the other side of the river. They moved here for the purpose of being a little closer to the children's school. But Ali's kin has always been right here.

Every morning Mariam wakes up her elder brother: "Wake up that you may bathe and have breakfast."

Today Sunday these three are going to the bushes near the Sigi river to drop down mangoes (by casting stones). They are pedalling bicycles. Ali and John are good at this work but Mariamu doesn't know how to bring down mangoes as she is still a small child. Well, this indeed is their habit, that is doing different things, all three together.

There at the side of the river is a big mango tree. Before dropping mangoes, it behooves them to request permission from the tree's owner. So, they went to Mr Kasimu's and knocked on the door. Shortly his son opened it.

"Everything okay (literally, you have no problem)?" they greeted him. "Is your father home?"

"He is in the yard" the boy replied.

So, they circled around the house, also the yard wall, and they knocked on the back door. The old man opened the door.

They greeted him "I grip your feet, elder."

And he replied "It is welcomed, I am pleased." He continued "I think you have come to request permission for the mangoes", because this is not the first time children have come for the sake of mangoes. He told them "Okay, each of you can drop three mangoes. Okay?"

All three smiled, flashing (literally, showing) their teeth and replying "Yes, elder!" They thanked the old man by bowing to him. With great joy, they left, heading for that mango tree.

More Scenarios for Practice

Below are a few suggestions for scenarios you can imagine and write about on your own for further practice. Beyond that you will likely have scenarios of your own to write about.

- Shopping at a market: asking prices, buying by weight or quantity, identifying the produce or asking what something is, etc
- Visiting a game park: describing the terrain, picnicking (what are you eating?), identifying the fauna as well as the flora or asking what something is, etc
- Attending a soccer game: describing the parts of the playing field, naming the player positions, naming their uniform parts, etc
- What do you do after you wake up in the morning?

Another useful thing to do is to translate back from Swahili to English the previous practices.

TIP: While in East Africa look for Swahili books in bookshops including books for children and students, including stories. Some of these could be valuable resources for studying Swahili AND they should be cheap to purchase ;-)

An On-going Project

This is an excellent way to practise written Swahili: constructing your own Swahili dictionary, small at first but always growing. Here is a starting model:

KAMUSI YANGU, MY DICTIONARY

Maelezo ya mafupisho, explanation of abbreviations*:*
*n. = **nomino**: jina la kitu*, noun
*v. = kivumishi: neno la kueleza **n**.*, adjective
*t. = ki**t**enzi: neno la kutenda*, verb
*e. = kielezi: neno la kueleza **v**. au **t**. au vilevile **e**.*, adverb
u. = kiunganishi: neno la kuungana maneno, conjunction
*mf = **mf**ano*, example
*kar. = neno la **kar**ibu: maana yake ni karibu*, related / synonym
*nyu. = neno la ki**nyu**me, maana yake ni ya kinyume*, antonym

***chanuo**(-,ma) n. kitu kinachotumiwa kuchana nywele [kar. kitana]*

***dereva**(-) n. mtu aendeshaye gari [nyu. abiria]*

***dogo** v. mf: milimita ni n**dogo** kuliko mita [nyu. kubwa]*

jana e. siku kabla ya leo [nyu. kesho]

kiatu(ki,vi) n. kitu kinachovaliwa mguuni [kar. ndara]

mwalimu(mw,w) n. mtu afundishaye shuleni [nyu. mwanafunzi]

mtu(m,wa) n. binadamu [kar. mwanamume; nyu. mnyama, mdudu]

na u. mf: moja *na* moja ni mbili [nyu. kasoro, bila]

ona t. kupata picha kwa macho [kar. tazama]

TIP: Ask your local acquaintance or colleague to explain some word:

Tafadhali nieleze maana ya _____ (a Swahili word), please explain to me the meaning of _____.

Make note of the answer and use it to make another entry in your above personal Swahili dictionary!

23 Index table of Noun Groups

This table summarizes all prefixes, etc which are governed by noun groups (singular, plural, pronoun, adjective, object, relative) and is thus very useful for selecting them for use in word construction (AND as always for revision). They are sorted by [1]G(rou)p, then by the source index shown in superscript at the beginning of the [2][Comment] Eg column, then by [3]Prefix.

[3]Noun Group Prefix	pg	T	S P	[1]Gp	[2][Comment] Eg
__adj	55				adj Foreign-origin Eg *kitabu safi*, clean book [not *kisafi*] p55 *vitabu safi*, clean books [not *visafi*] p55
Kuna- pron	191				pron Eg *kuna watu mjini*, there are people in town p192
Mna,	191				pron Eg *nyumbani mna watu*, there are people in the house *mna sukari humu*? is there sugar in it? *mna maji kisimani*? is there water in the well? *mna samaki ziwani*? are there fish in the lake? *mna watu sokoni*? are there people in the market? P192
ya-	193				pron Eg *yafaa tuende*, it is befitting we go

³Noun Group Prefix	pg	T	S P	¹Gp	²[Comment] Eg
					haifai kuchelewa, it is not proper to be late haiwezekani, it is not doable *haidhuru*, literally it means 'it does no harm', and is translated as 'it is okay' P193
ni-^{pron}	172	TI			^{pron} *wa*, be, Eg *mpishi ni muhimu hotelini*, a cook is important in a hotel p172
si-^{pron}	172	TI			^{pron} Neg. *wa*, be, Eg *mpishi si muhimu dukani*, a cook is not important in a shop p172
-ko-^{4.R}	144			G	^{4.R} Eg *Kusoma kunakotosha*, reading(s) which suffice(s) p144
-ku-^{5.O}	133			G	^{5.O} Eg *ninakuona*, I see it p133
kw-^{adj}	54			G	^{adj} e&i-adjective Eg *kufanya kwema*, good doing(s) p54 *kufanya kwingine*, other doing(s) p54
ku-^{adj}	53			G	^{adj} Eg *kucheza kuzuri*, nice playing(s) p53
ku-^{noun}	37			G	^{noun} Eg *kusema*, talking pg38, *kusamehe*, forgiving pg38
--^{noun}	38			G	^{noun} Eg *kusoma*, reading(s) p38
kutoku-^{noun}	38			G	^{noun} Eg *kutokusema*, silence pg38

³Noun Group Prefix	pg	T	S P	¹Gp	²[Comment] Eg
kuto- *noun*	38			G	*noun* Eg *kutosamehe*, unforgiving pg38
ku-*pron*	67			G	*pron* Eg *kunatosha*, it suffices p67
-ko-*4.R*	139			Pl	*4.R* Eg *Mahali kunakotosha*, place(s) which suffice(s) p144
-po-*4.R*	143			Pl	*4.R* Eg *Mahali panapotosha*, place(s) which suffice(s) p143
-mo-*4.R*	139			Pl	*4.R* Eg *Nyumbani mnamotosha*, house interior(s) which suffice(s) p144 *Nyumbani mnamotosha*, house interior(s) which suffice(s)
-ku-*5.O*	133			Pl	*5.O* Eg *ninakuona*, I see it p133
-mu-*5.O*	133			Pl	*5.O* Eg *ninamuona*, I see them p133
-pa-*5.O*	133			Pl	*5.O* Eg *ninapaona*, I see it p133
pe-*adj*	53			Pl	*adj* e&i-adjective Eg *mahali pe(e)ma*, good place(s) (-e- dropped from the adjective) p53 *mahali pe(i)ngine*, other place(s) (-i- dropped from the adjective) p53
pa-*adj*	53			Pl	*adj* Eg *mahali pazuri*, nice plac(e)s p53
-ni *noun*	36			Pl	*noun* Eg *kikapu*, basket, results in: kikapuni, in(side) basket pg36
-_*noun*	36			Pl	*noun* Eg *mahali*, place(s) p36

³Noun Group Prefix	pg	T	S P	¹Gp	²[Comment] Eg
ku-[pron]	67			Pl	[pron] Eg *kunatosha*, it (e.g. some place) suffices p67
m-[pron]	67			Pl	[pron] Eg *[mnatosha*, it (e.g. interior space) suffices p67
pa-[pron]	67			Pl	[pron] Eg *panatosha*, it suffices p67
-ye-[4.R]	140		S	Pp	[4.R] All Persons Eg *Mtu anayetosha,* person who suffices p140
-o-[4.R]	140		P	Pp	[4.R] All Persons Eg *Watu wanaotosha*, persons who suffice p140
-ni-[5.O]	134		S	Pp	[5.O] 1st Person Eg *ninanipenda*, I love myself p134
-tu-[5.O]	134		P	Pp	[5.O] 1st Person Eg *ninatupenda*, I love us p134
-ku-[5.O]	134		S	Pp	[5.O] 2nd Person Eg *ninakupenda*, I love you (singular) p134
-wa-[5.O]	134		P	Pp	[5.O] 2nd Person Eg *ninawapenda*, I love you (plural) p134
-m(w)-[5.O]	134		S	Pp	[5.O] 3rd Person Eg *ninampenda*, I love her / him p134
-wa-[5.O]	134		P	Pp	[5.O] 3rd Person Eg *ninawapenda*, I love them p134
we-[adj]	48		P	Pp	[adj] e&i-adjective Eg *wavulana we(e)ma*, good boys (-e-dropped from the adjective) p48 *wavulana we(i)ngine*, other boys

³Noun Group Prefix	pg	T	SP	¹Gp	²[Comment] Eg
					(-i- dropped from the adjective) p48
m-*adj*	48		S	Pp	*adj* Eg *mke mzuri*, pretty wife p48
wa-*adj*	48		P	Pp	*adj* Eg *wake wazuri*, pretty wives p48
mw-*adj*	48		S	Pp	*adj* Vowel-adjective Eg *mvulana mwangalifu*, careful boy p48
m-*noun*	23		S	Pp	*noun* Eg *mtoto*, child *watoto*, children p23
wa-*noun*	23		P	Pp	*noun* Eg *mtoto*, child *watoto*, children p23
mi-*noun*	24		P	Pp	*noun* Eg *mtume*, prophet *mitume*, prophets p24
mwa-*noun*	23		S	Pp	*noun* Eg *mwalimu*, teacher *walimu*, teachers p23
Mwi-*noun*	24		S	Pp	*noun* Eg *Mwislamu*, Muslim *Waislamu*, Muslims p24
we-*noun*	24		P	Pp	*noun* Eg *mwizi* or *mwivi*, thief *wezi* or *wevi*, thieves p24
n-*pron*	68	Tl	S	Pp	*pron* 1st Person Eg *n*atosha*, I suffice 68
ni-*pron*	65		S	Pp	*pron* 1st Person Eg *ninatosha*, I suffice p65
si-*pron*	81	Pr Tl	S	Pp	*pron* 1st Person Eg *sitoshi*, I don't suffice p81

³**Noun Group** Prefix	pg	T	S P	¹Gp	²[Comment] Eg
tu-^pron	65		P	Pp	^pron 1st Person Eg *tunatosha,* we suffice p65
tw-^pron	68	Tl	P	Pp	^pron 1st Person Eg *tw*atosha,* we suffice 68
m-^pron	66		P	Pp	^pron 2nd Person Eg *mnatosha,* you suffice p66
m-^pron	69	Tl	P	Pp	^pron 2nd Person Eg *mw*atosha,* you suffice 69
u-^pron	65		S	Pp	^pron 2nd Person Eg *unatosha,* you suffice p65
w-^pron	69	Tl	S	Pp	^pron 2nd Person Eg *w*atosha,* you suffice 69
a-^pron	65		S	Pp	^pron 3rd Person Eg *anatosha,* she / he suffices p65
wa-^pron	65		P	Pp	^pron 3rd Person Eg *wanatosha,* they suffice p65
-cho-^4.R	142		S	T	^4.R Eg *Kitu kinachotosha,* thing which suffices p142
-vyo-^4.R	142		P	T	^4.R Eg *Vitu vinavyotosha,* things which suffice p142
-ki-^5.O	132		S	T	^5.O Eg *ninakiona,* I see it p132
-vi-^5.O	132		P	T	^5.O Eg *ninaviona,* I see them p132
ch-^adj	50		S	T	^adj e-adjective Eg *kisu chema,* good knife p50

[3]Noun Group Prefix	pg	T	S P	[1]Gp	[2][Comment] Eg
vy-[adj]	50		P	T	[adj] e-adjective Eg *visu vyema*, good knives p50
ki-[adj]	50		S	T	[adj] Eg *kitabu kizuri*, nice book p50 vowel-adjective Eg *kisu ki*(i)ngine, other knife p50
vi-[adj]	50		P	T	[adj] Eg *vitabu vizuri*, nice books p50 vowel-adjective Eg *visu vi*(i)ngine, other knives p50
ch-[noun]	30		S	T	[noun] Eg *chumba*, room *vyumba*, rooms p30
vy-[noun]	30		P	T	[noun] Eg *chumba*, room *vyumba*, rooms p30
ki-[noun]	30		S	T	[noun] Eg *kiti*, chair *viti*, chairs p30
vi-[noun]	30		P	T	[noun] Eg *kiti*, chair *viti*, chairs p30
ki-[pron]	66		S	T	[pron] Eg *kinatosha*, it suffices p66
vi-[pron]	66		P	T	[pron] Eg *vinatosha*, they suffice p66
-zo-[4.R]	143		P	U	[4.R] Eg *Tenzi zinazotosha*, poems which suffice p143
-o-[4.R]	143		S	U	[4.R] Eg *Utenzi unaotosha*, poem which suffices p143
-u-[5.O]	133		S	U	[5.O] Eg *ninauona*, I see it p133
-zi-[5.O]	133		P	U	[5.O] Eg *ninaziona*, I see them p133

[3]Noun Group Prefix	pg	T	S P	[1]Gp	[2][Comment] Eg
nj-*adj*	53		P	U	*adj* e-adjective Eg *funguo njema*, good keys p53
n-*adj*	52		P	U	*adj* Eg *fagio nzuri*, nice brooms p52
m-*adj*	52		S	U	*adj* Eg *ufagio mzuri*, nice broom p52
ny-*adj*	53		P	U	*adj* Vowel-adjective Eg *funguo nyingine*, other keys p53
mw-*adj*	53		S	U	*adj* Vowel-adjective Eg *ufunguo mwingine*, other key p53 *ufunguo mweupe*, white key; *funguo nyeupe*, white keys] [*ufunguo* mwema, good key p53
ny-*noun*	33		P	U	*noun* Eg *uwanda*, plateau, plain *nywanda*, plains [sometimes *nyanda*] p33
nd-*noun*	34		P	U	*noun* Eg *ulimi*, tongue *ndimi*, tongues p34
ul-*noun*	34		S	U	*noun* Eg *ulimi*, tongue *ndimi*, tongues p34
w-*noun*	34		S	U	*noun* Eg *wimbo*, song *nyimbo*, songs p34
n-*noun*	33		P	U	*noun* Eg *uyoga*, mushroom *nyoga*, mushrooms p33 *ungu*, pot (native) *nyungu*, pots p33

³Noun Group Prefix	pg	T	S P	¹Gp	²[Comment] Eg
_-noun	33		P	U	noun Eg *utenzi*, poem *tenzi*, poems p33
u-noun	33		S	U	noun Eg *utenzi*, poem *tenzi*, poems p33
ma-noun	34		P	U	noun Eg *uvuno*, harvesting *mavuno*, harvest p34
mb-noun	34		P	U	noun Eg *The* uw- is dropped and a prefix *mb-* is attached: *uwinda*, hunting *mbinda*, huntings p34
uw-noun	34		S	U	noun Eg *The* uw- is dropped and a prefix *mb-* is attached: *uwinda*, hunting *mbinda*, huntings p34
u-pron	67		S	U	pron Eg *unatosha*, it suffices p67
zi-pron	67		P	U	pron Eg *zinatosha*, they suffice p67
-yo-4.R	141		P	V	4.R Eg *Miti inayotosha*, trees which suffice p141
-o-4.R	141		S	V	4.R Eg *Mti unaotosha*, tree which suffices p141
-i-5.O	132		P	V	5.O Eg *ninaiona*, I see them p132
-u-5.O	132		S	V	5.O Eg *ninauona*, I see it p132

³Noun Group Prefix	pg	T	S P	¹Gp	²[Comment] Eg
my-^{adj}	49		P	V	^{adj} e-adjective Eg *mikuyu myema*, good sycamore / fig trees p49
mi-^{adj}	49		P	V	^{adj} Eg *miitu mizuri*, beautiful forests p49
m-^{adj}	49		S	V	^{adj} Eg *mwitu mzuri*, beautiful forest p49
mw-^{adj}	49		S	V	^{adj} Vowel-adjective Eg *mkuki mwangavu*, shining spear p49
mi-^{noun}	26		P	V	^{noun} Eg *mmea*, plant *mimea*, plants p26
m-^{noun}	26		S	V	^{noun} Eg *mmea*, plant *mimea*, plants p26
mu-^{noun}	26		S	V	^{noun} Eg *muhogo*, cassava plant *mihogo*, cassava plants p26
mw-^{noun}	26		S	V	^{noun} Eg *mwembe*, mango tree *miembe*, mango trees p26
i-^{pron}	66		P	V	^{pron} Eg *inatosha*, they suffice p66
u-^{pron}	66		S	V	^{pron} Eg *unatosha*, it suffices p66
-yo-^{4.R}	141		P	xFF	^{4.R} Eg *Matunda yanayotosha*, fruits which suffice p141
-lo-^{4.R}	141		S	xFF	^{4.R} Eg *Tunda linalotosha*, fruit which suffices p141
-li-^{5.O}	132		S	xFF	^{5.O} Eg *ninaliona*, I see it p132

³Noun Group Prefix	pg	T	S P	¹Gp	²[Comment] Eg
-ya-⁵·⁰	132		P	xFF	⁵·⁰ Eg *ninayaona*, I see them p132
me-ᵃᵈʲ	49		P	xFF	ᵃᵈʲ e&i-adjective Eg *maembe me(e)ma*, good mangoes (-e-dropped from the adjective) p50 *maembe me(i)ngine*, other mangoes (-i- dropped from the adjective) p50
__ᵃᵈʲ	49		S	xFF	ᵃᵈʲ Eg *dafu zuri*, nice unripe coconut p49
ma-ᵃᵈʲ	49		P	xFF	ᵃᵈʲ Eg *madafu mazuri*, nice unripe coconuts p49
j-ᵃᵈʲ	49		S	xFF	ᵃᵈʲ Vowel-adjective Eg *debe jangavu*, shining can p49
ja-ⁿᵒᵘⁿ	28		S	xFF	ⁿᵒᵘⁿ Eg *jambo*, issue / problem / matter *mambo*, issues / problems / matters p28
ji-ⁿᵒᵘⁿ	28		S	xFF	ⁿᵒᵘⁿ Eg *jicho*, eye *macho*, eyes p28 *jina*, name *majina*, names p28 *jino*, tooth *meno*, teeth p28
me-ⁿᵒᵘⁿ	28		P	xFF	ⁿᵒᵘⁿ Eg *jino*, tooth *meno*, teeth p28
ma-ⁿᵒᵘⁿ	28		P	xFF	ⁿᵒᵘⁿ Eg *tunda*, fruit *matunda*, fruits p28

[3]Noun Group Prefix	pg	T	S P	[1]Gp	[2][Comment] Eg
_ _[noun]	28		S	xFF	[noun] Eg *tunda*, fruit *matunda*, fruits p28
li-[pron]	66		S	xFF	[pron] Eg *linatosha*, it suffices p66
ya-[pron]	66		P	xFF	[pron] Eg *yanatosha*, they suffice p66
-*yo*-[4.R]	142		S	xFV	[4.R] Eg *Nyanya inayotosha*, tomato which suffices p142
-*zo*-[4.R]	143		P	xFV	[4.R] Eg *Nyanya zinazotosha*, tomatoes which suffice p143
-*i*-[5.O]	125		S	xFV	[5.O] Eg *ninaiona*, I see it p133
-*zi*-[5.O]	133		P	xFV	[5.O] Eg *ninaziona*, I see them p133
nj-[adj]	52			xFV	[adj] e-adjective Eg *karafuu njema*, good clove(s) p52
m-[adj]	52			xFV	[adj] Eg *mboga mbaya*, bad vegetable(s) 52
n-[adj]	51			xFV	[adj] Eg *nyanya ndogo / ngumu / njazi / nzuri*, small / hard / plentiful / *nice tomato*(es) p51
_ _[adj]	52			xFV	[adj] Eg *ndizi kubwa*, big banana(s) p52
ny-[adj]	52			xFV	[adj] Vowel-adjective Eg *chupa nyangavu*, shining bottle(s) p52 *karafuu nyingine*, other clove(s) p52 *karafuu nyororo*, soft clove(s) p52

[3]Noun Group Prefix	pg	T	S P	[1]Gp	[2][Comment] Eg
_ _[noun]	32			xFV	[noun] Eg *nyanya*, tomato *nyanya*, tomatoes p32
i-[pron]	66		S	xFV	[pron] Eg *inatosha*, it suffices p66
zi-[pron]	66		P	xFV	[pron] Eg *zinatosha*, they suffice p66

Elimu haina mwisho

There is no limit to education

Appendix A: Pseudo-homophones

This appendix shows collections of pseudo-homophones (near-homophones) which potentially cause confusion, in Swahili as well as in other languages e.g. in English, the words in_s_idious (meaning treacherous in an unapparent way) and in_v_idious (meaning unpleasant), with a <u>single letter</u> difference, are a source of confusion, at least when first encountered, and it takes effort to sort out the confusion but sorted out they must be. And so, it is also the case with Swahili.

We start off with an introductory example of three verbs, followed by a number of others presented alphabetically: [verbs herein are given in their English infinitive forms i.e. with a "to" in front so that they can be visually distinguished from non-verbs]

inua, to lift up
inuka, to get up
inama, to bend down

The interesting thing about the above set of pseudo-homophones is that they all involve body actions. This is not always the case, as will be seen in the examples below.

The above set needs to be memorized in order to be differentiated and used correctly. This is easier said than done, unless of course you have a good ability to memorize. But most of us, I assume, would find it a challenge to memorize all the pseudo-homophones sets presented here, in addition to others as encountered. One technique that may help memorization is to expand the words of a set into short phrases or sentences, preferably inter-related e.g.

*"**Inuka**, halafu **inama**, halafu **inua** kitu hiki"*, "Get up, then bend down, then lift up this thing"

Some may find it easier to memorize illustrative sentences such as the above.

More sets of pseudo-homophones:

adabu, good manners *adhabu*, punishment *thawabu*, reward *dhahabu*, gold
adhimu, to honour *nidhamu = adhamu*, discipline *nadhifu*, tidy
aghalabu, often / mainly / most *angalau*, at least / not even [cf. *walao*, at least]
ambulia, to benefit / to receive *ambukiza*, to infect
andika, to write *bandika*, to join together / to set *tandika*, to lay out *tundika*, to suspend
azima, to borrow / to lend (also *kopa*, to borrow) *azimu = azimia = amua*, to decide
banda, barn [cf. *bandari*, harbour] *ganda*, peel / to coagulate / to freeze [cf. *gamba*, shell / scale] *kanda*, to knead [cf. *kinanda*, stringed musical instrument] *panda*, joint / to climb / to sow [cf. *andaa*, to prepare] *randa*, carpenter's plane / to gambol *sanda*, shroud *tanda*, to spread over [cf. *kitanda*, bed] *ukanda*, belt *uwanda*, plateau / plain
bao, board game / score *mbao*, timber / plank *ubao*, board
baraka, blessing *haraka*, haste

waraka, document
batili, to make worthless *bahili*, miser [cf. *hili*, this (xFF); *Kiswahili*, Swahili] *stahili*, to deserve *stahimili*, to be tolerant [cf. *himili*, to bear] *stahi*, to respect *stadi*, expert
chinja, slaughter *chanja*, grid-iron / to cut / to vaccinate *changa*, young / to collect *mchanga*, young person / sand *changamsha*, to exhilarate *changanya*, to mix / to confuse
chonga, to sharpen / to carve *chunga*, to tend / to sift [also *chekecha*, to sift; *kung'uta*, to sift / winnow] *chungwa*, orange *chungu*, bitter / ant / native pot (cf. *kichuguu*, ant hill) *chungua* = *chunguza*, to inspect *chungulia*, to peep / to look after
chuma, iron / to pick (e.g. flowers) *chuna*, to skin *chanua*, to bloom *chano*, wooden tray *chana*, to scrape / to shred / to comb [also *kun(w)a* = *kwangua* = *paa*, to scrape]
dharau, to scorn *dharura*, emergency *hudhuria*, to attend *hadhara*, rally *hasara*, loss *hasira*, anger
elewa, to understand / to know *eleza*, to explain / to describe *elea*, to float / to be lucid [cf. *enea* = *sambaa* = *tapakaa*, to spread out] *eleka*, to carry on the hip *elekea*, to be headed for / to be inclined to *elekeza*, to guide [cf. *ezeka*, to thatch; *ezua*, to unthatch]

faraja, relief [as in the saying *baada ya dhiki, faraja*, after hardship, relief – more in Appendix D: Idioms, Proverbs, Teasers] *furaha*, joy *fahari*, grandeur *ufasaha = fasihi*, elegance especially of literary style [cf. *sihi*, plead] *ufanisi*, effectiveness / efficiency
futa, to erase *mafuta*, oil *tafuta*, to look for
hadi, until *haja*, need [cf. *hoja*, issue / concern] *haki*, justice / right(s) [vs *hakika = yakini*, certainty; *yamini*, right hand] *hali*, condition [cf. *bali*, but] *halisi*, real *halali*, lawful *hamu = ghamu*, craving *hasa*, especially, properly *hisi*, to feel / to figure out *hata*, even / until *hati*, writing / document [cf. *makala*, write-up; *taarifa*, report] *haya*, shyness
hitimu = timi(z)a = isha, to complete *himiza = sisitiza*, to urge
kaburi, grave *kiburi*, pride
kanga, shawl, sarong *kanga*, guinea fowl [cf. *kororo*, crested guinea fowl; *mnyororo*, chain; *mnyoro*, intestinal worm] *kaanga*, to fry
katibu, clerk *kitabu*, book *katiba*, constitution *maktaba*, library
kitanda, bed *kiwanda*, work yard
kiti, chair *tikiti*, melon *msikiti*, mosque
kijivu, grey [cf. *mvi*, grey hair]

jiwe, stone   *njiwa*, pigeon
komba, bush baby   *kombe*, bowl   *kombo*, crooked / acquittal / scrap   *konda*, to slim down   *konde*, fist
kuku, hen   *kikuku*, bracelet   *kuukuu*, very old
kuta, to meet / to find (out)   *ukuta*, wall
laini, soft, smooth   *laiti*, if only
lamba, to lick   *labda*, perhaps
lemaa, to maim   *kilema*, a cripple [*mlemavu* = *kiwete*, a disabled person]   *lemea*, to press on / to oppress [also, *dhulumu*, to oppress]
maarifa, knowledge [cf. *taarifa*, report]   *maarufu* = *mashuhuri*, famous   *marufuku*, forbidden   *maalum(u)*, well-known / special   *taalamu*, educated
mahali, place   *mahari*, dowry   *mandhari*, view   *madhumuni*, purpose   *muhuri*, seal [cf. *nembo*, coat of arms; *bendera*, flag]
maliasili, natural resources   *rasilimali*, capital (financial)
mlozi, sorcerer / almond tree   *mluzi*, whistle (sound)
mwanzo = *chanzo*, beginning [*chanzo* also means first draft / principle]   *mwanzi*, bamboo tree   *mwanya*, gap   *mwamba*, rock [e.g. *Mwamba wa Bismarck*, Bismarck Rock, at Mwanza, the Tanzanian port at the southern end of Lake Victoria]   *mwambao*, shore

mwanga, light *mwangwi*, echo
mwezi, moon / month *mwizi* = *mwivi*, thief
nauli, fare *kauli*, statement [cf. *kauri*, cowry shell, ceramic]
onea = *tesa* = *sumbua*, to harass [cf. *teka*, to pillage / to draw water] *onya*, to warn
nyanya, tomato *nyinyi*, you (plural) *nyonya*, to suck(le) *nyoya*, feather / hair *nyunya*, to drizzle
pa, to give *paa*, to ascend / to scrape off / gazelle / roof (of a native hut)
pafu, dead lung (e.g. in a butchery) cf. *pumu*, lung *pofu*, eland *povu*, froth
pakua, to unload / to serve food *pekua*, to pry / to scratch
panga, to arrange / to hire / machete *upanga*, sword *kipanga*, bird of prey *mpangaji*, tenant *pango*, cave / lair *pangusa*, to wipe
punje, grain *punde*, shortly / little *punda*, donkey *punga*, to wave [cf. *mpunga*, rice plant] *pungua*, to reduce *pumba*, husk
rithi, to inherit *ridhi*, to please *ridhika*, to be pleased *ridhisha*, to satisfy *ridhiki*, to be dissatisfied *radhi*, contentment / pardon [cf. *maradhi*, illness]
sayari, planet

tayari, ready *bahari*, sea *fahari*, grandeur
shtaki, to accuse *shtuka*, to be startled
staajabu, to be astonished *staarabu*, civilized
tamani, to covet [cf. *tamaa*, greed; *shika tamaa*, to hope; *kata tamaa*, to despair; *tama*, end; *shika tama*, to despair] *tumaini*, to hope [*tarajia*, to hope for]
tangaza, to announce *angaza*, to shine
tegemea, to depend *egemea*, to lean on *tegemeza*, to support
teleka, to cook by putting pot on fire *teleza*, to slip *telekeza*, to abandon
tetea, to advocate *teketea*, to be burnt / to be destroyed *tetemea* = *tapa*, to tremble
thabiti, resolute *thibitisha*, to establish *udhibiti*, control *dhihirisha*, causing to show / to be clear
tunda, fruit *tundika*, to suspend [cf. *tindika*, to fail] *tundu*, naughty / hollow
tubu, repent *tibu*, to treat *tiba*, medicine *matibabu*, medical care
tukia, to happen *tokea*, to appear / to happen *toweka*, to vanish *tokomea*, disappear
twaa, to receive / to take *tua*, to alight *kua*, to grow up

ukungu = *kungu*, fog
kungu, fruit (small) with... (refer to the Dictionary in Volumes 2 and 3)
mkungu, banana fruit stalk
uvungu, hollow e.g. under bed
ukumbi, vestibule / hall
(*u*)*kundi*, group
ukindu, 'raffia' of wild palm
kinda, offspring of animals

umba, to create [cf. *umbali*, distance]
umbo, shape
unda, to construct
muundo, structure

unga, flour / to join [cf. *ungama*, to acknowledge; cf. *kimbunga*, hurricane; cf. *mgunga*, acacia]
ungu, pot
ungo, tray
kiungo, joint / link / condiment [cf. *kiunga*, orchard / suburb]
muungano, union
tunga, to string / to compose [cf. *tunza*, to look after / to reward]
mtungo, arrangement / fish strung together

vivu, lazy
wivu, jealous
mvuvi, fisherman

vua, to fish / to take off (clothes) [cf. *mvua*, rain; *pua*, nose; *ua*, flower / courtyard; *bua*, plant stalk; *dua*, prayer; *jua*, sun / to know]
vuja, to leak
vuka, to cross (a river) / to have escaped [cf. *fuka*, to emit / to fill (a hole)]
vuma, to blow hard (wind) / to rumble (low sound) / to be famed
vuna, to reap
vuta, to pull [cf. *futa*, to erase]

wali, cooked rice
awali, first
swali, question
mwali, flame / bride
mwalimu, teacher
jedwali, schedule

yumba, to sway [cf. *umba*, to create]
jumba, mansion

nyumba, house
chumba, room [cf. *mchumba*, fiancé(e)]
fumba, to puzzle
kumba, fence [cf. *kumbatia*, to embrace]
pumba, husk [cf. *mpumbavu*, fool]
kitumba, bud / bag
mtumba, bale [cf. *tumbako*, tobacco]

zizi, cattle pen
mzizi, root
zizima, to become cold
ziwa, lake
maziwa, milk

Appendix B: Nouns/Verbs Made Up From Each Other

In this appendix: (1) A matrix of derived (made up) nouns is presented in order to be able to see patterns of how nouns are made up. This profile is a good representation of such transformations. Thus, these patterns are useful for making up other nouns, usually with success but even when not their intended result is likely to be understood and be corrected by the listener. (2) The reverse verbs-from-noun is presented.

TIP: Make a habit of mentally checking a word as to whether it is derived, keeping in mind that sometimes the derivation is visually obvious, sometimes not as much e.g. *tuhumu*, suspect, and *tuhuma*, suspicion, whose derivation is visually obvious, as compared to *ongoza*, lead, and *mwongozo*, guidance, which is less obvious, even less so being *vua*, fish, and *mvuvi*, fisherman, vaguer still *nya*, defecate, and *kinyesi*, stool, and the vaguest *fa*, die, and *kifo*, death, or *ja*, come, and *ujio*, coming! The benefit of being able to tell a possible derivation is that the size of the Dictionary (Volumes 2 and 3), which only shows a very limited number of derived words, effectively increases significantly.

The patterns (of changes with respect to verbs) are shown hyphenated and bolded. They are shown from simplest to complex:

Verb [F] denotes foreign origin	Noun
No change is made, noun is used as-is:	
kosa, err / lose	*kosa*, error
Changing the ending vowel to -*a*, -*i* or -*o*:	
jaribu, try	*jarib-i-o*, attempt [-*i*- is euphoniously added]
omba, request	*omb-i*, request
shiriki / shirikiana, share	*shirik-a*, corporation [see cooperation below]
sikitika, grieve	*sikitik-o*, sorrow
tandika, lay out	*tandik-o*, spread e.g. bedding
tuhumu, suspect	*tuhum-a*, suspicion
tatiza, mystify	*tatiz-o*, problem

Verb [F] denotes foreign origin	Noun
vuna, reap	*ma-vun-o*, harvest [*ma-* is prefixed as this is always plural]
Changing the ending vowel to –(*i*)*zi*:	
andama, follow	*andam-izi*, following
ongea, converse	*ma-onge-zi*, conversation [*ma-* is prefixed as this is always plural]
tembea, stroll	*tembe-zi*, stroll
Prefixing *m-* or *mw-*:	
enda, go	*mw-enda*, goer
jaza, fill	*m-ja-mzito*, pregnant [*zito*, heavy]
teua, select	*m-teua*, nominator
zeeka, age	*m-zee*, old person / elder [*-ka* is dropped]
Prefixing *m-* / *mw-*, and suffixing or changing the last vowel to: *-a* / *-(i)ji* / *-ka* / *-le-* / *-ni* / *-o* / *-shi* / *-vi* / *-wa* / *-zi*:	
andama, follow	*mw-andam-izi*, follower, successor
andika, write	*mw-andi-shi*, writer [*-k-* is euphoniously dropped]
angaza, shine	*mw-angaz-a*, light / port hole / publicity
athiri, affect [F]	*mw-athiri-ka*, affected person
changa, collect	*m-chang-o*, collection
enda, go	*mw-end-o*, motion *mw-enend-o*, conduct [from *enenda*, a variation of *enda*] *mw-end-eleo*, progress [*-ele-* inserted]
fanana, resemble	*m-fan-o*, example [*-an-* dropped]
fuga, rear (animals)	*m-fug-o*, livestock
kaza, fasten	*m-kaz-o*, pressure
ongoza, lead	*mw-ongoz-o*, guidance
shinda, win	*m-shinda-ni*, competitor *m-shinda-ji*, winner
shtaki, accuse	*m-shtaki-wa*, accused
tetea, advocate	*m-tete-zi*, advocate
teua, select	*m-teu-le*, nominee
tunga, compose	*m-tun-zi*, composer [*-g-* is euphoniously dropped]

Verb [F] denotes foreign origin	Noun
tunga, string together	*m-tung-o*, stringing of
uguza, treat sickness	*mw-ugu-zi*, nurse [one -z- is redundant]
vua, fish	*m-vu-vi*, fisherman
zaa, bear / deliver (off-spring)	*m-za-zi*, parent
Prefixing *ki-*, the last vowel is changed to -*i*,-*o* or -*si* /*ji* /*zi*:	
fanana, resemble	*ki-fan-i/o*, match
fa, die	*ki-f-o*, death
lima, cultivate	*ki-lim-o*, agriculture
nya, defecate	*ki-ny-esi*, stool [-*e*- inserted]
ongoza, lead	*ki-ongoz-i*, leader
pa, give	*ki-pa-ji*, talent (God-given)
pata, get	*ki-pat-o*, income
zaa, bear / deliver (off-spring)	*ki-za-zi*, generation
Prefixing *u-*, usually the last vowel is changed to -*i*, -*o*, -*fu/vu* or -*ji* / *vi* / *zi*:	
fuga, rear (animals)	*u-fuga-ji*, livestock keeping
fungua, open	*u-fungu-zi*, opening
ja, come	*u-j-io*, coming [-*a*- changed to -*i*-]
kosa, err / lose	*u-kos-efu*, failure [-*e*- inserted]
kuza, expand	*u-kuza-ji*, development
lima, cultivate	*u-kulima*, agriculture [no change in ending]
nyenyekea, be humble	*u-nyenyeke-vu* / *u-nyenyeke-o*, humility
ongoza, lead	*u-ongoz-i*, leadership
pungua / *punguza*, reduce	*u-pungu-fu*, reduction
shiriki / *shirikiana*, share	*u-shirikian-o*, cooperation [see corporation above]
tafuta, look for	*u-taf-i-t-i*, research [-*u*- changed to -*i*-]
tunga, compose / string together	*u-tung-o*, composition *u-tun-zi*, penship [-*g*- dropped]
tenga, set apart *tengwa* / *tengana*, be separated	*u-tengan-o*, separation

Verb [F] denotes foreign origin	Noun
vua, fish	*u-vu-vi*, fishing
zoea, be used to	*u-zoe-fu*, experience

In the reverse direction, verbs too are made up from nouns, often of foreign origin e.g.

Noun [F] denotes foreign origin	Verb
No change is made, noun is used as-is:
adili, ethics [F]	*adili*, act morally
Changing the ending vowel to -*i* or -*u*:
dhana, thought [F]	*dhan-i*, think
hutuba, sermon [*hotuba* is a variation] [F]	*hutub-u*, lecture
Changing the middle vowels to -*i*- or -*u*-:
athari, effect [F]	*ath-i-ri*, affect
habari, information [F]	*h-u-b-i-ri*, inform
hadhara, rally[F]	*h-u-dh-u-ria*, attend [note the -*i*- preposition]
safari, journey [F]	*saf-i-ri*, travel
Changing both the middle and the last vowels to -*i*- or -*u*-:
baraza council [F]	*bar-i-z-i*, convene
shaka, doubt [F]	*sh-u-k-u*, doubt
Using verb transformations [see section 5.8]:
neema, comfort / bounty	*neemeka*, be well-off
udhaifu, weakness [which itself is made up from *dhaifu*, weak] [F]	*dhoofika*, become weak
usingizi, sleep	*singiza*, pretend; with prep: *singiz̲ia*, fictionalize
wakili, representative	*wakilisha*, represent
Using prepositions [see section 10.2]:
tope, mud	*topea*, to sink (in mud)

Note: sometimes, a verb and an associated noun are <u>both</u> directly adapted from a foreign language, in which case one is not derived from the other in Swahili e.g. (1) verb *hukumu*, judge and noun *hakimu*, judge, which in turn gives us *mahakama*, courts [*ma*- prefix is attached as it is always plural in usage]; note that the latter is a noun-to-noun derivation; (2) verb *abudu*, worship and noun *ibada*, prayer – or, verb *ashiria*, signal and noun *ishara*, signal; (3) verb *ajiri*, employ and noun *ujira*, wage [cf. *ajira*, employment]

Appendix C: Wide-use Verbs

In Swahili there are a few verbs that are used in idiomatic ways that result in a wide range of meaning. These verbs are as follows, in order of most wide-use to less-wide, along with examples under each verb to illustrate wide-use:

toa, offer / produce / show / remove
toa hadithi, tell a story
toa jibu, solve
toa makosa, fix errors
toa sharti, to state requirements / conditions
toa shauri, advise
toa siku, schedule a day
toa ukali, show (literally) fierceness or (meaningfully) bravery

The "remove" meaning of this verb is used, in its infinitive form, to negate other verbs e.g.
kusema, say or saying
_kuto_kusema_, not say or silence [_kuto_ is a shortened form of _kutoa_]
Negation of the infinitive / gerund was covered in section 3.8 GERUNDS [G]: Kusoma- Kusoma, reading(s).

piga, hit / strike
piga chapa, print
piga domo, brag
piga hema, pitch tent
piga hodi, knock on door
piga kikumbo, shove
piga kura, vote
piga magoti, atone
piga maji, imbibe
piga marufuku, ban
piga pasi, iron (clothes)
piga ramli, divine

tia, put

tia chuoni, enrol in college
tia ndani / pamoja na, include
tia nanga, cast anchor [But also, *weka nanga*]
tia rangi, paint [But also, *paka rangi*]
tia weko, weld

pata, get

pata hasara, incur loss
pata kufanya, accomplish
pata kujua, get to know

kata, cut

kata roho, die
kata shauri, decide
kata tamaa, despair [cf. *shika* q.v.]

weka, keep / put / set

weka akiba, reserve / conserve
weka heshima, honour
weka hukumu, defer ruling

ona, see

ona kelele, hear noise
ona kiu, be thirsty
ona njaa, be hunger

shika, hold

shika tama, despair
shika tamaa, hope [cf. *kata* q.v.]

Appendix D: Idioms, Proverbs, Teasers

Swahili has its own idioms and also, like other languages, idioms translated from another language and East Africa being at one time under British rule idioms from English are more likely to be used than all other foreign languages. The same can be said of proverbs. On the fun side, it has teasers which are frequently oral exchanges where one person describes something cryptically and the other person has to decipher. Here are a number of representative examples:

Nahau, idioms

angua kicheko, drop laughingly [to **burst out laughing**]

amekula chumvi nyingi, has eaten a lot of salt [**elderly**, much **experienced**]

bega kwa bega, shoulder to shoulder [in **cooperation**]

changa moto, collect fire [a **challenge**]

chemsha bongo, boil the brain [a **quiz**]

funga safari, fasten journey [to **embark** or **decide**]

funga ndoa, fasten marriage [to **marry**]

huduma ya kwanza, first service [**first aid**]

katisha njia, have the road cut [to take a **shortcut**]

kufa moyo, dying heart [to **despair**]

kwenda haja, go to need [to '**go**' ;-)]

mbio kuzidi risasi, faster than a bullet [**high speed**]

mikono mitupu, empty hands [**mission unaccomplished**]

mtu wa chuma, person of steel [a **tough** person]

njia (ya) panda, joint roads [**crossroads**]

pata jiko, get a kitchen [to **marry**]

tega masikio, ready the ears [to **listen carefully**]

unga mikono, join hands [**seal a deal**]

vaa miwani, wear glasses [having glazed eyes i.e. be **drunk**]

vunjika moyo, be **heart-broken** [as in English]

Methali, proverbs

Many of the chapters in this book begin with a proverb headline q.v.
Here are some more:

Ahadi ni deni, a promise is a debt (it has to be honoured, for one's credibility)

Akufanye kwa dhiki ndiye rafiki, one who does for you in (your) hardship is indeed a friend (a friend in need is a friend indeed)

Asifuye mvua imemnyea, one who praises rain has been rained on

Asiyefundishwa na mamaye hufunzwa na ulimwengu, one who is not taught by his mother is taught by the world (will be straightened out)

Asiyekubali kushindwa si mshindani, one who does not accept being defeated is not a sportsperson

Baada ya dhiki faraja, after hardship relief (there's a bright light at the end of a tunnel)

Ponda mali, kufa kwaja, crush wealth, dying comes [can't take it with you!]

Shukrani ya punda ni teke, gratitude of a donkey (an ingrate) is a kick

Siku za mwizi ni arobaini, days of a thief are 40 (you can get away with it for only so long)

Tamaa mbele, mauti nyuma, greed ahead, death behind (trouble follows greed)

Umoja ni nguvu, utengano ni udhaifu, unity is strength, separation / division is weakness

Vitendawili, actions two-ways (teasers)

The practice is that one person announces *"Kitendawili!"*, a teaser! The listener responds *"Tega!"*, trap (i.e. trick me). The first person then proceeds to state one (see examples below) and then commands *"Tegua!"*, untrap (i.e. solve). The other person then gets to answer. One of the first teasers I recall a classmate / friend teased me with was *"Kila niendapo ananifuata"*, wherever I go he follows me. Answer: *"Kivuli!"*, shadow! Note: the inanimate shadow is given an animate pronoun, the "a" in *ananifuata*. Often, a human substitutes the object of the riddle e.g. in the fifth one below, *mwanangu*, my little child, represents the riddle's object, *ngoma*, drum. These substitutions are quite common, and the riddle-solver has to un-substitute while solving.

Kitendawili, teaser	*Jibu,* answer
Ajenga ingawa hana mikono, he builds though he has no hands	*Ndege*, bird
Bibi hatui kamwe mzigo wake, lady never alights her load	*Konokono*, snail
Hausimami, hauchoki, doesn't stop, doesn't tire	*Moyo*, heart
Kamba yangu ndefu, haifungi kuni, my rope (is) long (but) does not bundle up kindle	*Njia*, road
Ninapompiga mwanangu watu hucheza, when I hit my child people play	*Ngoma*, drum
Nyumba yangu ndogo lakini ina wapangaji wengi, my house is small but it has many tenants	*Ganda la kiberiti*, matchbox
Nzi hatui juu ya damu ya simba, flies don't alight on lion's blood	*Moto*, fire

Appendix E: Correspondence

Correspondence makes for a significant volume of Swahili text. Primarily these are letters, of both the personal and business varieties, and of both print and electronic media. In East Africa, text messages are much used, given that cell phones are in wide use. Of these types and/or medium, any differences would be in the formality and grammatical correctness, being less formal in the personal type especially text messages e.g. a business correspondence would be towards the upper end of this spectrum, texting towards the lower. In this appendix, we will not deal with texting as its usage varies very widely and is very informal.

First, we take up **formal** correspondence:

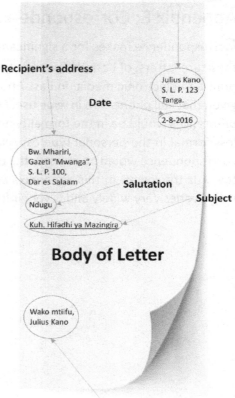

S.L.P. = *Sanduku la Posta*, Post Office Box
Date format: DD-MM-YYYY
Bw. Mhariri, Mr. Editor
Gazeti "Mwanga", "Mwanga" Newspaper
Ndugu, Brother
or *Dada*, Sister [in socialist Tanzania*]
Kuh., short form for *kuhusu*, concerning**:
Hifadhi ya Mazingira,
Preservation of the Environment

Wako mtiifu, your obedient

[*Elsewhere: *Bwana*, Sir, or *Bibi*, Madam; **or *Yah.* short form for *yahusu*, it concerns]

Formal eMails would follow the above model. However, friendly / informal correspondence would be different from the above as follows:

Salutation: *Kwa rafiki yangu*, to my friend
Hujambo? You're okay?
Hali yako? Your state (well-being)?

Closing: *Salama kwa wote nyumbani*, greetings to all at home
Rafiki yako, your friend

Appendix F: Widely-used *Ki-* Prefix

Prefix ***ki-*** is widely used to make up **nouns** and **adverbs**. This appendix presents, in one place, several examples illustrative of this use of ***ki-***. Previously, this was covered separately in sections 3.4 THINGS [T]: Kitu-Vitu, things(s), 3.11 Making Up Nouns and 6.1 Making Up Adverbs, but here one can compare and contrast the resulting nouns and adverbs side by side:

adv = adverb

n = noun

(dim) = diminutive

(syn) = synonym

Note the <u>euphonious</u> modifications!

From noun roots			
jumba, mansion	***kijumba***	n	(dim) cabin
mfalme, king	***kifalme***	n	(dim) petty king
		adv*	royally
		n	royalness
mji, town	***ki<u>jij</u>i***	n	(dim) village
mtoto, child	***kitoto***	n	(dim) small child
		adv*	childishly
mti, pole	***ki<u>jit</u>i***	n	(dim) stick
mtu, person	***ki<u>jit</u>u***	n	(dim) runt
mvuli, shady place / *uvuli*, shade	***kivuli***	n	(syn) shade
mwana, son / child	***kijana***	n	youth
mzee, old person	***kizee***	n	(syn) old person
		adv*	like an old person
Mzungu, European	***kizungu***	adv*	like a European
tako, buttock	***kitako***	n	(syn) buttock
		adv*	on the haunches

*Reminder: any of these adverbs can be used with -*a*, of, to make up an adjective e.g. *farasi wa kifalme*, a royal horse. [See section 4.3 Making Up Adjectives.] Note: an original adverb prefixed with *ki-* remains an adverb but having a specialized meaning e.g. adverb *sasa*, now, prefixed with *ki-* is adverb *kisasa*, modernly: *anafikiri kisasa*, she thinks modernly. Furthermore, as stated above, it can be used to make up an adjective e.g. *anatumia vifaa vya kisasa*, she is using modern tools.

From adjectival roots			
pofu, blind	*kipofu*	n	blindness
		adv	blindly
From verbal roots			
cheka, laugh	*kicheko*	n	laughter
funga, close	*kifungo*	n	fastener
		n	prison
kohoa, cough	*kikohozi*	n	cough
nywa, drink	*kinywaji*	n	beverage
ongoza, lead	*kiongozi*	n	leader
pa, give	*kipaji*	n	gift
tenda, do	*kitendo*	n	deed
tua, alight	*kituo*	n	stop
ziba, block	*kiziwi*	n	deaf person

Appendix G: -*po*- infix / suffix

This infix or suffix can initially be confusing, so we devote an appendix to sort it out. -*po*- occurs in the following situations:

Sec.		Relative (where)
10.3 10.9	all tenses	*mahali pali**po**kuwa na matunda mengi*, the place **where** there were many fruits
10.3	Timeless tense	*kanisa aenda**po** ni Mtakatifu Antoni*, the church **where** he goes is St Anthony
		Conditional (when, whenever)
10.4	when	*ali**po**fika nyumbani akanipiga simu*, **when** she reached home she called me
10.4	whenever	*kila nitaka**po**kuja nitakaa*, [adverb] **whenever** I will come I will stay
10.4	Timeless when	*afika**po** hupumzika*, **when** he arrives, he rests
10.4	Timeless whenever	*kila aja**po** kwetu hunywa chai*, **whenever** he comes to us he drinks tea
		Object (it)
10.1	*wa na*, have	*nina**po** mahali*, I have **it**, the place
		-*po/ko/mo* (...is/are + Place)
10.8	all tenses	*watu wa**po** mlangoni*, people **are** at the door
10.7.3	old *li* tense	*watu walio**po** mlangoni*, people who **are** at the door
		*anakwenda Tangata kili**po***, he is going Tangata **where** it is
		-*o -ote* (any, anywhere, wherever)
8.7	any	*mahali **po pote***, [adjective] **any** place
8.7	anywhere	*unaweza kukaa **po pote***, [adverb] you can sit **anywhere**
8.7 10.4	-*po*-, when +anywhere	*nitaka**po**kwenda **ko kote** nitaendesha baisikeli*,

		[adverb] **when** I will go **anywhere** I will ride the bicycle
		*nienda**po** **ko kote** huendesha baisikeli*, [adverb, timeless tense] **when** I go **anywhere** I ride the bicycle
8.7 10.3	*-po-*, where + wherever	***po pote** alipokwenda*, [adverb] **wherever** he went
		*mnyama hukojoa **po pote** apenda**po***, [adverb, routine tense] an animal urinates **wherever** it pleases
	ndi- (emphasis)	
21.2	*-po-*, when	*ndipo*, **that's** when
	-po-, there	*ndipo*, **it's** there

Caution: A *-po-* is not necessarily the infix 'when'. It could be the beginning of the verb itself e.g. *ali**po**toa*, when he produced, where *-po-* is the infix 'when', versus *alipotoa*, he ruined, where it is part of the verb ***potoa***. Fortunately, there are only a very few cases like this.

Index

Mwenda pole hajikwai,
A careful walker does not stumble

Mwishoni, bahati njema, rafiki yangu!
In the end, good luck, my friend!

Made in the USA
Las Vegas, NV
10 February 2024